ASTROLOGY
AND ITS PRACTICAL APPLICATION

BY

E. PARKER

TRANSLATED FROM THE DUTCH

BY

COBA GOEDHART

D1602666

NEWCASTLE PUBLISHING CO., INC.
NORTH HOLLYWOOD, CALIFORNIA

1977

A NEWCASTLE BOOK
FIRST PRINTING APRIL 1977
PRINTED IN THE UNITED STATES OF AMERICA

PREFACE.

Whether Astrology is a science or not is a question which can only be discussed when we know what is meant by science. For many of the dogmas that to-day go officially by that name will hardly seem to be such to a thinking person, seeing that — considering their continual modifications and changes — they seem to result from groping rather than knowledge.

No one who takes the pains to compare them can deny that there is a relation between Astrology and the science of to-day.

When for instance we examine the most primitive plant and animal forms, the so-called *radiolariæ, diatomœ* etc. (cf. *Haeckel "Kunstformen der Natur"*) and also the *Chladnic figures,* formed in fine sand along magnetic lines of power under definite vibrations, does it not seem as if the latter had come to life in the former? Snow crystals too, sections of flowers, flowers themselves, trees, ferns — even the parts of our own body (lungs, heart, organs of hearing etc.) show this wonderful mutual correspondence.

Might not this indicate that these plant and animal forms have their origin under definite vibrations, built up of definite materials?

Would it really be impossible to prove that those vibrations come to us *through the celestial bodies* as nuclei in Cosmic vibrations — seeing that so much has been found (the 'Od' of Reichenbach, and other similar 'substances') that proves in fact that *something emanates* from the celestial bodies?

Can it be maintained much longer that matter should exist apart from *spirit* which sends out its vibrations to set the *matter moving,* when, on one hand we learn that our *muscles* work according to the command from the centre of the mind conveyed to them by the *nerves,* and on the other hand we believe that *all things* are made by *the Word* that was *with God* and *was God?*

Flammarion's work "La pluralité des mondes habitués" has this passage: *„this law of unity which gives to many minerals a definite geometrical shape, and to every one of the worlds a fixed form and a similar motion; which in space groups together systems of worlds round Mother-Suns and in the lap of dense matter a group of single molecules round a centre of affinity. It is this law that has formed the system of the bloodvessels, of the bones of man and animals according to the same model as the leaves of plants and the ramifications of trees."*

And *Kant* also has said in his *"Träume eines Geistersehers"*: *"It will be proved that in this life already the human soul is indissolubly connected with the immaterial entities of the spirit-world."*

In truth, *much can be found* by him who earnestly wishes to *seek.* But first the attitude of *scoffing negation* must give place to that of *impartial interest.*

This book has been written for those who take an interest in Astrology because of the important place it has occupied in human thought for ages and who would like to be acquainted to it more intimately.

In order not to frighten away the laity I have kept to the *main points* when choosing the subdivisions and the calculations that require to be dealt with, but at the same time I have tried to set these forth *as completely and clearly as possible*. All details of value for closer study, but confusing to the beginner have been omitted.

May that which is given bring to the reader the realisation of the powers working in the Cosmos, the connection of all that exists, and prompt him to further research into the occult teachings.

Differences of opinion, additions, explanations etc. arising *after serious perusal of this work* will be gratefully accepted.

E. PARKER.

AMERSFOORT, July 1927.

the clouds of sense roll back and show the form devinely fair

CONTENTS.

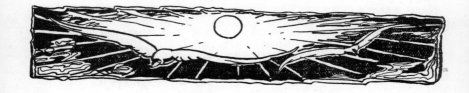

I

INTRODUCTION.

As the *Sun* by its influence regulates on earth the *seasons,* the *division of the day* etc., and the influence of the *Moon* may be seen e.g. in the *tides,* so do other celestial bodies also exercise a definite influence upon everything on earth, not only on the material but also on the *spiritual* plane.

The principal influences known up to this moment come from the Sun, the Moon, the planets (Mercury, Venus, Mars, Jupiter, Saturn, Uranus, Neptune) and the Signs of the Zodiac.

All these being constantly in motion form ever changing positions in relation to each other and in relation to us; these positions we put down in a horoscope-figure in order to conclude from them under what influences we are. As we undergo those influences on this *earth,* the horoscope must have the earth (place of birth) for a centre.

Those in ignorance of Astrology take this as a proof that its students deny or forget that our system is heliocentric i.e. that the Sun is its centre, and therefore assert that Astrology is an illusion. But it is well to remember, that the Egyptians, with whom Astrology was honoured as the *divine science,* knew already that the Sun is the centre of our system, whereas Western peoples without Astrology for centuries supposed that the Sun revolved around the earth!

When we are born we each come separately into contact with the said forces, and though all through life we are under their influence, yet that first contact is strongest and of the most consequence for our characters. The position of the stars at the moment of our birth, our birth-horoscope, indicates what will be our characters, our inclinations, and our circumstances in life. It is no mere chance that we prove to be exactly as the constellations led us to surmise, nor are we objects without a will of our own which happen to receive that special imprint of the stars. The cogs of the wheels interlock — we could not be born on this earth under these circumstances (necessary to our development) unless those special positions in the skies were formed.

Like makes like conscious.

The theory of heredity is not thrown over by Astrology as some people think, but in a measure is confirmed by it. When investigating horoscopes we find that in a family some special signs are dominant.

It is necessary for a precise delineation of a horoscope to know the exact place and date of birth; for, every degree of longitude and every

2

minute makes a difference. This accounts for the great distinction sometimes found between twins.

The elements of the horoscope are three in number, viz.

1. *The Signs of the Zodiac.*
2. *The Houses* (being the twelve fields into which the circle of the horoscope is divided).
3. *The Planets.*

For convenience' sake we shall in the following pages include the Sun and the Moon under the word "Planets".

II

Synthetic Account of the Zodiacal Signs.

The signs of the Zodiac are 12 in number, viz.

♈ *Aries* (Ram) ♎ *Libra* (Balance)
♉ *Taurus* (Bull) ♏ *Scorpio* (Scorpion)
♊ *Gemini* (Twins) ♐ *Sagittarius* (Archer)
♋ *Cancer* (Crab) ♑ *Capricorn* (Goat)
♌ *Leo* (Lion) ♒ *Aquarius* (Waterbearer)
♍ *Virgo* (Virgin) ♓ *Pisces* (Fishes)

To form a better idea of their various natures we shall divide them into groups and mutually compare them.

First we distinguish between the *cardinal or principal signs* (♈, ♋, ♎, ♑), the *fixed signs* (♉, ♌, ♏, ♒) and the *mutable or changeable signs* (♊, ♍, ♐, ♓) which by fours form a cross and which we shall now examine in detail.

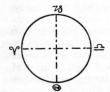

The Three Crosses.

The Cardinal Cross.

This is formed by the signs ♈—♎ and ♋—♑. These four mutually have these 'cardinal' properties in common: the *consciousness of self* and—in a way—of *responsible authority* over others. People born under these signs always feel more or less called to lead their fellow-men, to help them in word and deed, to educate them and where necessary to *further their evolution.* With ♈ and ♎, the positive sings this inclination is shown *in the world,* with ♋ and ♑, negative, it can better be seen *in intimate circles* or along lines that strike one less. But as ♈—♎ and ♋—♑ are opposite to one another much difference can be found in their similarity.

Aries being a *Mars-sign* is fond of active work, personal example, this type intervenes immediately and settles things quickly. When ♈ sees something that is wrong he directly bustles about to fight it and he will not be content unless he reaches his aim. When his fellow-men are of the same opinion as he, but lack the courage and the power to contend on his side, he is willing to do their share of the work, being satisfactorily supported by their sympathy in his endeavour. Thus ♈ is the "champion" as well as the "Lamb taking away the sins of the world".

Libra, the *Venus-sign* is naturally opposed to all strife, because it adheres to the principle that everywhere the supreme consciousness can balance equally all opposites. That is why ♎ is sure to give the advice to read much, to study much, not to disapprove of a thing too quickly, but to try and find the sunny side of things unpleasant, and therefore with others be ready to bring about the desired solution together. But above all: *"together",* for then the least chance of one-sidedness exists. „Jede Konsequenz führt zum Teufel", all extremes are wrong, but to walk in the path of the *golden mean* brings blessing and happiness—that is Libra's line of work.

Cancer, preeminently *the Mother-sign* will first pay attention to the education of and care for his or her own children, or, failing these, those who are looked upon as most intimately related. With this sign *feeling* is the principal thing. ♋ will always try to reach others through feeling, and is therefore most successful with children and sensitive people. ♋ will try to get somebody to do a thing "in order to please him (♋)" and keep him from doing a thing because "he (♋) would be made miserable by it", all of which as a matter of fact holds good in intimate circles only. When in the world some injustice is done, ♋ will not call the doers thereof to account, but pass them by in indignant silence and demonstratively show compassion with the victims in order to induce the culprits to turn from sin.

Capricorn in opposition to ♋ may be called the *Father-sign;* here the dominance of Saturn renders the outlook on life more or less melancholy and serious. ♑ very soon knows that life is not easy and that only steady, hard work renders it bearable. He will also prompt others to perform their duties punctiliously—at least if they come to ask advice from him or if his position towards them is that of a superior (father): for this negative sign is not apt to interfere with other people's business, neither does it itself suffer interference. But knowledge and experience are willingly placed at the disposal of those who seek earnestly and much patience and tact is also shown to those who are younger.

The Fixed Cross.

This is formed by the signs ♉, ♌, ♏ and ♒ and all these are distinguished by care for spiritual or material store, *a fixed possession,* from which can be spared to others or taken for oneself to enable or to accelerate to carry out plans. The positive pair ♌—♒ show this *in the world,* whereas the negative couple ♉—♏ keep their "capital" calmly to themselves and enlarge it until it proves to be possible to expend it usefully in some wise.

4

Taurus, as an earthly sign, will make up his possessions of *'earthly'* metal (money), because practical life proves that even the best plans fail, if they are not backed up financially. Being ruled by Venus—although negatively—makes those born under this sign subject to altruistic, artistic or religious feelings, so that they are always willing to stand by enterprises of that kind financially. ♉ is averse to all complications; motive, aim and means must be simple and true, before he is wishing to give help honestly and in good faith. Things beyond the comprehension of a ♉ man are ignored; but when they are pressed upon his attention, he is likely to oppose them as firmly (fixedly) as on the other hand he might support them.

Scorpio however follows the principle that *knowledge is power* and that in order to gather knowledge one should not be afraid of complications. He usually feels most attracted to things not generally known; things hidden from the majority but which might be of great importance to anyone able to work with that knowledge. ♏ also knows that there is danger lurking in knowledge just as in every other power, and so is often very reticent. He likes to put others to the proof and when they come up to his expectations he grows indulgent and helpful and evinces much respect for anybody morally stronger than himself. On the other hand to those whom ♏ looks upon as his inferiors, his attitude will be disparaging, although this will find expression more negatively than positively.

Leo feels himself first of all the ruler, the *patron* of all enterprises in which he takes part. Therefore his "capital" consists of organising power and an inspiring love for enterprise. Leo is the sovereign head, the representative person, the tie that binds the various workers and seekers together and who gives them some "grip". It goes without saying that ♌ requires a certain amount of respect, and submission from those workers in order to increase his sway and this in a less developed ♌ leads easily to pedantry and despotism, but in the more evolved is used to promote success of the aim in view.

Aquarius, the opposite of ♌, is of more 'democratic' tendencies and finds its greatest power in solidarity and friendship of those of the same mind. The "working capital" of ♒ is "brotherhood", which provides a constant inspiration to the workers when depressed. To ♒ all others are important and interesting but he will admire most those who have progressed furthest in living the brotherhood ideal. Like all airy signs ♒ is ideal by nature, but more even than the other three signs he tries to put his ideals into *practice*. But since ideals are usually „dreams of the future", more than the other airy signs ♒ will experience opposition—a thing which of course does not alter the "fixedness" of the conviction.

The Mutable Cross.

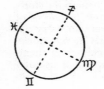

This cross is formed by the signs ♊, ♍, ♐ and ♓. The cardinal signs represent the word "initiative", and the fixed signs "capital" whilst the mutable signs symbolise *"work"*. Although every one of course has to work to a certain extent, the cardinal signs do so principally in order to become predominant and the fixed signs in order to seize some desired power. The mutable signs alone like work *for its own sake* and could not live without it. Here also is the distinction between + and — the *positive* signs ♊ and ♐ doing their work on the positive plane; the *negative* ♍ and ♓ being bound to the negative. The difficulty of the mutable or changeable signs lies in their inability to keep to the point; their interest goes also out to things outside their line and they always like to do things to which they are not called. This leads either to *genius* or to *failure*.

Gemini, the positively ruled sign of Mercury the "messenger of the Gods", has naturally an interest in everything; all "messages" of all "gods" are important and interesting to the ♊ man. He is sure to be wherever anything can be learned or picked up, and he continually studies and works out the problems he meets with. However little "education" a ♊ type may have had, he will make the impression of being generally well-informed. His knowledge is often scant and superficial, but shows that his mind has been active in all those directions and has formed an image of the whole. Though ♊, being an airy sign has its strongest point in the department of *thought*—reflection, deduction, execution—yet on the material plane nothing turns up without inducing ♊ to try his hand at it. For solid, practical work this type is less fit.

Sagittarius, as a fiery sign, always occupies itself with an ideal. The difference between ♐ and ♊ is, that ♊ with all his work does not know for certain what it will lead to, whereas ♐ has the inspiration of a definite thought always prompting him to action. Jupiter the ruler of ♐ gives him confidence that his ideal must in the end be victorious and that all circumstances must cooperate for good. This comforting certainty does not leave him even in the darkest times, and it is this characteristic that procures him a large number of friends willing to help him overcome critical junctures. Sagittarians like to stand in *full life;* they want space for their activity and listeners for their theories. As a rule they are more or less *philosophical,* but being one of the "changeable" signs, they are also able to fall into the opposite extreme and behave like *frolicsome foals* (♐ the Centaur as a matter of fact is closely related to the horse).

Virgo as a negative factor will be less creative than analytic and constructive in his work. Where there is neglect or destruction ♍ puts his hand, arranging everything systematically and constructively. That is why under this sign we find so many workers in laboratories, nurses and housewives. ♍ is the ministering angel of the cardinal and fixed signs which can always depend on the due execution they give of their orders and the care of any properties entrusted. As however Mercury rules this sign, though negatively, the ♍'s are usually endowed with *good brains* and *artistic inclinations;* but it is not always given to them to show this openly. In any case they look upon their knowledge and their art only as a means of serving others.

Pisces, the watery sign, reacts first of all to *"perceptions" of the feelings.*

6

Where a ♓ type feels that sorrow and misfortune are, he has but one longing, *to help*. Neither the desire for knowledge of ♊, nor the inspiration of ♐, nor the critical activity of ♍, but general human *compassion* is here the motive of all actions. The "Fishes" usually pursue their course quietly and are often not valued particularly highly by their fellow men, because they look upon themselves as "unworthy". *One gets to know the fishes when in need,* for the Fish himself only feels in his element when he can look after and console others. As, however, society at present has no room for such natures, a ♓ is apt to hide behind an other sign of his horoscope or not to take himself quite seriously in order to prevent others doing so. It is seldom or never that a "fish" dares to live out fully what he feels to be in him.

The Four Elements.

Another division of the zodiacal signs is according to the different elements—fire, earth, air, water—to which they belong.
The *fiery signs* are ♈, ♌, ♐:
the *earthy signs* ♉, ♍, ♑;
the *airy signs* ♊, ♎, ♒;
the *watery signs* ♋, ♏, ♓.
In this way therefore four *triangles* are formed each of which consists of one cardinal, one fixed and one mutable sign.

The Fiery Triangle.

Fire is in every philosophic and religious system, also in Christianity, the symbol of the *divine spirit,* the active, male, creative principle of live. The fiery signs are therefore all of them *positive;* they all have the consciousness that they have something divine in them and cannot but bear witness to it in the material world. Fire is called "the *Creator, Sustainer* and *Destroyer"* and when we regard the fiery trinity ♈—♌—♐ we easily recognise these three qualities.

Aries the cardinal sign naturally is the one in which the Divine Spark expresses itself as *Creative Power.* Aries is the Creator of new things, the pioneer, he who rings in a new era („a new *spring* and a new sound"). For that reason it is the first sign of the zodiac and the beginning of a new cycle, not only on the material plane, but also on a higher one (Easter, Resurrection). So it will be understood that Aries people though they are only the material expression of the Aries principle and even as such not pure, for it is influenced in many other ways, always promote new things likely to grow and expand, and always strive honestly and independently.

Leo as a fixed sign gives more the realisation of the mighty fire that not only creates but also *sustains.* He feels himself a ruler 'by the grace of God,' disposing of the weal or woe of those around him, claiming their admiration and adoration. ♌ is therefore, as a rule, more or less kingly, which in this material world may be expressed by the lowest, most childish despotism as well as by the noblest magnanimity. Leo is the radiant one, the giver; and it is a fact that a ♌-type—inasmuch as he is not transformed by other influences —is the example of a *sunny*, kind human being who can help others to keep their joy of live and energy—merely by his cheering presence.

Finally, *Sagittarius* in his mutability will not find satisfaction either by himself starting new things (♈), or by autocratic conduct in his own circle (♌). He does not recognise the ideal supporting him, as something "new" but as the real, the only true one that has always been, although it may seem to have been temporarily somewhat hidden among other things. ♐ feels convinced that he will find the same principle also in others, if he is able to *destroy* their self-sufficient calmness, their superficial prejudices and succeed in extracting what is good from their way of thinking. Therefore ♐ is by nature the philosopher, the explorer in spiritual and material things, the tutor and the missionary. He keeps a keen eye on every possibility of propagating his ideas. No blank in a conversation but ♐ begins to speak; no unexpected meeting but if possible ♐ starts enthusiastically on some topic of philosophic interest. If however the lower side of this sign is expressed, it produces those noisy people who continually talk about their success in sports and love, about their clubs and their flirtations.

The Earthy Triangle.

To man the *earth* is the acme of *solidity*, in both a figurative and literal sense *the ground under his feet*. The earthy signs ♉, ♍ and ♑ produce a being who believes in solidity, in palpable reality and in aims which are practically attainable. And as it is certain that we cannot get rid of matter except by controlling it, it is quite necessary that the element of earth should be represented in the Zodiac. There is, however, an ascending line in these three earthy signs beginning with the *fixed* sign, which is typically earthy.

Taurus, the Bull, symbolises the earth principle best. It is the bull who helps us to plough the fields in order that seed may be sown for a new harvest; the bull (or the cow) is the most important part of the husbandman's stock of cattle, in short the bull is indispensable to agricultural life. ♉ feels that he is one with the earth and for that reason evinces a great love for all that it produces. He feels safe in the lap of *"Mother Earth"* and, confident of her good care, he is of good cheer and liable to humour and jollity. "Were we not born under Taurus?" (Twelfth Night, Shakespeare.)

Just as the principal value of the earth is its capability of bringing the seeds entrusted to it to their full growth, so does the ♉-type realise that this earthly body exists as a temple containing higher things which must attain development through that very limitation.

Virgo as a mutable or changeable sign naturally feels that con-

8

nection between spirit and matter too, but owing to Mercury's influence is not so firm of conviction and devotion. ♍ is constantly concerned with the care of the "temple" for the sake of the "spirit"; then feels dissatisfied because he discerns so little of the spirit and therefore tries to lose himself in spiritual problems. The figure of *Martha* in the Bible is characteristic of ♍, very busy with earthly activities but nevertheless taking an interest in un-earthly matters, at the same time somewhat discontented at not being able to give much time to the latter. Virgo's powers of observation are as great in spiritual matters as in earthly, but it is worthy of notice that ♍ is more prone to lose sight of the principal line than of the smaller details. This type is therefore more fit to achieve conscientious work under the guidance of e.g. a cardinal sign, than to be himself the responsible leader.

Capricorn as a cardinal sign, realises that he cannot remain passive and inactive, but that he must be up and doing in order to get *out* of matter onto higher planes. But he who wants to conquer matter, suffers most by its resistance. If therefore ♑ is not strongly enough equipped, finally, after all his striving for higher things, he will become not the ruler *of* matter, but *in* matter i.e. not a *wise man,* but one *in a high position;* he will be able to show no inner, but only outer power.

The old name of ♑ is "makara", which means pentagon and is among other things the symbol of man. In the *Secret Doctrine,* where much of importance may be found about this sign, attention is drawn to the fact that this sign is related to the birth of the spiritual Microcosmos and the death or dissolution of the material universe, its passing into the spiritual (Secr. Doctrine part II p. 718). And if we bear in mind that Christ also was born when the ☉ was in ♑ (December 25) we may to some extent understand what mysteries are hidden in this zodiacal sign that once brought a "God-man" to birth.

The Airy Triangle.

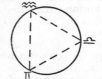

The element *air* symbolises man's *thoughts,* his *mental power.* It is the positive power which raises him *above the animal,* and it is noticeable that not one of the airy signs has an animal as a symbol. The air is the element most "apart from the earth" and thus people under this influence have the least inclination to earthly things. Usually the airy signs show an extraordinary disdain of earthly logic, and this is in some degree proved by ♊, but chiefly by ♒.

Gemini the first airy sign, is mutable, *changeable,* just as our first independent thoughts are always unstable and changeable. Gemini is however at the same time the sign most desirous of all-round development, and is apt for the time being to embrace the most contradictory theories which it leaves so soon as others seem better. The rapidity of thought is the inner side of ♊. For no sign is so sharp, so quick at repartee as this one; and even although difficulties may arise through superficiality of perception, a ♊ is able to disentangle himself very quickly! The *duality* of ♊ manifests itself in the first place in the nervous system: both extreme gladness and deep despondency are to be found in him (like the air which is easily rarified and condensed).

Libra, a cardinal sign, aims at the *balancing* of various existing thoughts. Where differences of opinion exist, ♎ takes the initiative to bring both parties together; listening first to one then to the other, ♎ considers how to bring the two into harmony. When he has an idea of his own, he always wishes to know what others think of it; not in order to reject his idea but to make it more balanced. When someone does not dare to express his opinion, ♎ will urge and stimulate him; he likes to point out the line the other has to follow in order to attain greater clarity, but he bewares of exerting too strong a pressure lest the other's personality should be influenced. This *prudence,* this tendency to approve of two different things at one and the same time easily tends in actual life towards that *indecision,* lately called by a scientific name "ergophoby" and the cardinal being is only shown by the power of *setting others to work for himself.*

Aquarius, the fixed airy sign as such is averse to all indecision. He has his fixed ideas, his *convictions firm as a rock* and acts accordingly, no matter whether all the world gape at him and disapprove. He considers his sudden impulses to be suggestions from above which he must obey unconditionally. When ♒ is morally far enough developed he may indeed gather wisdom, and the water which the "Waterbearer" pours from his jug onto the earth may truly be *water of life.* But for that reason it is doubly necessary to an ♒ *to keep himself under control.* He usually enjoys great popularity among his acquaintances and as a rule has much influence with them; so the *nature* of that influence will be of much importance. Like all fixed signs ♒ gives a tendency to self-assertion and it is noteworthy that with all its good qualities this sign has so little belief in the spiritual equality of others. It is advisable for ♒ — though it may seem paradoxal to him and his admirers — to see that his ideas and conceptions are as broad as possible.

The Watery Triangle.

The element *water* is the *negative, female* principle and symbolises *feelings, emotions,* therefore in the three signs forming this triangle, the element of feeling is prominent. "The sea is always full and spreads its waters on all sides" (Zohar)—and the watery signs are particularly sensitive to the sea of emotions in which they live, and readily contact others along the line of feeling.

Cancer, the cardinal sign shows this most conspicuously. Cancerians stress feeling as an *educational factor* and wish to act on this in the circle of their acquaintances. Their own way of observing and working exhibits the same principle "plus fait douceur que violence"; slow but sure, respecting others *but not yielding one of his own ideas.* ♋ goes ahead with his work imperceptibly making people act as he wishes. That this does not happen openly and that a ♋ even does not like to hear that he is influencing others, must be ascribed to the fact that ♋ loves to live in peace with all the world and is well aware that to exercise power openly often raises antipathy—and often brings about the reverse of the object desired.

♋ will help his people forward and patronize them, but in exchange desires their gratitude and respect just as he himself also displays unbounded gratitude and adoration for those to whom he owes his life, his position etc. Therefore ♋ is the sign of filial love, patriotism, attachment to tradition and relics, the sign of *reverence* and *submission.*

Scorpio, the fixed *watery* sign is under the influence of the *fiery* planet Mars which as a matter of course denotes strife between these opposing elements. Scorpio is therefore the sign where *feelings are put to the test,* where they must be purified in order to become of real, lasting worth. In practical life ♏ appears to us as the tempter, the seducer who puts to the test our feelings and our moral *"firmness"* and is temporarily able to overshadow our thoughts completely. When however the solution has been found, when the soul has stood the test, it rises as *re-born,* more powerful than ever. This sign therefore is connected with all kinds of occult mysteries and powers, as well as with sin and riotousness. This type *never* is *destitute of will;* the will may be used in every case, it is always a prominent feature of the ♏ character. And in this lies hidden the possibility of correction even from the worst depths.

Pisces, as a mutable sign, moves on the rise and fall of the sphere of feeling as a fish does in the water. More than any other this type is sensitive, *open to impressions and moods instigated from without.* If the surroundings are quiet and sympathetic, ♓ can be happy, satisfied, even *exceedingly jolly;* if, on the other hand those around him are nervous, agitated and restless he is at a loss how to act and makes a mess of things. And yet the ♓-type is so pleased to be of service to others; if only one knows how to play on his *feeling,* he will be found willing to do anything; for this watery sign lacking the support of the "cardinal" and the "fixed", is the most *feminine* of the twelve. And though the character it associates with is of great importance for each mutable or changeable sign, for ♓ it is most certainly of the highest importance. ♓, in order to find himself, must lose himself completely—but *not in somebody else*—which unfortunately often is the case.

III

The Houses of the Horoscope.

The houses of the horoscope denote the *different sections* of what we call our course of life such as our hobbies, pastimes, our relations with others, our own home etc. That with different people different parts occupy the most important place in life, is the consequence of the fact that in every horoscope another stress falls on these *"houses"*, as will be shown in some later pages of this book.

The *1st House* being connected with the first zodiacal sign ♈, denotes the *temperament* and to some extent also the health of the person concerned, his little ways (good and bad), in short his manner as shown to his fellow-men. If this house is important through position of planets, or through a strong ♈ influence, the manner is blunt, firm and *self-conscious,* the appearance being at the same time rather striking.

The *2nd House,* running parallel to ♉ the second zodiacal sign, denotes *earthly possessions,* personal property and the way this is increased and used. If this house occupies a prominent place, financial affairs will play a great part, for better or for worse according to the nature of the planets placed in it or being its ruler.

The *3rd House* connected with ♊, symbolises the way in which ideas from outside are received and assimilated, *education* therefore, and the results of it in the *family circle.* On the material plane the ♊-like movability shows itself in the taking of little trips and journeys which, however short, do not fail to enrich experience. A strong position of this house makes people intelligent, quick in movement, quick of expression.

The *4th House* corresponds to ♋ and represents the sphere of domesticity, *place of birth, family-tradition.* If this house is favourably occupied, domestic conditions are satisfactory and *at the end of life* pleasant memories will cause a cheerful mood. The relation to whichever of the parents who was most motherly by nature (apart from sex) is indicated by this house.

The *5th House* is the house of ♌ and symbolises both cordial relations with the other sex and enterprises undertaken at one's own risk and responsibility. ♌ must reach whatever his *heart* desires and therefore the fifth house shows us the actions and activities springing from *self-confidence* and *authority.* The *children* too, who fall under this heading of course, are indicated by this house.

12

The *6th House* correspondends to ♍ and is the house of the orderly and critical work that *seems insignificant and is yet so very important.* Under this heading come one's servants, domestics etc. who must be superintended continually in order that the work may go smoothly. Our first and foremost servant however, is *our own material body,* and this house gives details about its condition. If it is favourably occupied, everything tends to success and health is good; inharmonious occupation on the contrary indicates disappointments in the work and a weak constitution.

The *7th House,* opposite the 1st, brings contact with *the other pole,* with him or her who will be our partner or our husband (wife) and this house (♎) will by its conditions indicate whether those relations will be harmonious or not.

The *8th House,* opposite the 2nd, symbolises the *spiritual capital* gained; but since this does not show much before *death* or before a great trial has been passed through, this ♏-house is often called the house of death. It also indicates the material advantages or disadvantages in store for us after the death of our partner or of our relatives.

The *9th House,* opposite the 3rd, indicates the way in which inner considerations are confirmed, augmented and propagated in the world. As ♊ is the one who *is* educated, ♐ *wishes to teach and educate himself* and therefore this house denotes in what way one tries to expand one's own consciousness and that of other people. Not only spiritual but also *material explorations* come under this heading, aircraft for example. It is noteworthy that with airmen, motorists etc. the *philosophical* tendency of the 9th House usually degenerates into a *superstitious liking for all kinds of mascots.*

The *10th House,* opposite the 4th, is the house of *social position, calling,* place in the world. If this house is important in the horoscope, the person concerned belongs to the prominent people of society, to the *"upper ten".* Here moreover the relation with the most *"fatherly"* (♑) of the parents, the one who has cared most for *social* success, comes into prominence.

The *11th House,* opposite the 5th, denotes what impression the native's ♌-enterprises make on others, in other words the *friends* obtained in life. If the occupation of this house is favourable, friends will be ready to help and trustworthy, and have a great share in striving for and reaching the aim.

The *12th House,* corresponding to the sign ♓ and being opposite to the 6th House, leads man to *self-examination.* Not the mote in the eye of another (♍) but the beam in one's own eye should be found; and where the 6th House shows the native's servants, in this house he has to do all the work *himself.* Therefore the task of the 12th House often proves severe, but the most difficult battle is crowned by the most glorious victory. Happy the man who learns the lesson of this House well, he will be a blessing to his fellow-men.

IV

The Planets.

Deep within us blossoms, the Life, *the will to live,* seeking expression and radiating its essence in the **Sun;**
and as a reflex of the radiated light the *emotions* precipitate, as the **Moon** reflexes on the earth the light of the Sun.

But in order to guide the primitive tendencies man needs a *clear mind* of which **Mercury** is the messenger.

Thus the idea *harmony* awakes in man, who after having adjusted the balance within himself, aims at *harmonising his "self" with that of others, the opposite pole* **(Venus).**

Unfortunately, the ideal materialises; where peace was sought, *discord* and *strife* arise; man expelled from paradise must toil in the sweat of his brow **(Mars).**

Until *justice, mercy* and *philanthropy* awaken in man and the Prodigal returns to his Father—**Jupiter.**

Then the *earnestness* grows in man, wisdom, which discerns the simple principle in the most complicated forms, and he understands that the greatest power is hidden in the restraint of **Saturn.**

Not until we have reached *that,* can we endeavour to rule that which now rules us, the *supernatural knowledge* which comes to us through **Uranus—,**
and finally approach the *Sublimely-Divine,* in the sphere of **Neptune.**

The Sun (☉).

As the Sun is the *heart* and the *generator of our solar system,* so in our horoscope the Sun is the *pushing power of our earthly life.* It represents all that aspires, and the Sign in which it is placed manifests our *Individualities* [1]). As primitive man inclines to worship the Sun, so the ☉ in the horoscope indicates what we admire most and in what direction we prefer to strive. Also the house in which the ☉ is placed, is of very great importance in our development.

If the ☉ is favourably posited i.e. if it is placed in congenial signs or houses or if it receives strong harmonious aspects, then the circumstances are favourable for the development and the expression of the inner side; if, on the other hand the ☉ is posited in less harmonious houses or signs and is afflicted by one or more planets there will be clouds before its face, so that the flow of vital power is only felt in part.

One has more *self-confidence;* more *vitality,* more *influence on others* in proportion to the strength of the Sun; one is then less liable to influences from outside because one gives so much energy oneself. That is why the ☉ is weak in the signs naturally given to self-sacrifice and meekness. A "sunny" man does not know the word "sacrifice"; he gives of his own fulness because he cannot but do so, and the very giving procures him joy and ever increasing growth. *Leo* is above all sunny, radiating, rich, proud, generous; the ideal ruler who guides the good and the wicked by the force of his being, the strength of his warm heart.

The Moon (☽).

When the Sun has set and the earth is left in darkness, the Moon appears in the sky to hold like a mirror the rays of the descended Sun before our eyes. That is why the ☽ in our horoscope symbolises contemplative, sensitive thought; and the sign in which it is placed determines the nature of our emotions, of our *personality.* In the same manner as the ☽ gives the memory, the reflection of the Light that was, so through its influence we have our memory, our remembrance and the "longing" for what we have already experienced as pleasant, which is connected with it. In the case of children and people in the state of nature who live exclusively on their emotions, the ☽ therefore has much influence.

A strong position of the ☽ strengthens the memory and increases the ability to sense the feelings, moods and thoughts of the surroundings which are then used for spiritual enrichment.

Whereas "Sun"-people are able to help many of their fellowmen,

---

[1]) The two words "individuality" and "personality" are often used in quite a different sense; the latter is sometimes taken to be the real self and the former something characteristic added to it, some distinguishing detail. If however we bear in mind that the word *"individuum"* originally had the same significance as *"atom"*, and the word *"persona"* meant *"mask"* or *"part"* (rôle), we feel justified in our conception of the two ideas.

those with a harmoniously placed Moon *are themselves greatly helped by them.* Through their sensitiveness (negative) they unconsciously appeal to the protection of those more positively inclined, and therefore are able to go through life fairly easily. If, however, the ☽ is weakly or inharmoniously posited; it makes the native liable to domination by *the less developed.* For the ☽ favours indeed the growth of all that the ☉ germinates, but it also furthers the spreading of all kinds of poisonous gases.

This dual nature which both *gives* and *takes,* characteristic of the ☽ is found also in the sign ♋ which it rules; here too we find the wish to retain and yet to give everything; the mother who has given her child of her inmost being, but cannot renounce the child. (Cf. The Secret Doctrine, the relation between Moon and Earth.)

Mercury (☿).

This planet being nearest the Sun, appears to our eye as the messenger of the light and life of the Sun; as the Secret Doctrine (part II p. 669) says "Leaving the king of heaven (the Sun) I come to you, mortals, to help you".

☿ therefore brings us the light of the Sun in the form of *logical mind, pure mind* through which we, mortals, are able to illuminate our store of ☽ experiences, to arrange and order them so that we may get some idea of their nature and the way in which they may be used. As, however, the effect of this "light" depends on what *"is lighted"* (i.e. the experiences) it is evident that ☿ is called a "changeable" or "adaptable" planet. See for example the verse:

"There were six men of Hindostan
To learning much inclined
Who liked to see the elephant
Though all of them were blind", etc.

One bumps up against the elephant's body and receives the impression of a large, heavy wall; another feeling the trunk comes to the conclusion that the creature resembles a snake; the third comes in contact with a leg and calls the elephant a tree and so forth.

Similarly we do not *all get the same mental insight* from ☿ as we do get *the same instinct of life* from the ☉, but what we receive *adapts itself to that which we have obtained already.*

The sign through which the ☿ influence reaches us indicates the way in which our mind works and what attracts it most. And it goes without saying that this planet feels most at home in the signs ♊ and ♍ the nature of which is *observant* and *discriminating;* in ♊ its positive effect manifests in ability to observe and survey, in ♍ its negative side in arranging, ordering, purifying.

16

Venus (♀).

Venus is looked upon as *"the occult sister, the 'alter ego' of the Earth"*. (The Secret Doctrine part I p. 387) and as such instils into us also the longing for a *"twin-soul"*, an"other self"; inspires feelings of love, affection and companionship. So ♎ too, the sign which ♀ rules (positively) is *two in one,* the *two* scales without which the balance has no reason for existence; a *unity* in distinction to the pronounced duality of the signs ♊ and ♓.

What we love is *good* in our eyes, but *beautiful* also; is not „Ich liebe dich" immediately followed by „mich reizt deine schöne Gestalt" (Erlkönig)! And so this accounts for ♀ giving, together with the feeling of love, the sense of beauty, harmony and rythm and a taste for works of art in which various contrasts are balanced.

If ♀ is strongly placed in a horoscope, it bestows great *sensitiveness* with regard to both people and things, it gives the intuition to place a thing exactly where it should be, to give to people that of which they are most in need.

In ♉ the sign where the negative side of ♀ is ruler, the opposite comes to the fore; here *receptivity* for inspiration is present, and the instinct to continue to adore what once was admired or accepted. ♎ (positive) is he who adapts and re-adapts according to ever changing circumstances —if afflicted: whimsicalness; ♉ (negative) the faithfulness to the chosen person or thing notwithstanding all change—if afflicted: stubbornness.

Mars (♂).

Mars, the *"Stronghold of God"*, *"Saint Michael"* the fighter against evil, bestows on us a feeling of honesty, integrity and the *moral courage* to defend our insight and our beliefs against people of different opinion. He propagates ideas of Truth and Light, defeats falsehood and darkness (the dragon), in short at all times he stands for the Right.

As *Prometheus* he brings us the fire of the Sun, and since by means of fire infinitely delicate instruments are made he is also a furtherer of evolution.

Martial energy leads to *deeds,* and *experience is the best teacher.* The martial battle teaches us what we are worth, to what degree our theories (☿) and our ideals (♀) are not only a beautiful dream but our inalienable possession.

The idea of *propagation,* inherent in ♂, becomes also *physical propagation* in the material world and thus ♂ is the planet of passion in contrast to ♀ the planet of ideal love.

A strongly posited ♂ denotes a great longing for manifestation and creation; if ♂ is weakly or inharmoniously placed this is perverted into despotism and egoism; the battle is fought *for the sake of fighting* and instruments ingeniously devised are used for *destruction* of what is good and useful. The sign ruled by the positive side of ♂ is ♈, the Ram, apt to attack everyone who waylays his herd; the pioneer, fighting in the foremost ranks; the negative side of ♂ manifests in ♏ the sign of *inner* battle, of inner destruction and construction.

Jupiter (♃).

Jupiter is represented to us in Greek mythology as the *"father of the gods"* in "The Secret Doctrine" as "Father Ether" and since ether permeates everything in the Cosmos, it is evidently the fatherly creative and sustaining force.

Therefore ♃ in our horoscope symbolises belief, faith in *Providence, omnipresent,* through which we receive all we need. People with a strongly posited ♃ do not worry, they keep their faith and optimism under all circumstances, a thing which in itself is favourable for those among whom they live. ♃ inspires thoughts of plenty and happiness, divine worship and charity ("All mankind become brothers, where thy gentle wings may rest", again "Brothers, above the starry canopy, there must dwell a loving Father"; Lied an die Freude, Schiller).

As ether is omnipresent, ♃ is also the all-wise, the righteous, the merciful one. He is however at the same time the "God of thunder and lightning" („Jupiter Tonans") and at the sight of deeds of injustice will be filled with indignation and wrath which speedily seize suitable means to punish the criminal.

In ♐ the positive side of ♃ is operative and indeed this sign most reflects the character of ♃, in its idealistic religious-philosophic aspect. In ♓, now placed under the rule of ♆ we again find the negative side of ♃ whose *omniscience leads to complete forgiveness.*

Saturn (♄).

Satan (♄) is the Watcher on the Threshold of the Temple of the King; he stands in Solomon's porch, he keeps the keys of the sanctuary (The Secret Doctrine part II p. 285). ♄ is the last of the 7 planets belonging to our system, the circumference of that realm of which the Sun is the centre, it is the planet of *limitation,* of temptation and purification and therefore its effects in our lives are felt to be hindrance, opposition, trial. "He binds in fetters and limits all things" and *through that very limitation* gives us a clear conception of what lies before us.

♄ takes away from us our social ballast, our friends, our deceptive pleasures and leads us willingly or unwillingly into solitude, where the "Voice of the Silence" may be heard.

Therefore ♄ is the friend of those who thirst for insight and intensification of life; but to those who seek *themselves* and turn away from higher things, he is the inexorable judge able to compel and to destroy— until in the end man comes to understand his language and blesses the iron hand that has guided him. For not until we have understood ♄ can we cross the threshold.

♑ is the sign which corresponds to the positive ♄-nature. It is the sign of the solitary seeker, difficult to understand, limited in his hope, limited in his courage to live, who usually only surmises and does not fully appreciate the strange Angel in his heart. On the other hand, in ♒ ruled by the negative side of ♄ there is some inkling of what ♄ can give when once he has become our friend, and a vague idea that ♄ cannot be such a bugbear as he appears; thus ♅ is admitted as co-ruler.

Uranus (♅).

Although ♄ has robbed his father ♅ of the dominion of the world, as Greek mythology put it, although matter has conquered spirit in the material world—yet spirit exists and is ever in matter, being its inspirer, motive power, and *ruler,* though unknown and not understood. Although according to our false idea matter is omnipotent, it is subject to laws which are beyond material conceptions, for the concrete power of observation can only see results, not *causes.* In order to discern the latter one must look further than ♄, *the angel of manifested worlds* and enter the sphere of ♅. This sphere may be approached by the path of *feeling* as well as that of *intellect,* but this can only be achieved when the motives are sufficiently purged of material desires. Unless this purification has been undertaken, those who follow the line of feeling will only attain anarchism and immorality; whilst those who follow the intellectual line will be blocked in their theories about atoms, electrons, nerves etc., if they have not first passed the threshold watched by ♄.

Therefore neither *"affinity of soul"* and similar means of making *personal-material* circumstances more pleasant, nor *electro-dynamic* or *occult* hypotheses avail, so long as *social advantage* or *personal power* is the aim sought; on the contrary so long as these hold sway ♅ leads to most undesirable consequences.

We find the same difficulty in the sign ♒ where the result of ♅'s influence is *good* if ♄ has been *conquered,* and *bad* if the *selfishness* peculiar to Saturn hinders the higher evolution of ♅ ideas.

Neptune (♆).

Even more remote from us, figuratively as well as actually, is the sphere of ♆, the ruler of "water", the all-pervading space out of which everything came into existence, when "the Spirit of God moved upon the face of the waters" as we read in Genesis. "Water" is generally regarded as the element of feeling, the feminine element. The Secret Doctrine draws attention to the word Mater (mother) from which the letter M is derived. It originates in 𓈖, an Egyptian hieroglyph for "water", called *the universal matrix* or *the great Depth.*

Being the ruler of this element ♆ renders those who are able to react to its influence, exceedingly sensitive to impressions from outside; and the more primitive, the more unconscious, the *less pronounced* they are, the greater that sensitiveness will be. Water as the source of all that exists, contains within itself also the origin of every thought, every action; therefore ♆ is somewhere called the *"God of the faculty of judgment"*.

Therefore ♆ may lead to that height of "knowing" and "understanding" where "all is forgiven"; but with the many who are not free from earthly-mindedness (♃), ♆'s influence is shown only in vague, ecstatic, sceptical, uncontrolled states, which—according to the development of the person concerned—may lead to *religious mania, intemperance, dancing mania,* or *indulgence in narcotics*. An experienced eye will recorgnise even in these perversities the typical ♆-impulse to *dissolution, unity, divinity*.

♓ is the sign ruled by ♆ and here, too, we find the longing for collective upliftment in a vaster, loftier consciousness, although actually the person concerned would *have to sacrifice himself* completely (cf. the ideals of christianity which is so strongly affected by ♓). In a lower aspect, however, a ♓-type will thoughtlessly throw himself away (sacrifice himself) for inferior aims.

V

How to calculate a Horoscope.

Standard time — Local time — Summer time — Greenwich time.

The Ephemerides (astronomic tables) necessary for the calculation of horoscopes are found in

Veen's tables for calculating the horoscopes of those born between the years 1847 and 1926[1]).

We shall try to explain as simply as possible with the aid of these tables how to calculate horoscopes, leaving out some corrections which make the calculation unnecessarily difficult.

When after further study the student is able to calculate exactly, he will perceive that the miscalculation of some seconds of time or arc-minutes made by our method is of no particular importance in judging a horoscope.

The application of our method is likely to help many who have no talent for mathematics but who may often prove to have a good discernment in astrology.

We know that wherever we live, in the middle of the day the Sun is in the *meridian*. Every place has its own line of meridian. The more eastward a place is on the earth, the earlier the sun will rise and the sooner it passes the meridian of that place. In places situated east of our dwelling-place it is later than with us — the sun there rose earlier.

To indicate a place on earth *the meridian of Greenwich* is taken as zero or standard meridian. If the time at Greenwich is 12 o'clock at noon, at a place 5 degrees east of Greenwich it will be 20 minutes later. The reason is that every circle, therefore also the circumference of the earth contains 360 degrees and the earth revolves around its axis in 24 hours. Therefore it moves 15 degrees in 1 hour, or 1 degree in 4 minutes. A difference in time of 4 minutes must thus be reckoned for every degree East or West of Greenwich.

For the whole of Holland we have assumed it to be noon when the Sun reaches its highest point (culminationpoint) in the meridian of Amsterdam. Amsterdam is situated 5 degrees to the East of Greenwich.

---

[1]) Published by P. Dz. Veen, Amersfoort (Holland).

So the clocks throughout Holland indicate 5 × 4 minutes that is 20 minutes later than at Greenwich.

In Germany the *Standard time* is taken to be the time of the highest position of the Sun (its culminationpoint) in the meridian of Görlitz, situated 15 degrees to the East of Greenwich. Therefore throughout Germany the clocks indicate 60 minutes later than at Greenwich.

It will be clear that by accepting a *Standard time* in a large country such as Germany, extending beyond 17 degrees of longitude, the precise *local time* — that is the time calculated according to the Sun's culminating in the meridian *of the place* — may be very different from the accepted Standard time of the whole country.

The next table indicates the difference in time between the *local time* and times before or after Greenwich time of some of the important towns in England.

Time Correction before (sub) or after (add) Greenwich time.

		min. sec.			min. sec.			min. sec.
London	sub.	0.0	Leeds	sub.	6.9	Bridgewater	sub.	12.—
Boston		0.0	Warwick		6.20	Cardiff		12.40
Lewes		0.0	Newcastle		6.28	Edinburgh		12.42
Grimsby		0.0	Bradford		7.—	Swansea		15.54
Brighton		0.36	Salisbury		7.10	Barnstaple		16.—
Hull		1.21	Birmingham		7.36	Plymouth		16.32
Lincoln		2.8	Poole		8.—	Glasgow		17.11
Windsor		2.22	Cheltenham		8.16	Paisley		17.40
Reading		4.—	Wolverhampton		8.28	Falmouth		20.—
York		4.18	Worcester		8.48	Dublin		24.52
Portsmouth		4.24	Manchester		8.59			
Rugby		4.24	Bristol		10.24			
Doncaster		4.30	Shrewsbury		11.—	Cambridge	add.	0.23
Nottingham		4.33	Chester		11.34	Folkestone		4.43
Leicester		4.48	Carlisle		11.44	Norwich		5.12
Sheffield		5.56	Liverpool		12.—	Dover		5.20
Southampton		6.2	Newport		12.—	Yarmouth		6.55

Smaller places situated at the same Longitude have the same difference in time between Greenwich as that given in the table.

In the *U. S. of America* we find:

1. *The eastern-time-zone.* Here the Standard-time is regulated to the meridian of 75° westward of Greenwich, which is 75 × 4′ = 5 hours earlier than Greenwich-time.

In this zone are situated the following towns e.g.

Baltimore 77° W.

Washington 77° W.

Philadelphia 75° W.

New York 74° W.

Boston 71° W.

2. *The central-time-zone.* Here the Standard-time is regulated to the meridian of 90° Westward of Greenwich, which is 90 × 4′ = 6 hours earlier than Greenwich-time.

In this zone are situated the following towns e. g.

Columbia 92° W. Cincinnati 84° W.
Chicago 87° W. Detroit 83° W.

3. *The mountain-time-zone.* Here the Standard-time is regulated to the meridian of 105° Westward of Greenwich, which is 105 × 4′ = 7 hours earlier than Greenwich-time.

In this zone is situated Denver 105° W.

4. *The pacific-time-zone.* Here the Standard-time is regulated to the meridian of 120° Westward of Greenwich, which is 120 × 4′ = 8 hours earlier than Greenwich-time.

In this zone are situated the following towns e. g.

San Francisco 122° W.
Los Angeles 118° W.
Salt Lake City 112° W.

Each of these time-zones contains fifteen degrees of longitude, being the distance which the sun passes through in one hour.

In a town situated on the Meridian of 75°, 90°, 105°, 120°, such as e. g. Philadelphia 75° W., Standard-time is the same as localtime; but in Chicago which lies 87°, that is 3° eastwards of the 90° Meridian, the difference of the Standard- with the local-time is 3 × 4′ = 12′.

In most of the countries of Europe since 1916 we have had a so called Summer-time during the summermonths [1]). It is evident that the stars do not take this arbitrarily changed time into account and therefore, when the Summertime at birth is given, this must be reduced to the *exact* local *Solar time.* Before proceeding to calculate the horoscope of a person born in the summermonths since 1916, one has to make sure whether or not the time given is the artificially fixed Summertime.

Veen's Tables give the positions of the planets — including Sun and Moon — for Greenwich at 12 o'clock at noon. Obviously in order to arrive at the exact positions in the Birth-Horoscope, the moment of birth must be reduced to Greenwich time.

[1])
1916. May 21st, 2.0 a.m., to October 1st, 2.0 a.m.
1917. April 8th, 2.0 a.m., to September 17th, 2.0 a.m.
1918. March 24th, 2.0 a.m., to September 30th, 2.0 a.m.
1919. March 30th, 2.0 a.m., to September 29th, 2.0 a.m.
1920. March 28th, 2.0 a.m., to October 25th, 2.0 a.m.
1921. April 3rd, 2.0 a.m., to October 3rd, 2.0 a.m.
1922. March 26th, 2.0 a.m., to October 8th, 2.0 a.m.
1923. April 22nd, 2.0 a.m., to September 16th, 2.0 a.m.
1924. April 13th, 2.0 a.m., to September 21st, 2.0 a.m.
1925. April 19th, 2.0 a.m., to October 4th, 2.0 a.m.
1926. April 18th. 2.0 a.m., to September 19th, 2.0 a.m.

We were born at a certain place on the earth. This place is the centre where Cosmic law affects us.

In a birth-horoscope the centre of the circle of the horoscope represents our place of birth at the moment of birth around which the Sun, Moon and planets in the Zodiac revolve. Their positions are described in a circle.

At our birth, to the *East* of our native place, a sign of the Zodiac was rising. To the *West* one was setting.

The line from East to West is the line of demarcation between that which is visible and invisible, i.e. which has set.

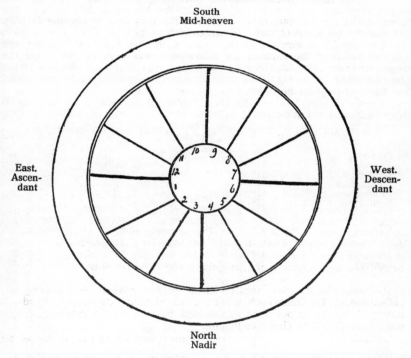

The *Rising Sign* is called the *Ascendant;* the *Setting Sign* the *Descendant.*

The *South-point* or point of culmination of the Sun in the Meridian of our native place is called *Mid-heaven (Medium Coeli);*

the *North-point Nadir,* or *Imum Coeli;* here the Sun is at midnight. Each quadrant of 90 degrees is subdivided into three parts of 30 degrees, therefore we divide the horoscope into twelve equal parts, called *the twelve houses of the horoscope.*

The six lines dividing the Horoscope-figure into twelve parts *(houses)* *are assumed* to be drawn with the native place as centre.

The *Houses* represent the native's *earthly circumstances.* Each house provides the key to a special *subdivision* of them, as mentioned on pp. 11—13.

The earth revolves upon its axis in 24 hours, therefore all 12 Zodiacal Signs and the Planets pass the horizon of a definite place on the earth in 24 hours. Thus on the *Eastern horizon,* every two hours another Sign arises which is called the *Rising Sign.*

The first House begins with the Rising Sign, the 10th is to the left of the Meridian, the 9th to the right of the Meridian, the 7th is in the West above the horizon. In the annexed diagram of a horoscope (p. 23), the Houses are indicated by the numbers 1 to 12.

The points of contact of the lines with the circle are called the *angular points* of the Houses, the *Horns* or *Cusps.* In order to insert the degrees of the Zodiacal Signs on the Cusps, the *Tables of Houses* which are calculated according to *Placidus'* method [1]) are used; they can be had for different degrees Northern and Southern Latitude.

Veen's Tables 1847—1926 give Tables of Houses of 10, 40 and 50 degrees Northern Latitude.

---

[1]) *RAPHAEL'S TABLES OF HOUSES FOR GREAT BRITAIN CONTAINS*
TABLES

for Plymouth	50° N. 22';		for Belfast	54° N. 34';
Taunton	51° N. 1';		Newcastle-on-Tyne	54° N. 59';
London	51° N. 32';		Ayr	55° N. 28';
Buckingham	51° N. 59';		Glasgow	55° N. 53';
Birmingham	52° N. 28';		Dundee	56° N. 28';
Nottingham	52° N. 57';		Aberdeen	57° N. 9';
Liverpool	53° N. 25';		Inverness	57° N. 29';
Hull	53° N. 45';		Wick	58° N. 27';
York	53° N. 58';		Orkney Isles	59° N. 0';

RAPHAEL'S TABLES OF HOUSES FOR NORTH LATITUDES. 2°—59°.

for Madras	13° N. 0';		for Tokio	35° N. 39';
Bombay	19° N. 0';		Algiers	36° N. 48';
„	20° N. 0';		Athens	37° N. 58';
„	21° N. 0';		Lisbon	38° N. 48';
Mandalay	21° N. 59';		Pekin	39° N. 54';
Calcutta	22° N. 33';		New York	40° N. 43';
Canton	23° N. 12';		Rome	41° N. 54';
Amoy	24° N. 27';		Sofia	42° N. 42';
Benares	25° N. 19';		Toronto	43° N. 40';
Lucknow	26° N. 51';		Belgrade	44° N. 48';
Agra	27° N. 10';		Montreal	45° N. 30';
Delhi	28° N. 40';		Geneva	46° N. 12';
Cairo	30° N. 2';		Buda Pest	47° N. 29';
Alexandria	31° N. 12';		Vienna	48° N. 14';
Jerusalem	31° N. 46';		Paris	48° N. 50';
Nagasaki	32° N. 45';		Prague	50° N. 5';
Bagdad	33° N. 20';		Petrograd	59° N. 56';
Cabul	34° N. 30';		(Helsingfors)	

These Tables are serviceable *for all places in or near these Latitudes, and in any part of the world.*

W. Foulsham & Co., Ltd. 10 & 11. Red Lion Court, Fleetstreet. E. C. 4. London.

In order to calculate a horoscope we must know what the *Sidereal Time* was at the place and moment for which that horoscope is required. The sidereal time indicates how long *ago* it is at that moment that the *vernal point* passed the meridian of that place.

The average Sidereal Time for 12 o'clock local time is on:

	Jan.	Feb.	Mrt	Apr.	Mei	Jun.	Jul.	Aug.	Sep.	Oct.	Nov.	Dec.
1	18 43	20 45	22 36	24 38	2 36	4 39	6 37	8 39	10 42	12 40	14 42	16 40
2	18 47	20 49	22 40	24 42	2 40	4 43	6 41	8 43	10 45	12 44	14 46	16 44
3	18 51	20 53	22 44	24 46	2 44	4 47	6 45	8 47	10 49	12 48	14 50	16 48
4	18 55	20 57	22 48	24 50	2 48	4 51	6 49	8 51	10 53	12 52	14 54	16 52
5	18 59	21 1	22 52	24 54	2 52	4 54	6 53	8 55	10 57	12 55	14 58	16 56
6	19 3	21 5	22 56	24 58	2 56	4 58	6 57	8 59	11 1	12 59	15 2	17 00
7	19 7	21 9	23 00	1 2	3 0	5 2	7 1	9 3	11 5	13 3	15 6	17 4
8	19 11	21 13	23 3	1 6	3 4	5 6	7 5	9 7	11 9	13 7	15 10	17 8
9	19 15	21 17	23 7	1 10	3 8	5 10	7 9	9 11	11 13	13 11	15 13	17 12
10	19 19	21 21	23 11	1 14	3 12	5 14	7 12	9 15	11 17	13 15	15 17	17 16
11	19 23	21 25	23 15	1 13	3 16	5 18	7 16	9 19	11 21	13 19	15 21	17 20
12	19 26	21 29	23 19	1 22	3 20	5 22	7 20	9 23	11 25	13 23	15 25	17 24
13	19 31	21 33	23 23	1 26	3 24	5 26	7 24	9 27	11 29	13 27	15 29	17 28
14	19 35	21 37	23 27	1 29	3 28	5 30	7 28	9 30	11 33	13 31	15 33	17 31
15	19 39	21 41	23 31	1 33	3 32	5 34	7 32	9 34	11 37	13 35	15 37	17 35
16	19 43	21 45	23 35	1 37	3 36	5 38	7 36	9 38	11 41	13 39	15 41	17 39
17	19 46	21 49	23 39	1 41	3 40	5 42	7 40	9 42	11 45	13 43	15 45	17 43
18	19 50	21 53	23 44	1 45	3 44	5 46	7 44	9 46	11 48	13 47	15 49	17 47
19	19 54	21 57	23 48	1 49	3 47	5 50	7 48	9 50	11 52	13 51	15 53	17 51
20	19 58	22 1	23 52	1 53	3 51	5 54	7 52	9 54	11 56	13 55	15 57	17 55
21	20 2	22 4	23 56	1 57	3 55	5 58	7 56	9 58	12 00	13 59	16 1	17 59
22	20 6	22 8	23 59	2 1	3 59	6 2	8 00	10 2	12 4	14 3	16 5	18 3
23	20 10	22 12	24 2	2 5	4 3	6 5	8 4	10 6	12 8	14 6	16 9	18 7
24	20 14	22 16	24 6	2 9	4 7	6 9	8 8	10 10	12 12	14 10	16 13	18 11
25	20 18	22 20	24 10	2 13	4 11	6 13	8 12	10 14	12 16	14 14	16 17	18 15
26	20 22	22 24	24 14	2 17	4 15	6 17	8 16	10 18	12 20	14 18	16 20	18 19
27	20 26	22 28	24 18	2 21	4 19	6 21	8 20	10 22	12 24	14 22	16 24	18 23
28	20 30	22 32	24 22	2 25	4 23	6 25	8 23	10 26	12 28	14 26	16 28	18 27
29	20 34		24 25	2 29	4 27	6 29	8 27	10 30	12 32	14 30	16 32	18 31
30	20 38		24 30	2 33	4 31	6 33	8 31	10 34	12 36	14 34	16 36	18 35
31	20 42		24 34		4 35		8 35	10 38		14 38		18 38

As the *Ecliptic* — the circle in which Sun, Moon and Planets apparently move — forms a certain angle with the *Equator of the earth,* the division of the Zodiac in the Twelve Houses of the Horoscope is not equal.

We observe the ecliptic as an arc which meets the Horizon at an angle and this causes an unequal division of that arc and therefore of the Signs in the Twelve Houses of the Horoscope. This division depends on the Geographical Latitude at which the birth took place.

The 12 Signs and 12 Houses coincide with each other at the Equator, but as soon as we go north or south (i.e. are at Northern or Southern Latitude) we see irregularity which increases towards either the North or Southpole. Consequently along the sectors of the houses (30°) which we assume to be drawn across the earth, we perceive greater and smaller parts of the Zodiac pass, according as we move further from the Equator.

A Sign which is not intersected by any of the Cusps is called an *intercepted* Sign. And near the Poles three signs may be intercepted in one House, whereas another sign might reach over a couple of Houses.

Fo fill in the Zodiacal Signs and the degrees on the Cusps we can make use of the Table of Houses calculated for the latitude of the birth-place. There we find next to the *Sidereal Time* which we have calculated by reducing the local time of the hour of birth to sidereal time, the Cusps of the Houses 10, 11, 12, Ascendant (1), 2, 3. The opposite Signs and the same degrees are placed on the opposite Cusps of the Houses 4, 5, 6, Descendant (7), 8, 9.

In order to distinguish them we write the *intercepted Signs* over the arc of the House. To fill in the planets we refer to the example specimen on p. 28.

The Aspects.

The ☉, ☽ and planets may influence each other *harmoniously* or *inharmoniously* according to their position in respect to each other or the *aspect,* as it is called, which they form with each other.

A *harmonious aspect* is formed when they are at a distance from each other of *120* degrees i. e. when they are placed in the same degree of Signs belonging to one element (see p. 6); as there are e. g. ☉ in 10° ♈, ♂ 10° ♌, ♃ 10° ♐; (☉ △ ♂ △ ♃) or
☽ 2° ♎, ♀ 2° ♒, ♅ 2° ♊ (☽ △ ♀ △ ♅).
A harmonious aspect is also formed when 2 planets are at a distance of 60 degrees i. e. when they are placed in the same degree of Signs, belonging to two differents element which harmonise, such as *Fire* and *Air, Earth* and *Water.*
e.g. ♂ in 21° ♈ and ♀ 21° ♊ (♂ ✶ ♀) or ☽ 15° ♓ and ♃ 15° ♉ (☽ ✶ ♃).

An inharmonious aspect is formed by planets at a distance from each other of 90° or 180°, i. e. in the same degree of Signs belonging to the same 'cross' (see p. 2), such as the *cardinal signs,* the *fixed signs,* the *mutable signs.*
e.g. the ☉ in 6° ♈ is in inharmonious aspect to ♃ 6° ♋ and so to ♂ in 6° ♎ (☉ □ ♃ ☍ ♂).

We distinguish the following aspects:

conjunction or coming together i.e.	at	0	degrees	'distance
semi-sextile	„	30	„	„
sextile	„	60	„	„
square	„	90	„	„
trine	„	120	„	„
inconjuction	„	150	„	„
opposition	„	180	„	„

The way in which the aspect manifests depends on the nature of the planets aspecting each other.

A *conjunction* (☌) may be either *harmonious* or *inharmonious.*
It is obvious that e.g. ♀ and ♂ in one House will not be able to live in complete harmony, whereas ☿ and ♀ will harmonise especially in aesthetical matters.

A *semi sextile aspect* (⊻) causes all kinds of *plans* to rise according to the nature of the planets aspecting each other, plans which cannot at the time be carried out.

A *sextile aspect* (*) makes the proposed aim clearer than does the semi-sextile, but not until the struggle for life begins, symbolised by the square aspect, will the scheme be realised effectually.

A *square aspect* (□) expresses continuous *competition;* first one, then the other is master.

The *trine aspect* (△) brings *harvest,* — the result of former work, — close near the door.

The *inconjunction* (⊼) indicates troubles, objections to what is reached.

An *opposition* (☍) renders it difficult to maintain *inner balance.* It leads to the necessity to forego some physical possession (the nature of which is indicated by the Houses); the loss often leaves an dissatisfied feeling, a regret, that one has not tried sufficiently to arrive at a mutual understanding.
If something is expelled instead of being brought into harmony, the task remains for the next incarnation.

In order *to judge character* by means of the horoscope, we limit ourselves to the aspects of conjunction (☌), sextile (*), trine (△), square (□) and opposition (☍).

The astrologers set limits of influence (Orbs) to the aspects and call e.g. ♂ 4° ♈ in □ aspect to ☿ 6° ♑, or ☽ 12° ♎ in △ aspect to ♃ 15° ♒ [1]). These orbs should be taken not larger than 6 degrees when the planets recede, and 10 degrees when they approach each other.

As the earth revolves upon its axis, the *Signs* move from East to West.
The Planets move by their own progression in the Signs from East to West in the *Day-section* of the Horoscope and from West to East in the *Night*-section.

Should a harmonious and an inharmonious aspect act *simultaneously,* the inharmonious manifestation may to a great extent be neutralised by the harmonious action.

---

[1]) The effect is somewhat modified if an aspect falls in one of the last degrees of one sign and one of the first degrees of another; for instance a square aspect between two planets -one of which is placed in 29° ♊ and the other in 2° ♎ will not be very inharmonious, as these signs are congenial (air signs)'; on the other hand a trine aspect in 1° ♉—28° ♌ (earth and fire) is not quite harmonious. Such Orbs must be assumed to be less, not more than 3°.

VI

Specimen of Calculating a Horoscope.

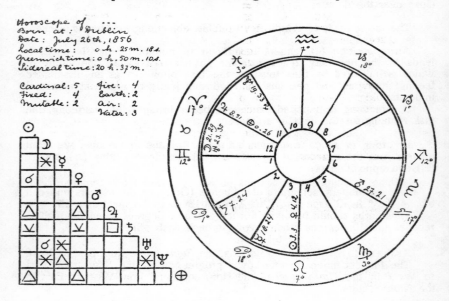

Horoscope of ...
Born at: Dublin
Date: July 26th, 1856
Local time: 0 h. 25 m. 18 s.
Greenwich time: 0 h. 50 m. 10 s.
Sidereal time: 20 h. 37 m.

Cardinal: 5   Fire: 4
Fixed: 4   Earth: 2
Mutable: 2   Air: 2
Water: 3

The birth took place at Dublin.

Dublin lies 53° 20′ Northern latitude and 6° 13′ Westward of Greenwich.

The time at Greenwich is 24 m. 52 sec. later than at Dublin (see list p. 21). At the moment of birth it is therefore

$$0 \text{ h. } 25 \text{ m. } 18 \text{ s.}$$
$$\text{add} \quad \underline{24 \text{ m. } 52 \text{ s.}}$$
$$0 \text{ h. } 50 \text{ m. } 10 \text{ s. Greenwich-time.}$$

We must now look up what *sidereal time* it was at the moment of birth 0 h. 25 m. In the table (see p. 25) we find for July 25th. S. T. 8 h. 12 m. The birth

took place at 0 h. 25 m. *local time*. At the moment of birth it was therefore
8 h. 12 m.
add 12 h. 25 m.
20 h. 37 m. sidereal time.

In Veen's Table of Houses for 50 degrees northern latitude which we may use, for the greater part of Ęngeland [1]) we find the sidereal hour 20 h. 37 m. nearest to 20 h. 38 m. Next to it we find the cusps of the houses in the columns 10, 11, 12, Ascendant, 2, 3.

The opposite signs and degrees are on the opposite cusps [2]).

We thus find the signs and degrees on the cusps of

	10th	house	7°	♒		4th	house	7°	♌
	11th	„	3°	♓		5th	„	3°	♍
	12th	„	17°	♈		6th	„	17°	♎
Ascendant	1st	„	12°	♊	Descendant	7th	„	12°	♐
	2nd	„	1°	♋		8th	„	1°	♑
	3rd	„	18°	♋		9th	„	18°	♑

We now fill in the signs and degrees on the cusps of the houses *on a horoscope form* (see above p. 28).

If we then compare the succession of zodiacal signs we see that in the 12th house the sign ♉ is lacking and in the 6th house the sign ♏, opposite ♉ therefore we put the symbols of these signs *aslant* in the houses, to show that these signs are not traversed by the cusps of these houses, but are *intercepted* signs (see p. 25).

We now calculate the positions of the planets at the moment of birth.

The Sun (☉) see Standard-Sun-Table in Veen's Tables 1847-1926 p. 1.

is placed July 20th 27° 20' Cn (♋)
July 30th 6° 53' Le (♌)

In the table: *Differences in minutes for the year 1856* we find that for 1856, after Febr. 29th we must add 27 minutes to the positions mentioned in the Standard Sun Table.

---

[1]) See footnote p. 24

The Table of Houses for 10° *Northern Latitude* of Veen's Tables may be used for places of *Southern Latitude* by adding 12 hours to the Sidereal Time of the moment of birth. What we get then is the Sidereal Time, and we must take then the opposite signs on the Cusps. The Asc. of the Table becomes the Descendant etc.

[2]) We should bear in mind that opposite

Aries	— Ar (♈)	lies	Li (♎)	— Libra
Taurus	— Ta (♉)	„	Sc (♏)	— Scorpio
Gemini	— Ge (♊)	„	Sa (♐)	— Sagittarius
Cancer	— Cn (♋)	„	Ca (♑)	— Capricorn
Leo	— Le (♌)	„	Aq (♒)	— Aquarius
Virgo	— Vi (♍)	„	Pi (♓)	— Pisces

We get thus for the Sun's position on July 20th 1856   27° 47′ ♋
and on July 30th 1856   7° 20′ ♌

The motion of the Sun in 10 days is therefore   9° 33′
                in 1 day „   „   0° 57′
                in 5 days „   „   4° 45′

The Sun's place on 20th July 1856 is   27° 47′ ♋
„   „   motion in 5 days is   4° 45′
„   „   place on 25th July (noon Greenwich) is thus 2° 32′ ♌

It is very simple to find how much the motion is in the hours and minutes before and after 12 o'clock noon at Greenwich by using the Table of Logarithms printed on the last page of this book.

As we have seen before, the Sun moves in one day 0° 57′. We now look up in the Table of Logarithms the place where the column 0 degree and 57 minutes (the day's motion on July 25) intersect and find . . . . Log. 14025

The logarithm number of 12 hrs. 50 m. we find at the intersection of the columns 12 and 50 . . . . Log. 2719

We add and find the sum Logarithm 16744

Now we look up in the Table of Logaritms the number 16744 and find the nearest Log. 16670, which is placed at the intersection of the columns 0 degrees and 31 minutes, this is thus the motion of the Sun in 12 hours 50 minutes.

So we must add:
1) the position of the Sun on July 25th noon Greenwich   2° 32′ ♌
2) the motion of the Sun in 12 h. 50 m.. . . . . . . 0° 31′
                                 3° 3′ ♌

The **Sun** (☉) is therefore at the moment of birth placed in 3° 3′ ♌.

The **Moon** (☽) was on July 25th (noon '56) (see Veen's Tables) 14° Ta (♉)
and on July 26th (noon '56) („   „   „   ) 28° Ta (♉)
The motion of the Moon from 14° ♉ to 28° ♉ in 24 hours is therefore 14°. The motion in 12 hrs. 50 m. will easily be learned with the aid of the Table of Logarithms.

We know that the Moon's motion from July 25th to July 26th is 14° 0′ i.e. Logarithm 2341
the Logarithm for 12 hrs. 50 m. is 2719

We add and find the sum Logarithm. 5060

We look up in the Table of Logarithms the number 5060 and find the nearest Log. 5061 which is 7° 29′.

The position of the Moon on July 25th (noon Gr.t.) is . 14° ♉
we must add the motion in 12 hrs. 50 m. or . . . . . 7° 29′

The **Moon** (☽) is therefore at the moment of birth placed in 21° ♉ 29′

Mercury's (☿) place, (see Veen's Tables)   noon 20/7 '56   9° ♋
„   „   „   noon 30/7 '56   26° ♋

Mercury's (☿) motion in 10 days 17°, or in 1 day
1° 42′ and in 5 days 8° 30′

  „   „   place, noon 20/7 '56 . . . . 9° ♋
              add motion in 5 days . . . . . 8° 30′
  „   „   place, noon 25/7 '56 . . . . . 17° 30′ ♋
Log. 1° 42′ (1 day's motion) . . . . . . = 11498
Log. 12 hrs. 50 m. (Time of birth) . . . . = 2719
☿'s motion in 12 h. 50 m. . . . . . = Log. 14217 = 0° 54′
☿'s place noon 25/7 '56 . . . . 17° 30′ ♋
   add motion in 12 h. 50 m. or . . . . . 0° 54′
Mercury's (☿) place at the moment of birth . . = 18° 24′ ♋

Venus' (♀) place, noon 20/7 '56 . . . . 27° ♋
  „   „   noon 30/7 '56 . . . . . . 10° ♌
  „   motion in 10 days 13°, or in 1 day 1° 18′ and in 5 days 6° 30′
  „   place, noon 20/7 '56 . . . . . . 27° ♋
       add motion in 5 days . . . . . 6° 30′
  „   place, noon 25/7 '56 . . . . 3° 30′ ♌
Log. 1° 18′ (1 day's motion) . . . . = 12663
Log. 12 hrs. 50 m. (time of birth) 2719
♀'s motion in 12 h. 50 m. . . . . . = Log. 15382 = 0° 42′
♀'s place, noon 25/7 '56 . . . . 3° 30′ ♌
add motion in 12 h. 50 m. . . . . 0° 42′
Venus' (♀) place at the moment of birth . . . 4° 12′ ♌

Mars' (♂) place, noon 1/7 '56 . . . . 15° ♎
  „   „   noon 1/8 '56 . . . . 0° ♏
  „   motion in 31 days 15°, or in 1 day 29′ and in 25 days 12° 5′
  „   place, noon 1/7 '56 . . . . 15° ♎
       add motion in 25 days . . . . . . 12° 5′
  „   place, noon 25/7 '56 . . . . 27° 5′ ♎
Log. 0° 29′ (1 day's motion) . . . . . . = 16960
Log. 12 hrs. 50 m. (time of birth) 2719
♂'s motion in 12 h. 50 m. . . . . . = Log. 19679 = 0° 16′
♂'s place, noon 25/7 '56 . . . . 27° 5′ ♎
add motion in 12 h. 50 m. . . . . 0° 16′
Mars' (♂) place at the moment of birth . . = 27° 21′ ♎

Jupiter's (♃) place noon, 1/7 '56 . . . . . . 8° ♈
  „   „   noon, 1/8 '56 . . . . . . 9° ♈
  „   motion in 31 days 1°, or in 1 day 2′, in 25 days 50′
  „   place, noon, 1/7 '56 . . . . . 8° ♈
  „   place, noon, 25/7 '56 . . . . . 8° 50′ ♈
Log. 0° 2′ (1 day's motion) . . . . . . = 28573
Log. 12 hrs. 50 m. (time of birth) 2719
♃'s motion in 12 h. 50 m. . . . . . = Log. 31292 = 0° 1′
Jupiter's (♃) place at the moment of birth . . = 8° 51′ ♈

Saturn's (♄) place, noon, 1/7 '56 . . . . . . 4° ♋
„ „ noon, 1/8 '56 . . . . . 8° ♋
„ motion in 31 days 4°, or in 1 day 8′, in 25 days 3° 20′
„ place, noon, 1/7 '56 . . . 4° ♋
„ place, noon, 25/7 '56 . . . . 7° 20′ ♋
Log. 0° 8′ (day's motion) . . . . . = 22553
Log. 12 hrs. 50 m. (time of birth) . . . 2719
♄'s motion in 12 h. 50 m. . . . . . = Log. 25272 = 0° 4′
Saturns' (♄) place at the moment of birth = 7° 24′ ♋.

Uranus' (♅) place, 1/5 '56 . . . . 20° ♉
„ „ 1/9 '56 . . . . 25° ♉
„ motion in 120 days 5°, in 1 day 2½′,
in 86 days (1/5—25/7) . . . = 3° 35′
Uranus' (♅) place at birth . . . . . . = 23° 35′ ♉

Neptune's (♆) place 1/5 '56 . . . . 20° ♓ Retrogr.
„ „ 1/9 '56 . . . . 19° ♓
„ „ 28/6 '56 . . . . . = 20° ♓ [1]) Retrogr.
„ „ 1/9 '56 . . . . . = 19° ♓
„ motion in 64 days (28/6—1/9), 1°; in 1 day = 1′ Retrogr.
„ „ in 27 days (28/6—25/7). . . . = 27′ „
Neptune's (♆) place at birth . . . . . . 19° 33′ ♓ „

The place of the **Part of Fortune** (⊕) is:
the longitude of the moon add to the longitude of the ascendant,
subtract from the sum the longitude of the Sun.
The Moon is in the Zodiac. . . . . 1 sign 21° 29′
The longitude of the Ascendant . . . . . 2 signs 12°
add . . . 3 signs 33° 29′
or . . . 4 signs 3° 29′
The longitude of the Sun . . . . 4 signs 3° 3′
subtract . . 0 signs 0° 26′
The **Part of Fortune** (⊕) is therefore 0° 26′ past 0° Aries or 0° 26′ ♈.

[1]) When a planet *appears* to move *backward* in the zodiac, it is called *retrograde*. See *Retrograde tables* in Veen's Tables (1847—1926).

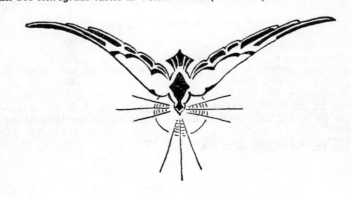

VII

How to judge the Nativity.

Having now a horoscope before us together with a list of aspects, we may start *judging* them. The three principal points to be considered are *Sun, Moon* and *Ascendant,* also the *Houses* in which the former are placed. Moreover every Sign, every House occupied by more than one planet exerts a great influence upon the character and life of the native. What determine the meaning of a House are the Sign on its cusp, the planets posited in it and the ruling planet of that Sign[1]). If there be no planet in a House of which one wishes to know further particulars, then its *ruling planet* and the *Sign* in which that planet is placed, must also be judged.

If therefore, a person having ♊ on the Cusp of the 10th House, and no planets in that House, wishes to know what prospects he has in his profession, he must note the position of *Mercury* — in this case the ruler of the tenth House — that is to say the *House, Sign* and *Aspects* in which ☿ is placed.

Harmonious aspects make for *cooperation* according to the nature of the planet which is harmoniously aspected, tinged by the Sign and the House in which the latter is placed. Inharmonious aspects make for frustration of some kind according to the nature of the inharmoniously aspected planet, tinged by the Sign and the House in which that planet is placed.

If a person has e. g. ☉ in 10, in △ aspect to ♃ in 6, he will easily hold a high social position being helped thereto by devoted and capable subordinates. If the ☉ is the ruler of the 4th house and ♃ in the 8th, this favourable influence is strengthened by pleasant domestic circumstances (4th house) and an inheritance (8th house) which renders him financially independent.

If on the other hand ♂ in 2 forms a □ aspect with the ☽ in 11, money will be rashly spent on all kinds of dubious pleasures in the company of friends (male and female).

If in that case ♂ rules the 6th and 1st houses, and the ☽ rules the 9th, health and personal dignity and spiritual development of the native will all suffer.

The influence of a planet placed near the cusp of a house usually begins to be felt in the *succeeding* house; thus e. g. ♄ in 12° ♎ may be judged to be in the 3rd house if 13° ♎ is placed on the cusp of the 3rd house.

---

[1]) See Ch. The Planets, p. 13—19.

Aries (♈) Ascendant.

The mien is brisk, sprightly and martial, and there is a good deal of enthusiasm for new plans and ideas. New thoughts, new schemes exercise a strong attraction and when once an idea has been accepted or grasped it will be propagated and put into practice with energy and insistence; *uncertainties* and less good sides being totally disregarded. There is usually not much patience to suffer that which is new to grow, and the subject much troubled by the native's *desire at immediate visible results.* Although the lead will willingly be taken in every kind of enterprise, yet it is advisable that some one in a higher position should keep the reins in hand and direct Aries' faculties of enthusiastic activity and originality in devising plans in the direction and the way which promises the greatest success. This person will also have to complete what Aries through haste forgets and rectify rash undertakings. Even when Aries' whole being is at rest — which does not occur often — his eyes will yet be actively engaged. Aries' manner is cheerful and optimistic; though, when disappointed, fits of despondency may occasionally occur. As a rule such a mood produces a *fit of rebellion against Fate,* sometimes manifested in a way which afterwards causes repentance. *Headaches* result from similar outbursts. (♈ corresponds with the head).

There is a good deal of irritability and very little is borne which offends the honour and self-respect of the individual. On the other hand the ♈-type in the heat of the battle (material or spiritual) scarcely notices that he is suffering great losses or has to bear up against great odds — being utterly engrossed in his fight. In this way a battle generally supposed to be a losing one may after all be won.

This characteristic will also be prominent when practising various branches of *sport,* a thing for which the Aries-type has a great liking. Every exaggeration should be avoided; it is advisable to rest at the least suggestion of overstrain.

Taurus (♉) Ascendant.

Makes for a quiet, calm and kind demeanour, prone to contemplation and meditation. This is very attractive, especially in youth before the specific characteristics of this type are fully developed. Later on when a difference of opinion arises, a ♉ becomes "too fixed" to give up his conviction.

Sometimes his placid manner alternates with *outbursts of great passion* and on certain subjects a stubbornness manifests which renders argument impossible.

Especially in youth the "Bull" gives great bodily strength, a compensation for possible afflictions in the horoscope with respect to health. When illnesses occur his strong constitution makes for recovery.

The character is honest and trustworthy; but there is a possibility of self-delusion, and it is only very intimate friends or those who are greatly admired who are allowed to express their faultfinding with this type or whose remarks are taken to heart. But once a fault has been recognised, it is immediately and readily removed — if that be possible.

Appreciation of what is beautiful in nature always remains keen and therefore helps the native materially to obtain solace and strength when life's circumstances prove to be unfavourable.

Gemini (♊) Ascendant.

Produces something *unbalanced,* something *dual* in manner and appearance. "Himmelhoch jauchzend—zum Tode betrübt"; now full of trusting optimism, now full of dejected doubt. Ever wishing for the good, but sometimes feeling impotent ever to reach it.

Both moods however are not of long duration; the inner nature is too active, there is too great a longing for new impressions to dwell on a special subject. On strangers and in society a very animated, even charming impression may therefore be made.

♊ as the Ascendant produces many pleasant relations, which are more or less superficial, *literary abilities,* and an extraordinary talent for *imitating* and *characterising* others. This type's manner is also characterised by the many *gesticulations* made when speaking.

As regards activities and pastimes in general, it is advisable for Gemini to have clear ideas and a sound judgment of his enterprises, before he talks about them with others or puts them aside. Otherwise his multifarious character easily degenerates into *halfness.*

Desire for knowledge rules ♊ from infancy onward and educators will often be driven into a corner by continual questions about the how and wherefore of things. In *department* of *religions,* this leads to conflicts. Childlike trust and faith are constantly being tested by the intellect; and if no satisfactory solution is found, a deep despondency arises, which is apt to make for the exact reversal of the original nature, viz. a complete disbelief in the Ground of all Things, and a mistrust of men.

Cancer (♋) Ascendant.

Manner as well as outward appearance is *backward,* shy, *modest,* sensitive, *irritable;* apparently meek, but really selfconscious and reticent; studious and receptive. Behind all seeming indifference a *strong feeling of selfhood* proves to be present, which is by no means easily persuaded to accept others' opinion and tends imperceptably to take the lead himself. Accuracy and care characterise every action; great stress is laid on an endeavour to do all work set as faultlessly as possible and also on acquiring every honour possible from the environment.

Fear of self-revealing often prevents pleasant intercourse and hinders the acquisition of knowledge. Although Cancer has a great desire to be the centre of attention, yet in various circumstances he is *timid* in public. It sometimes seems as if he lacks courage to face the world.

Strong external influences may cause a silent retreat when steadfastness would have been more courageous. Frequently an endeavour is made to attract attention by "being conspicuous through absence".

Undeniably Cancer has some *educational ability,* also the spirit of *helpfulness,* but it will always be difficult for him to disregard himself, and forego rightful gratitude and mutual affection.

In daily life ♋ manifests by his sensitiveness to happy and intimate beauty of sound, form and colour. Its great receptivity to impressions, moods and thoughts of the environment, makes possible some interesting experiments of an occult nature. With unsufficient selfcriticism jealous feelings toward those who are better off or with whom things go more smoothly, may arise; *suffering* with people will oftener be the case than to be *joyful* with them.

Leo (♌) Ascendant.

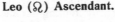

Manner and outward appearance have the high-spiritedness, dignity and "noblesse" of which the "Lion" is the epitome.

A pleasant, *radiating joy of life* emanates from Leo's whole appearance, especially when in congenial surroundings. Somewhat aristocratic or chic sets of people exercise a great attraction and are preferably sought, while great store is laid on occupying a prominent place among them.

When his mood is cheerful, the sunny, radiating side of ♌ is well expressed and his manner will then be characterised by hearty joyousness and regal hospitality, which may even react favourably upon the whole environment. Care should however be taken lest this ♌-attitude be assumed only in order to win praise or applause, since this would be a hindrance to the development of character.

His manner towards subordinates is *condescending and masterful;* obedience and devotion are expected and accepted as a matter of course, and when they are not given, his indignation will know no bounds. Intercourse with superiors is characterised by a correct courtesy which is however intended less as a homage to those people than as a means of making himself agreeable to them and thus gaining a possibility of being taken up by their set.

It is advisable for ♌ to stand aloof from people's opinions and to try and strive if need be alone, for whatever is regarded as good and noble. And the less his desire for gaining honour is indulged in, the greater will the things be which are ultimately accomplished.

As the heart is ruled by ♌, this type always has much feeling for his fellow-men, which manifests principally towards less developed people, younger people etc. who will be helped on with great devotion. When inner conflicts arise he will usually show a mask of pride or aloofness to those around him.

When the ☉ is placed inharmoniously, intimacy with others seldom arises. The people concerned will either be idealised and admired from a distance, or fear of being misunderstood may prevent the exposure of

the inner life. As a rule however personal relations will remain only superficial in order that ♌ may develop and work out his thought life the more
intensely — though in secret. But this leads to *selfcentredness* which is
neither advisable nor satisfactory.

♌ ought to try to keep his self-respect — not pride — as a vehicle
of invisible powers and lofty aspirations — not as a creature who is
himself perfect or almost perfect. Leo ought in all circumstances to retain
his healthy optimism and his warm sympathetic heart and then he may
offer his strength for humanity's service and make his sunny smile shine
alike for friend and foe.

Virgo (♍) Ascendant.

The observant and reserved mien and manner
bespeaks somebody noticing trifles and is somewhat
solitary by reason of his critical nature. Under all
circumstances, even towards intimates a certain "distance" is kept and never abandoned.

This separateness characteristic of ♍ is also evident in his fastidious-
ness, in being over-particular regarding surroundings, language, etc. He
carefully evades whatever might in any way distress or disturb him and
experiences very unpleasant sensations if others do not also keep to this rule.

♍ gives a particular propensity to discover little things that escape
other people's notice and nevertheless may sometimes prove of real
consequence. In business especially, this may of course come in useful.
Orderliness, love of regularity, systematic organisation of activities and
accurate administration tend to success along that line; ☿, the ruler of this
sign is *the* planet of "commerce".

A Virgo should however be on his guard against a tendency *to be so
absorbed in details* as to be in danger of *undervaluing great interests;* he
is apt too to criticise men and things so sharply and rashly, as to overlook
good points; and also to suffer from depression, bad temper and exaggerated
fear of illness.

Modern hygiene is quite in accordance with Virgo's bent; at the same
time it provides reasons—sought after by ♍ but bad for him—of being
uneasy about possible causes of illness. That uneasiness is less necessary
for this sign than for others, because his constitution usually is exceptionally
healthy.

It *is* good to distinguish the little things of life but they must not
rule us.

Libra (♎) Ascendant.

The outer appearance is *amiable, kind, polite.*
Libra greatly appreciates whatever is *beautiful, peaceful* and *harmonious,* and has an intense longing to be
himself in harmony with these things. Others' opinion
will always be considered though not of necessity
shared, and will even be attached publicly should occasion offer.

The part of *mediator* between antagonists will be willingly undertaken, and carried out with strict impartiality. Its very name "the Balance" emphasizes the Libra idea of balancing and considering, while ♀ as ruler brings a keen desire for concord and harmony. Readiness to help at the moments it is appealed to, is so great, that difficulties frequently arise later. The other sex especially cannot easily be refused, even though its wishes may be quite contrary to one's own convictions and though one will probably afterwards curse one's own willingness. It is advisable for Librans to try always *to be truly themselves,* and not to play some part deemed beautiful or important; not to say or do things which could not be said or done with the same conviction the next day.

To others who are quick in choosing, this "balancing" often gives the impression of indecision or even indifference, if not of laziness. They consider it colourless, vapid, callous; and only congenial people can appreciate the many things, weighed against each other and clearly classified in order to redress some balance which had been upset. ♎ is a *thinker,* not an irresolute person; ♎ as a cardinal sign likes to take the lead, leaving the minor details for others to do. If that does not work off smoothly, the balance is soon out of equilibrium. Libra is, however, prone to postpone matters that are not urgent, so that others often have to wait.

Libra learns from experience that it is very desirable to extend the dominion of rule and regularity to his own life, i.e. to rest at fixed times and never to overstrain himself, so that work will only be done when the power to work is present. Life on a well-balanced basis of "repose" enables people to do far more than if they were physically stronger.

Scorpio (♏) Ascendant.

Makes the native physically strong, although built somewhat disproportionately. His complexion is usually pale. Physical fatigue is easily overcome.

♏ makes the native *passionate* and *sensitive* especially in the period of youthful intensities. Selfcommand, sexual control and the upholding of his ideals may strengthen his willpower, and add to his energy in such a way as to enable him to reach much socially. Clear thinking will bring about the lower qualities to be sublimated in *productive work.*

In various departments of life rage may be aroused by the merest trifles, and will often find expression in most unreasonable reproaches.

Scorpio has great powers of observation; characters of unknown people are sometimes sensed at first sight and well defined, while things that the latter would rather keep silent or hide out of sight will often be speedily discovered. Their own nature is *very reserved,* and they confide only in very few people — probably because of disappointments and opposition experienced in early life.

The manner is usually somewhat serious and reserved, though by no means unkind. The nature of ♂, the ruler, manifests especially in the glance of the eyes which makes an impression on every one, while the whole appearance seems to send forth a power which makes for success.

♏ Asc. gives also a great deal of magnetic power. With some practice they will soon succeed in disposing of some of their own vital power to sufferers who arouse their sympathy. ♏ likes to enter into *lif's secrets;* both in other people's lives and in the problems of life and death everywhere in nature. The sensing of the *soul of things* and the knowledge of other people's difficulties are both typical of this sign.

Sagittarius (♐) Ascendant.

The *Archer* with his keen vision and his power of shooting gives the appearance of resolution of one who knows what he wishes and seeks earnestly for the best way in which to reach his aim.

♐ makes the native lively, sprightly in manner and very expressive. He likes to talk about subjects which he is thinking about and his whole attention will be absorbed in the subject or lecture in question, a fact made evident also by the many *intonations* of his voice.

♐ is the sign which corresponds to the 9th house. His whole life is consequently directed to attaining an expansion of consciousness; every discussion and speech aims at acquiring or approaching to more knowledge and greater understanding. His strong inner consciousness of human relations results in the same friendly manner being shown to all and sundry whatever their position in life, provided that they have not made themselves antipathetic by some action antagonistic to ♐'s ideals. For in that case will he continually and without scruple give vent to reproachful and provocative remarks; and the archer knows to hit the weak spots! He is always trying to spread his own ideas discussing or talking about them with every one likely to take an interest in them. Even in childhood this propensity manifests as the constant "wish to know", an insatiable *thirst for knowledge,* which cannot be put off, and which is only quenched when insight has been obtained. Love of *nature* and of *life in the open* is strong, while a certain free-religious feeling dominates the emotions.

Although at times solitude and seclusion are sought, in the long run they do not give satisfaction. Notwithstanding the fact that ♐ often is inwardly hurt by human prejudices, yet again and again he seeks human society, for to him nothing can have real value unless it is shared with others.

Capricorn (♑) Ascendant.

Produces a self-restrained, reticent manner which gives strangers an impression of aloofness or conceit. Great *love of work* and *ambition* are found, so that life for ♑ will be full of hard work. The work, however, will undoubtedly gain in quality if self and his own interests can be kept in the background. To others, especially younger people, he likes to act in a patronising and instructive manner, to which he has a right by virtue of his own development and his observant mind.

Trust, respect and appreciation on the part of others are greatly valued,

40

but on the other hand Capricorn does not easily give either trust or confidence. He has a constant fear of being opposed, cheated and slandered; ideas which often corrupt the atmosphere and hinder undisturbed joy. His capacities will show off best in more or less *official* callings, where direction and organisation are required. Capricorn's manner is sensible, decided and suggestive.

A peculiarity of this Ascendant is the keen sense of *formality* and of rank and standing in all departments of life, conceptions of "superiors" and "inferiors" being consequently very accurately and clearly denoted by conduct and conversation. But care should be taken not to be disturbed by outward show, lest excessive honour be paid to those who really are not worth it. As great care as possible is taken of his own appearance.

Sometimes the native assumes an attitude, *makes believe that more has been reached than could be achieved consciously and alone,* in order the sooner to be acknowledged by the public.

♐ knows that "to keep silent is to possess power", but also that by using big words others may be baffled and taken advantage of and made to do as he likes, though the exact meaning of what is said is not understood.

Aquarius (♒) Ascendant.

Makes the manner *cheerful, engaging* and *humane,* and rarely dejected. The ruler ♅, however, gives peculiar propensities. Good aspects arouse a great interest in occultism, mysticism and symbolism. These subjects are studied with pleasure and discussed, especially with a view to obtaining a clearer insight into man's inner nature and his place in the Cosmos, and not so much for the sake of the sciences themselves.

Intercourse with others will in general be easy. Connections will probably prove very favourable, both to social and moral well-being. Afflictions may cause more or less *eccentricity* and *self-will.*

♒ moreover often produces original and idiosyncratic views of people and things. The nature and essence of things are deeply probed. ♒ typifies the naturalist and judge of human nature. A certain love of ridiculing others cannot be denied and the native often enjoys observing and seeing through people's errors or follies although this is often done under the mask of artless coolness and friendly interest.

Pisces (♓) Ascendant.

Makes the native *over-sensitive, very susceptible to emotion.* Much more is felt than is warranted by one's own observation. Quite a lot of what is usually called "bad" or "wrong" is *understood,* and this produces a kind of docility which does not always act favourably on development. So the native will do well to learn to limit himself in all directions and be careful in choosing his friends, otherwise there is much likelihood of gossip and slander. The desire to comply with others' wishes makes Pisces *indulgent,* sometimes also *self-indulgent.*

"To know is to forgive" is characteristic which may be called a great virtue if it leads to effectual helpful conduct, but which becomes somewhat dangerous if one's own originally right ideas are lost and the result is not *lifting* but rather destructive.

♓ is *the still water running deep,* which is attracted by the unknown, by what is mystical. He is sensitive and prone to become easy-going, without knowing or asking whither?

The sign of Pisces produces a certain indifference to property. The native wishes for a simple life coupled with beauty both for himself and for all humanity.

♓ gives the appearance of activity but often accompanied by *timidity* which is to some extent a drawback to individual development. ♓ often keeps modestly in the background and leaves the conversation to others, the more so when the latter pretend to have more knowledge than they have. If, however, a question is dealt with in a scientific circle, a ♓-type is ready to give his own opinion and the result of his own industrious researches. No abstract theories, but practical remarks are then made in a critical, provocative way.

VIII

The Planets in the Twelve Signs.

The Sun in the Twelve Signs.

The Sun (☉) in Aries (♈).

(March 21—April 21).

The aim given by this position is *action, occupation* in every department of life. The activity of the spirit makes the native prone not only to become himself absorbed in various subjects but also — if found sympathetic or valid — to transmit them to others, *propagating* and *defending* them. He is apt to consider it his bounden duty to get his ideals widely accepted, if need be *by fire and sword,* like Mahomet (an Aries).

For this very reason it is good that an Aries-type should keep asking himself:

1) whether the ideas in question are really good and pure;
2) whether other convictions have no good in them nor a right to existence.

This self-control will save him from the fanaticism and rashness, to which an Aries-type is liable. His valuable spiritual qualities such as absence of prejudice, his courage, righteousness and enthusiasm may, however, if well directed greatly forward progress and betterment in general.

„Wohltätig ist des Feuers Macht
Wenn sie der Mensch bezähmt, bewacht;
Und was er bildet, was er schafft;
Das dankt er dieser Himmelskraft."
(Lied von der Glocke, Schiller).

A more developed Aries will always strive to be *"Fighter for the rights of Humanity"* sometimes we find a tendency towards *martyrdom*. (The *Lamb*, which is sacrificed). The imperturbable joy of life and a childlike carelessness, produced by this sign, explain why many of the frequent outbursts of passion and uncontrolled utterances are readily forgiven.

Aries is attracted by active life and is apt to return again and again to the people or things that have caused him disappointment.

The adoption of too rigorous or too decided measures by authority — parents, teachers and superiors in childhood — causes perplexity, stubbornness and waywardness where sometimes a single word might have produced the greatest meekness. Aries often overestimates his own strength, and for him usually experience is a hard school.

Intense admiration of the great, warm attachment and sacrificing devotion are all typical of this sign. *Friendship* indeed — more than love — is one of his dearest ideals, but he must beware of rashness and *prejudice*. For although usually "first impressions are the best", this is not always true with an Aries, since he especially is subject to many sudden changes of mood. First impressions are therefore often altered — either for better or worse.

☉ in ♈ makes for courage; an ♈ is easily a "fire-eater", a knight of the sword fighting with open visor, self-assertive; ever ready to stand in the breach for others and to go to the rescue at critical moments.

Affliction makes him irritable, rash, blunt, a ringleader who overestimates himself and is always ready for any enterprise.

Headaches, (fullbloodedness), apoplexy, inflammation of the brain, kidney-diseases (♉ ♎).

The Sun (☉) in Taurus (♉).

(April 22—May 21).

Like all earthy signs this type is very receptive of lofty motives and i eals which are so completely assimilated that they become identified with the person who works at them with the utmost power of will and perseverance.

These two characteristics *power of will* and *perseverance* are present, but do not manifest until *interest* and *ambition* are aroused; a thing which may happen slowly, seeing the "fixed"ness of this sign. Once a definite task has been grasped, no pains, no time, no energy will be spared to reach the goal. Peaceful, harmonious surroundings, are however, exceedingly necessary. For in an atmosphere of hurry and unrest Taurus' thoughts are apt to wander, and an attack of temper may spoil his pleasure of work.

On the other hand Taurus has a certain *sense of humour* which enables him to keep his courage in some straits and to see the good or comical side of the situation. This optimism arises from a strong inner consciousness of being led by a higher power which knows what is best for us.

Usually ♉ makes uncritical, trustful, obedient, conservative, gentle, and kind-hearted, but at the same time somewhat self-willed and stubborn, should differences of opinion arise. Taureans like to give to those poorer than themselves, but feel very bad when they themselves lack anything.

They have a great love of art, especially of *applied art;* and a vein of *strong, rich simplicity* often runs through it. Their highest ideal, both of art and of life, is calm selfconscious power coupled with the constant glow of holy ardour. Without proper control this calm assurance may however become rather phlegmatic and self-sufficient and then instead of regarding himself as a small, working part of the Cosmos, Taurus seems itself an important and independent unity. He should always remember that *in himself* man is of slight significance, but that he derives his value from the fact that he is an *instrument of higher powers,* which work through him in order to bring about a definite purpose. Once this is well understood and realised to the full, a source of possibilities is opened, destined to be very valuable either in a narrow sphere or in a wide one, provided sufficient activity and devotion are also present.

☉ in ♉ renders people old-fashioned and conservative, but tolerant; they like to consider a question thoroughly before they are willing to work hard for it, which however they will do and try to reach the goal once it has their approval. They are fond of the good things of earth and somewhat inclined to worship the *golden calf.*

If *afflicted,* Taurus easily becomes recalcitrant and obstinate, especially if his opponent proves to be as firm as he is.

Hoarseness, dry cough, inflammation of the throat, diphtheria, nasal catarrh, polypus, heart complaint (□ ♌), fainting fits, apoplexy; in 29° ♉ eye complaint.

The Sun (☉) in Gemini (♊).

(May 22—June 21)

Generally indicates an *expansive, adaptive nature.* The ego is fairly clearly conscious and tries to test himself by his environment. ♊ makes the mind very active, impressionable, intelligent and comprehending. An all-round development is more to Gemini's taste than depth and his chief object is to see, observe and know much, and to use this knowledge as well as possible. This sign likes to make comparative studies of all kinds of subjects from which the beginnings of many interesting essays, treatises etc. result.

It experiences great difficulty in finding theories or convictions which give lasting satisfaction. Again and again doubt arises; as the native's thought moves rapidly along various lines. Frequently a second subject takes the fancy before the first has been dealt with, a circumstance which produces *restlessness* and *nervousness* and at times even discontent and complaint of "lack of time". But had there been more time and opportunity, little more would indeed have been accomplished; interest in most things originates more in the desire to be able to say something to others about it than to form an independent opinion about them. The impression of being well-informed, usually made on others is due to the native's susceptible mind, his power of adapting various theories, his adroitness in imitating others and facility for imagery.

People and things which formerly exercised a great attraction are neglected when something else suddenly arouses his interest. There is a certain amount of *superficiality* in Gemini's mode of study and appreciation; that outer peculiarities are nevertheless sharply and quickly observed, — though the inner significance is often neglected. The consequence is that he is eager to make many contacts and desires to be abreast of everything which leads him unto all kinds of circles and connections. The experiences thus gained will be told to others in an engaging, pleasant manner so far as they may be supposed to contribute to the relater's popularity. Notwithstanding this changeability Gemini has a great *love of freedom*, and although knowledge be yet unsufficient, a decided wish to act according to his *own insight* and on his own responsibility. Speech and discussion is very easy; ♊'s own points of view are clearly explained and a sharp light thrown on those of others. But ♊ seldom makes his own point of view known before that of others has been heard and gauged, though this does not involve that this standpoint is less personal. Generally he does not like to concert with people of less development or those with less talent for languages unless he can outdo them on their own territory. And yet it is better to help those surrounding us as much as possible than haughtily to live in seclusion. Better to feel oneself the "Messenger" (☿) than the "inventor" of wisdom.

People with the ☉ in ♊ are many-sided, studious, all-round. They have a knack of saying things in an off-hand way, of making fools of other people, or of putting them off with fair words.

Affliction makes them unreliable, sceptical, talkative; prone to trim their sails to suit every wind.

Congestion of the lungs, consumption, bronchitis, pleurisy (♊ ☐ ♍), nervous disorders, scurvy, blood-illnesses.

The Sun (☉) in Cancer (♋).

(June 22—July 22).

The native's inner nature is distinguished by the two "Crab"-qualities: *receptivity* and *selection*.

Many moods are sensed, many theories thought over, and from all these, his own insight is constructed and strengthened; what is superfluous and unsympathetic being disregarded and rejected.

In actual life this is apt to lead him to *overvalue his "own" ideas* and to conduce to *oversensitiveness, timidity and reserve*. ♋ makes the mind very receptive and very impressionable. New thoughts are not heedlessly passed by, but duly considered, gauged, and seldom wholly rejected. For this reason Cancer has a reputation of being changeable in his ideas; also of having and showing different opinions about the same subject to different people according to the latter's personal influence or powers of persuasion. When his own conviction proves to be altogether opposed to that of the antagonist and when he does not consider his own eloquence equal to the defence of the standpoint adopted, he will usually agree outwardly, although underneath there will be much dumb discontent, sometimes even a smouldering rancour and consequently a certain amount of mistrust, a reserve towards strangers which is wrongly interpreted by many. Pronounced Cancer natures are not easy in intercourse and therefore seldom find some one who really understands them and to whom they can trust themselves completely.

Just as the "Crab", the chosen symbol of Cancer takes to itself for its development from its surroundings whatever it can use or needs, so Cancer takes great interest in all that happens in the world, in what is being thought and how things are worked precisely, in order to feed his own mind with this knowledge.

Cancer produces a good memory and great perseverance in so far as concerns the attainment of his goal, but often makes the native somewhat too engrossed in his own circumstances, ideas and feelings. ♋'s great love for his "own" concerns is also shown by the particularly strong tie which he has with family and relations, by his great respect for tradition, old family customs, heirlooms etc.

The Sun in ♋ fills the Individuality — the spirit — with the all-embracing loveprinciple, especially characteristic of this sign. The keynote of this sign's nature is the desire to tend and look after others and if other planetary influences in the horoscope render this quality less evident, closer scrutiny will surely reveal its presence.

♋ might be called the typical *mother-sign,* but just as it is often difficult for a mother to keep her love entirely pure of all egoistic desires, so in Cancer a very strong feeling of self frequently mingles with the feelings cherished for others. And just as a mother has first and foremost to learn that "*to educate is to make oneself superfluous,*" so the lesson for Cancer will be: "*love, without asking anything in return.*" For although ♋ seems to be willing to sacrifice much for another, he always — albeit sometimes unconsciously — counts on gratitude and expressions of gratitude, which often brings the contrary result. The sensitiveness natural to this sign, should not be regarded as a weakness to be treated with indulgence but as a means of communicating with others and of helping them with personal experience.

⊙ in ♋ causes people to like to live in the past and to talk about bygone days; it makes them economical, conservative and always on the look-out to buy things for "next to nothing."

Affliction makes them timid, restless; sometimes stingy, over-careful, and seldom inclined to give anything away without receiving something else (if possible better) in its stead.

Digestive disturbances, weak digestion, gastric fever, tumours, dropsy, illnesses of the breast, cancer, rheumatism, propensity to anaemia.

46

The Sun (☉) in Leo (♌).

(July 23—August 22).

Leo is the kingly, fixed fiery sign. As this sign is ruled by the Sun, a strengthening of the two natures follows. The element *fire* comes strongly to the fore and gives *light, warmth, radiance;* magnanimity, although some degree of despotism, easily follows; a desire not alone for inner greatness but also for outer honour. When harmoniously posited, this desire does not show in an unpleasant way, because feeling is not injured by it. Obviously a "sunny" man is respected in the world and is everywhere eagerly welcomed and appreciated. Under these circumstances the good side of Leo's nature shows to advantage; he loves to be the 'lion', the principal person and as such will be pleased to be of service to his fellow-men. Leo will readily listen to those who come to him for help or advice; and although his aid may not be quite free of a certain *self-satisfaction* it is not on that account less strong or *honest.* Leo's warm heart enables him to sympathise intensely, and whilst his inner strength can help on those weaker than he, his great trust in God and man often help many to overcome fear and doubt. To those who are indulgent to him, he is liberal, cheery and good tempered. He likes to see people around him joyful and happy and is willing to contribute his share to this end, even if some sacrifice be demanded of him.

But when less favourably posited, the desire for praise, honour and respect comes to the fore, and sometimes proves *annoying* if not sufficiently controlled, especially as Leo often lacks tact. The consequence of caring too much for *appearances,* will be that Leo's feelings are readily injured and his temper easily provoked. He is apt to fly into a temper and say things of which he repents later.

Leo is however too loyal not to get reconciled again, if need be taking the first steps, when his own temper or error proves to have caused the misunderstanding.

Although ♌ usually feels at home in a drawing room or in company of rank ("lion"), he really prefers kindly honest intercourse with people who really are indeed somebody, and have something to say. Sometimes he is interested in historic men whom he admires, especially in youth, fully intending himself to become as great and as famous (♌). And during that period many of his own actions may be traced to noble examples. *Patience* however is a quality which he needs to cultivate.

☉ in ♌ renders the native worthy, but also despotic, fond of starting things in a princely way and lording it over his neighbour at meetings.

Affliction makes him proud, vain, bombastic, prone to showing off.

Heart disease, palpitations, complaints of the spine, backache. In 6°Leo diseases of the eye.

The Sun (☉) in Virgo (♍).

(August 23—September 22).

A great aspiration for *purity and health* will be the motive and basis of every action and effort, even very hard work is no obstacle. On the contrary it affords great *satisfaction* to this type and his capacity of setting to work very practically and intelligently is an important factor in life. His mind is characterised by *a clear-cut view of the various parts of the whole*. His hygienic taste leads to know and practise accurately what is good and suitable for health.

Never easy-going for himself or others, ♍ constantly dissects and orders, putting aside what is bad or useless and criticising and finding fault. He will go so far as to split hairs and repel people in intercourse whilst by laying too much stress on the subdivisions, he will often lose sight of the main thing.

As has been said ♍ gives a discriminating, critical mind and a preference for detailed research in various directions. He must however be careful lest his criticism become *slashing* and his dissection *unnerving*, for by too much speculation and dissection, what is beautiful and moving is apt to be pushed into the background.

His manner of thinking is clear and logical, principles being pure and arguments plain, so that it will often be difficult for an opponent of an other temperament to find a rejoinder. Art also is regarded critically, but this does not hinder the existence of great feeling and appreciation for art; but he wants art to come up to certain requirements of *reason, fine humour or practical use*. He attacks everything exaggerated or sentimental. He does not like to hear remarks and objections to his *own* work and receives them in a disdainful manner. Altogether he undervalues the opinions of others, once he has formed his own judgment; ♍ is as exacting towards himself as towards others. Tolerance and even benevolence for all who are rather slight, although they pretend to be great, can best be strengthened by *conscious acknowledgement of faults and errors*. This recognition will help the native to overcome the "dissenting" habit caused by the complacency of his lower nature.

The habit of entering into detail will be retained rendering the individual critical of spiritual matters and anxious to obtain proofs which may be considered valid and sufficient by others.

☉ in ♍ makes for greatness in small things, always separating the chaff from the corn both in a material and in an abstract sense. Often in his criticism he fails to see the wood for trees.

Affliction makes Virgo censorious and sarcastic, materialistic and narrow-minded; whatever is not "useful" is despised as worthless.

Digestive disturbances, weak intestines, constipation, diarrhoea, dysentery, colic, peritonitis, typhoid fever, nervousness, weak lungs (□ ♊).

The Sun (☉) in Libra (♎).

(September 23— October 23).

Just as the *balance,* the symbol of ♎, ever strives towards equilibrium, so Librans always cherish a desire to attain *inner balance* which would free them from all earthly worries. Their concentration on higher things, on perfection might be compared to the *point of suspension* of the balance, one scale belonging to *mind*, the other to *feeling*. To find harmony in thought and feeling is their constant aim. From the source of latent knowledge the right way will be found and followed intuitively, the way to higher consciousness. In material, economic, and practical things it will not be difficult, once inner rest has been reached, to make a good "move" on life's chessboard.

♎ renders the native courteous, honest and aspiring; fond of order and rule; when well aspected able to organise and put things in their proper places; when afflicted exacting the latter qualities from others. Loss of balance and disquiet are extremely unpleasant to them. Librans have a great longing for *harmonious, and tasteful surroundings*, and *pleasant, agreeable relations* with family, connections and acquaintances. That is why it so easy for a ♎-person to talk to people appreciatively and kindly, and so difficult for him to refuse or upbraid. As a ♎-poet who knew himself well says:

> Happy and free and wise
> Is he who dares say "No!"
> That brief word, full of courage
> To every-one . . . .

They like to cooperate in order to improve social conditions or further domestic life. This *cooperation* is indeed the principal condition of the success of their enterprises. For however enthusiastically plans may be conceived, and motives felt, if no support and no pleasant cooperation with others can be arrived at, after some time ambition will flag and only disappointment and disgust will remain.

Whereas in some cases quite a large amount of work can be achieved through cooperation, at other times a certain *repugnance to work or action* will manifest itself. In that case the desire for ease prevails and with a friendly gesture others will be put to work; it is remarkable how willingly they do what Libra asks of them.

Those who are intellectually or artistically inclined will be attracted by all this, but to steady, dutiful workers ♎ is a constant source of irritation, although in the long run even they yield to the innocent, engaging manner of this sign.

Latent in Libra there is a strength of will moreover, which when once aroused and fully developed, will be capable of greater things than is usually imagined. His chief difficulty is however to be *his own master;* to learn to utilise his talents himself, to arrange his times for work and rest well and to regulate his whole life as best to further the growth of the Ego. He must therefore not indulge in his propensity to let things slide. We do not mean that his is a *careless life,* but that too little perseverance is shown once a direction has been taken; that in order to apply his constantly changing ideas, forethought is absolutely necessary. It is of such importance to see to things beforehand. Matters are liable to be postponed which should be settled promptly; and often the eyes are blind to existing difficulties and troubles which may even be wholly ignored. Libra's task is to learn not to be depressed and idle, but to tackle things. *Difficulties evaded continually return although in another form.* It is good for Libra to take the struggle for life of others as an example, and to exert himself to the utmost of his capacity to help those who are worse off than he is.

♎ makes for tolerance, but is liable also to lead to self-indulgence. The faculty of *character analysis* and of sensing *personal peculiarities,* in other words intuition, is pretty strongly developed.

People with the ☉ in ♎ are apt to weigh their words minutely; they are docile, lenient and in a dispute like to take the mean between two extremes.

When the position is *afflicted,* they are careless and subject to crazes, they assent to everything in order to keep friends with all the world which often leads them into trouble.

Kidney diseases, propensity to Bright's disease, pain in the loins, diabetes, skin-diseases, headaches (♄ ♈).

The Sun (☉) in Scorpio (♏).

(October 24—November 22)

One of the most prominent features is an *extraordinarily strong will,* and indefatigable power of work when it concerns some set purpose; further an *insatiable desire to know, to penetrate into everything* and find its *construction* and *principle of life.* Moreover fine intuition and at the same time strict, just judgment, so that other people's characters are usually analysed and intricate problems are soon made clear. *Scorpio does not disguise his opinion,* but those who come into contact with him, are soon made aware whether he finds them sympathetic or uncongenial. And as much as the former may count on profitable help and steadfast faithfulness, the latter will suffer severely through occasional caustic remarks, sarcasm and sometimes even pitiless wrath.

Scorpio has a remarkable faculty of detecting a weak point in the character of others and this gives him a certain feeling of solidarity, a confirmation: *"We are all sinners."* He should always bear in mind *that one must know the evil only in order to be able to transmute it into good,* and that it is wrong to detect a bad point merely to put it into the pillory, to condemn or scorn it. At any rate too much power must not be assigned to evil, seeing that the influence of good is ever stronger. The finger should be placed on the wound only in order to know where the cure has to be effected, but not in order to increase pain needlessly.

So ♏ should take care lest his interest in what is evil and abnormal should so absorb him that good is forgotten or neglected. On the contrary, the knowledge of "good" and "evil", natural to ♏, ought to be a stimulant, a means to arrive at loftier, better and purer insight, a way to raise himself and humanity. Then the symbol of the Scorpion with his sharp sting will be replaced by that of the *eagle* which soars to the Highest on mighty outstretched wings.

♏'s task is *to bring everything to the test of Truth,* and *put goodness and purity where meanness has been.* In that sense ♏ is the "Tempter", he who tests all that *is* good or *seems* to be good. If what is bad is only condemned, ♏ misses his regenerative effect and remains therefore incomplete. *Our heart ought not to be empty, but filled with good things.*

Scorpio cannot bear criticism of others, because according to his own opinion he always strives for the best. "Fully assured in one's own mind" is his motto. Nothing satisfies him so much as the consciousness of having served Truth to the utmost of his capacity.

In his higher aspect ♏ is as it were made to guide weaker people and *"convert sinners".* For this purpose tact and tolerance ought to be trained. ♏ should bear in mind that more is reached through gentleness than through hardness and that God, besides being *Infinite Justice,* is also *Infinite Love.* Even the worst man has a chance of bettering himself, and in this it is our duty to help him as much as possible.

⊙ in ♏ makes selfconscious, resolute, inquisitive, interested in occultism. Others will be tested and loiterers will not have an easy time of it.

Affliction makes the native passionate, masterful, jealous and gives very pronounced opinions, and a tendency to set snares for others. The saying: "I shall scourge you with scorpions" shows how terrible is the wrath of ♏.

Disturbances in the genital organs and the kidneys, sensitive to syphilitic infection, calculous in the kidney, gravel, gout, hemorrhoids, appendicitis, palpitations of the heart (□ ♌), tender nose and throat (8 ♉).

The Sun (⊙) in Sagittarius (♐).

(November 23—December 21).

Sagittarius is represented as being *half horse* and *half man* — *half material* and *half spiritual.* It is the human — spiritual — self which looks upward and bends the bow to a highly elevated mark; it is the body of the horse — material — that once will carry the spirit to that which he has seen as his ideal far away.

In this is comprised the lesson for Sagittarius. In this physical life he has to realise spiritual aspirations by means of his material faculties. So he must above all learn to listen; to listen to life's lesson and life's promptings.

The inner character, the foundation of Being resembles the "Archer", who *has the goal in front of him and keeps it in view,* firmly trusting some day to reach it. ♐-people have *high ideals* which they try to reach with *great enthusiasm* and *indefatigable activity.* They consider it their duty *to get on and to help others also* in their evolution. They are characterized by a wide love of knowledge and an extraordinarily active mind. They like to move in various spheres and contemplate the most divergent subjects. Everything is observed with great attention and they like to learn from people better informed than themselves. As ♐ loves to broaden his outlook, *he will busily discuss his own views with others* in order to see whether they should at certain points be modified or put aside; when ♐ argues it is not with a view to finding acceptance with his audience *à tout prix*. If by *logical reasoning* his opponent can prove himself to be right, ♐ will be the first to acknowledge and proclaim this new and better conception to any with whom he comes into contact. With this sign tolerance is innate; but those who propound rash and narrow-minded propositions will meet with severity and merciless criticism. In that case ♐ has a great desire boldly to proclaim his own view.

Interchange of thought, contact with the world are of prime importance for Sagittarius. He likes to be wherever he is near some sound, though it be but the ticking of a clock or the boiling of a kettle. In silence the wish to deliver a speech, or discover some point for discussion becomes imperative; in seclusion he often considers what subject he might deal with at the next opportunity.

The Archer must see a *goal* ahead, preferably one which is idealistic rather than practical. He is fond of defending enthusiastically free views of religion and indeed he is a warm pleader for any cause he has taken to heart. Consequently he enjoys fairly great popularity and great allowances are made for much which in others would be taken ill.

Sagittarians are fond of *freedom,* but often omit to deal with others in the same spirit, although they intend no harm. He likes to regard his friends as *pupils* and the relation is a pleasant one, so long as they are willing to listen to and learn from him, but when they begin to be refractory, he feels himself ill-used and is inclined to retire and pout in solitude for a time complaining being misunderstood. But his longing for discourse and society remains strong and it will not be long before the archer looks for another goal at which to shoot his arrows.

☉ in ♐ makes the native frank, free, idealistic, fond of talk — what the heart is full of, the mouth will talk about; ♐ is a good talker.

Affliction renders him audacious, extravagant, careless, prone to noise things abroad, and not to mince matters; changeable: to-day crying "hosannah", and to-morrow "crucify him"!

Sciatica, wounds in limbs through falling or cutting, paralysis of the legs, nervousness, propensity to pulmonary diseases (♀ ♍); in 8° ♐ eye-diseases.

The Sun (☉) in Capricorn (♑).

(December 22—January 20).

The character is endowed with those qualities which are so strikingly typified by the "Goat", climbing always higher and higher cautiously and alone from one summit to another. There is a strong inner urge for progress, spiritual as well as social; with, conscious or unconscious, the additional aim of thus enabling the native to exercise *authority* over others. In this he will usually meet with success, since weaker natures are sure to admire this way of acting. But people of the same nature or those who are keenly idealistic will be urged to resistance and opposition by it, which is apt to lead to less pleasant relations. That is why it is desirable for ♑ above all to strive for inner superiority, an increase of moral value which will overcome all unwillingness, jealousy or antipathy. Earnest perseverance, diplomatic reserve and great talent for diplomacy are qualities of ♑ which no doubt frequently contribute to a successful career.

♑ makes for great mental *earnestness, reliability* and inner *steadfastness.* The native is quiet, concentrated, comtemplative; diving deeper and deeper into every subject in the main is the line along which this Ego likes to develop and does develop most. *Philosophy* is studied by preference and especially pessimistic philosophy. There is a great predestination to see *fatality, inevitable fate* in everything and to regard man as a creature who on every side is limited.

And yet "the golden era" was governed by the ruler of ♑ which signifies that the ♄ limitation need not be unpleasant, if one subjects oneself to it *cheerfully and of one's own free will.* Harmonious aspects favour the supposition that in daily life Capricorn usually keeps his inclination to despondency in the background by a powerful, organising activity. Many ideals are then cherished and a quiet, strong hope prevails that they will surely be reached some day. Frequently a strong stimulant is added by the desire for honour and distinction.

Care should be taken if ♄ is afflicted for then ♑'s less good side comes to the fore, chiefly expressed by *discontent, admiration for and striving after outward power, honour and distinction;* greater respect for ceremony and ritual than for the thought hidden behind it. Capricorn is very apt to regard his own ideas as the only truth, which produces a certain kind of "spiritual loneliness". ♑ ought to beware of *onesidedness.* For where some definite idea is realised with much devotion and concentrated activity, a certain negation, an undervaluing of other people's conceptions easily arises. The native is adviced therefore to keep constantly in contact with people of different opinions; then right judgment will keep his mind free from dogmatism and prejudice and tend to influence the mentality helpfully.

Capricorn's great thirst for admiration and homage inclines to a certain *selfcomplacency,* which may lessen others' wish to admire his splendid work, splendid except for this self-glorification. This weakness naturally acts as a drawback to real progress, and should be overcome as soon as possible. Man achieves his highest attainments by the action of the Spirit, the Universal Spirit in whose operations all boastfulness and self-glorification naturally have no place. They only pertain to matter which is merely the "executive power", and as such frequently spoil much of what is accomplished. And that is ♑'s weak point: he is *so* absorbed in "executing" that he loses sight of the inspiring Principle in the long run.

☉ in ♑ renders the native diplomatic, reserved, a tireless worker. Much store is set by ceremony and etiquette, both with regard to himself and others.

Affliction makes him melancholy, morose with a sense of being ill-used, and not sufficiently appreciated, which easily degenerates into conceit.

Receptive to colds, predestined for rheumatism, skin diseases; slight taking of food, constipation, weak digestion (☍ ♋).

The Sun (☉) in Aquarius (♒).

(January 21—February 18).

Here we find *new ideas,* the *modern conceptions of art, humane phil-osophies;* the mind seeks the *soul* and the *essence* of all that exists and at the same time constantly aims at making others acquainted with what he has experienced of wisdom and beauty. Similarly Aquarius, the Water-bearer, pours upon the earth the waters of life which he has himself drawn.

His love of nature is ennobled by a wish to *understand it from a higher point of view,* to recognise in nature's expressions the working of sublime powers and ideals.

In everything Truth, the inspiration of omnipresent Truth is sought, the *life producing Cause* of all things, just as ♅ ruler of ♒ is the great *God of Causes* who stands behind Zeus (♃) behind Chronos (♄). It is not one and the same thing however to *sense* all this and to *put it into practice.*

There is a strong tendency towards scientific research especially of modern, finer technicalities and of "super-natural" forces. The human psyche also is a favourite subject for study and in both these departments many results may often be reached.

♒ gives the native the faculty of seeing through people's designs, he will speedily discern their nature and character and gauge their secret plans and feelings. He loves the study of nature — plants, animals and people — and of the supernatural world, occultism, astrology etc. In everything evolution, growth is admitted and his joy is to be able to observe it everywhere. His "knowledge of man" causes him to like to ridicule a person's peculiarities — and although this is usually done in a generous spirit, discord, misunderstanding and alienation may also often result.

He shows great readiness to be of service to those who ask for help or advice and he will often do good in silence, but for all that some degree of selfpleasing enters into these actions (♒ is, like ♉, ♏ and ♌ a *fixed* sign!).

☉ in ♒ produces idealists and reformers, knowers and friends of men, who sometimes like to make fun of their brothers („Was sich liebt, neckt sich!) (Those who love each other, tease each other).

Affliction renders the native rash, confused, eccentric. (11 is the fool's number! — Aquarius is the eleventh sign of the Zodiac).

Bad circulation, illnesses of the blood, palpitations of the heart, heart-burn, dropsy (with heart-diseases (♌) dropsy usually begins with the legs); bad eyes.

The Sun (☉) in Pisces (♓).

(February 19—March 21).

Pisces produces a very sensitive nature. The mind is extremely im-pressionable and constantly occupied trying to explain impressions as well as possible and to understand them, although this is more often along the line of *psychic-sensing* than that of *practical-science.* If we bear in mind the fact that the "Fish" is the symbol of Christianity and of Christ, the first great Christian, we shall readily understand that in every ♓-nature there is a little of that longing to understand and to forgive his fellow-men, to feel himself one with them and above all to succour those who are ill-treated by the world.

Sacrifice is the keynote of the character. There is a remarkable instinctive sensing of others' sorrow and joy, and at the same time a desire to aid those who suffer. For the life of the ♓ is full of suffering; his inner attitude is characterised by a vaguely sad idealism which nevertheless hopes for redemption and reconcilement. It is almost a matter of course that this attitude will not be appreciated by his environment and that people will often take advantage of his sensitiveness and humanity. In the midst of "ordinary" society or surroundings a sudden sensation of loneliness and discomfort is often experienced, a general feeling of not being at home there, a strong wish for a *"Land, das meine Sprache spricht,"* (Land which speaks my own language), a mood which sometimes overwhelms him very unexpectedly. And in these moods many *awkward* things are usually done for which only few people are able to account.

If however he is not afraid of other people's censures he will as a rule find himself the best way of getting out of difficult or unpleasant circumstances.

The sensing of thought being strong, it is probable that less significance will consequently be attached to *form,* and it is this very *emotionality,* this *undervaluing of outer observances* which render ♓'s social life so difficult.

The consciousness of his own imperfection makes him indulgent to others and the sense of his own unworthiness renders him willing to do any kind of work. This tendency also is often speculated upon by those who are less far advanced in their evolution.

It goes without saying that since ♓ is not understood, daily intercourse brings him disappointment, and that solitude is sought if the theories which he propounds do not meet whith approval. Well-meant words and action will probably be misinterpreted by the outer world, which again will tend to strengthen his love of seclusion.

The great difficulty for Pisces is to *give himself and yet to be his own self.* His great inclination to help, to support, in short to sacrifice himself, is easily abused by others which then leads to the loss of his own personality.

Giving should always be wholly spontaneous and not compulsory; it becomes more beautiful and helpful in proportion as the offering is free.

In his inmost being the native has an intense yearning to merge himself completely in others, to be absorbed in a universal brotherhood. Consequently he has the faculty of uniting himself with others on the mental and astral planes, in other words the power of sensing the thoughts and feelings of his environment (medium). It is however inadvisable for him to allow himself to go too far in this direction because without the help of logical differentiation, unwished-for and unfavourable consequences may easily occur, materially as well as spiritually.

♓ gives also occult tendencies; as well as a *natural predisposition,* there is often a *definite liking* for these things. The native has a firm belief in invisible forces and their influence on the human soul; and since in general far less store is set by the outer form than by that which is hidden behind it, it is easily comprehensible that ♓ should accept the existence of a "world of spirit". Moreover this sign of all signs gives most possibility of personal experience in this field.

♓ indeed produces a *loving nature,* but it does not render the native especially fit for *personal* attachments. On the one side there is a great thirst for confidence and devotion, on the other too little faith and trust. Thus lack of balance, *contrariness* arise which — when not sufficiently controlled — easily turn into the *exact opposite of what was idealised and intended from the outset.*

In this region feeling should be kept as pure and strong as possible; for this question, though difficult, is of too great importance to be carelessly passed over.

The strongest side of this character manifests in a harmonious peaceful atmosphere of humane, contemplative thought. Only there can the psychic sensitiveness develop in such a way as to prove that an "unpractical dreamer" may radiate a power far surpassing all wordly power, order and direction.

It is however necessary for Pisces to bring more line into his thought, to become more *conscious of himself* in order to better give spiritual and moral help.

A person with the ☉ in ♓ is of a quiet nature, often somewhat of a Cinderella in practical life who does not understand social life, nor does society understand her; who is sent from pillar to post, from Pontius to Pilate.

Affliction is apt to make Pisces unsociable, easily disconcerted, also an inclination to drink and excessive dancing may be found: a fish wants to swim!

A tendency to perspiration especially feet; very receptive to infections, typhoid fever, disturbances in the digestive organs (♉ ♍), intestinal diseases, consumption (□ ♊), neurasthenia.

The Moon (☽) in the Twelve Signs.

☽ in ♈. Feeling is usually the principal motive inducing all kinds of actions. These will be very spontaneous, very intense, and usually optimistic.

In spite of opposition a new plan is made with courage and energy; *sympathy for a question is considered a sufficient guarantee for the chance of success* and the native will often work disinterestedly at an idea that to others seems absolutely hopeless. And it often happens that others are inspired by this enthusiasm and thus far more is attained than was originally anticipated. Caution must however be recommended.

In the department of study, religion etc. feeling takes the lead; but the native should be on his guard lest when his feelings are deeply moved, his mind be too open to other people's ideas. For though later on more lucidity will follow, this lack of judgment is likely to have caused disappointment and disillusion which might have been prevented had there been less emotion.

The feelings are keen and intense. *"Everything or nothing"* is the motto.

Affliction renders restless, rash, independent of others' opinions.

Headaches (neuralgia), sleeplessness, baldness, catarrhal complaints, weak eyesight.

☽ in ♉ gives great *devotion* and *perseverance* in all enterprises, especially those which are considered particularly good and helpful for society. The feelings are deep and serious; health and finances are almost all that could be wished. The emotions are very impressionable, especially for *music*. There is a great liking and a great gift for music *(singing)*.

This position gives further love of art, and of all that adds beauty and sweetness to life. Sometimes pride, stubbornness and self-will are mingled. Then there is also some tendency to imagine oneself ill-treated and to feel offended when no harm was intended. Personal feeling should therefore be kept very pure, which will enrich and gladden the whole personality.

☽ in ♉ makes the native cheery, kind-hearted, well-disposed, fond of the good things of the earth, of solidity. Resourceful in unexpected difficulties.

Affliction renders him passionate, prone to exaggerate and deaf to reason when wrathful.

A weak throat, inflammation of the throat, croup, thrush, inflammation of the tonsils, goitre, in 29° ♉ eye-disease. Sexual disturbances (♂ ♏).

☽ in ♊ gives a desire for a busy varied life, in which much may be seen and learned. It gives the native great satisfaction to be of service at various places and in various directions. This position causes however a certain duality, changeable emotions, a restless seeking after truth. This gives rise to a great love of science and all kinds of art, but may however also conduce to superficiality or a continuous falling into extremes. ♊ should *"survey"* but not *"pass without seeing"* and learn to value things at their true worth, otherwise irresolution arises, through which good opportunities will pass unused.

☽ in ♊ gives a longing for knowledge, makes people resourceful. liberal-minded, adaptive, liable to sail with the wind.

Affliction produces restlessness and a confused mind, doubt, — an unbelieving Thomas.

Lung-catarrh, acute pneumonia, bronchitis, asthma, consumption of the lungs, rheumatism in arms and shoulders; nervous disorders.

☽ in ♋. Every feeling, every emotion is of value; everything experienced is of importance; all memories retained and often and willingly gone over again in thought. The *motherly feeling* shows to some extent in all relations, the wish to cherish, to look after — be it only in thought or with words. But just as a mother gives most love, so will she also have most expectations, be most *exacting* and suffer most when the child leaves her to go out into the world; she feels the parting most — if she forgets the child's own interests. Thus the slightest alienation or chill in intercourse will be a grievous experience; with insufficient selfcontrol there will be a chance of *"loving egoism"* and exacting admiration. Beloved people are idealised, but it should be considered whether in the end they profit by an image being made of them to which they cannot possibly live up; and whether this does not cause far more likelihood of sorrow and disappointment for both sides than ought to be the case. This position of the ☽ gives a certain conservatism of ideals, makes economical, careful, attached. Domestic life continues to have a great attraction in spite of the likelihood of conflicts.

☽ in ♋ makes the native subject to moods; kind, sociable, but inclined to be easy going, and not to exert himself seriously.

Affliction makes shy, timid, fearful even without a real cause. Afflictions of the ☽ in ♋ denote a not well balanced care for one's own and other people's interests. As the following verse says (as a nation the Dutch are under the influence of ♋):

"In matters of commerce the fault of the Dutch
Is giving too little and asking too much."

Digestive disturbances, anaemia, dropsy, fatness, swellings, inflation, tendency to cancer of the stomach, epilepsy (□ ♈).

————

☽ in ♌. Liable to overesteem himself, but also to increase his capacities. It is characteristic of the type to regard himself as the centre of his surroundings; and because he has much vital force and moral courage, many weaker people derive from him material or spiritual support. This is appreciated and shown in warm adoration and admiring affection, so that really much selfcontrol is wanted to keep "humble of heart". Honest sympathy and an open mind usually are prominent virtues, only sometimes they are coloured by a kind of *"false shame"* which partly hides feelings and thoughts when they are supposed to spoil some good impression to be made on others. But the noble kind-heartedness and magnanimous loyalty, the great feeling of responsibility for himself and others, in short all the "kingly" qualities which Leo gives to this character, impress us so favourably and pleasantly that we willingly forgive the more or less distinct self-conceit.

If the naturally overbearing manner can be sublimated and turned into a realisation of *inner dignity,* which cannot mix with people of less noble tendencies, then every temptation will be a source of greater power and more help, and thus conduce to greater usefulness in analogous difficulties of others.

Affliction makes proud, easily offended, conceited, and gives overmuch class feeling.

Heart troubles, bad circulation of the blood, impure blood, convulsions, faints, swoons, scrofula (□ ♉) backaches. In 6° ♌ eye-diseases.

☽ in ♍ gives *very minutely analytical feelings* and very decided personal taste. There is much love for the fine arts, especially for literature. Works of art are often inwardly enjoyed without its being much shown. Special inventions, subtle intricacies, minute classifications are much appreciated. Small differences in speech, dialect etc. are immediately noticed, the memory being especially strong for similar things. This accuracy manifests itself in every-day affairs, surroundings etc.

Inner enjoyment often leads to neglect of social duties, so that an egoistical impression will sometimes be made. But an inclination to be of service to others does exist, a wish to achieve much and be of help to many, to control and correct oneself and this at any rate is the first condition of true attainment.

This position gives the native a practical outlook on life, a correct discernment of the possibilities for progress and ability to make use of them.

☽ in ♍ renders the native fastidious, reserved, ever discriminating, separating the true from the false; fond of articles of use, of hygiene and the science of food.

When *afflicted* bickering becomes a mania, liable to lead to irritation and nervous overstrain.

Weak intestines, tendency to constipation, dysentery, colic, dropsy of the stomach, peritonitis, typhus, tumours in the stomach, gallstones, nervousness, pneumonia, consumption (□ ♊), eczema.

☽ in ♎ gives the feeling something humane and courteous which always pleads "extenuating circumstances" and admonishes to silence, if nothing good can be said.

There is a certain longing for much intercourse in the world and being well-known with the public. Appreciation of and intercourse with the other sex is also an important factor in life and in work. Feeling will usually prove a good guide in all kinds of action. But the native should strive to find happiness *in himself,* and not to let it depend on others.

In order to secure true and enduring peace both within and around the native, strengthening and inspiring him to greatest achievements he must attain tranquility in his own thoughts and harmony in his sensations, a thing more difficult to the balancing ♎ than it seems to be.

☽ in ♎ makes people inclined to postpone things, but kind, sympathetic, tolerant, fond of concord and appreciation.

Affliction brings crazes, a wavering mind, dependent.

Kidney diseases, propensity to Bright's disease, kidney abcess, uraemia, weak back, lumbago, stomach trouble (□ ♋), headaches (☍ ♈), sleeplessness (☍ ♈).

☽ in ♏. This position of the Moon makes the native very sensitive to emotional influences and consequently produces strongly pronounced sympathies and antipathies. These feelings should however not become too prominent, for this would cause the will either to slacken or be led into wrong channels.

♏ gives a certain *pride,* which is ashamed to accept defeat; and this is a good stimulant in a battle which is by no means easy.

There is much love for study of *occultism,* but with a view to the native's fanatical tendencies, a clear head should be kept particularly in this department.

This position moreover gives very peculiar moral and social ideas; special selfcontrol and a strong feeling of responsibility are needed to prevent unpleasantness. So these virtues should as much as possible be cultivated and it is advisable not to listen too much to the opinion of superficial acquaintances and partial friends.

Interest in and appreciation of the other sex is very great, but is usually limited to outward things: the desire for physical exercise and training of the muscles is easily overdone, when insufficiently supervised and becomes abnormal exhibition of strength which has a less favourable influence on the constitution. Moderation and deliberation in everything are urgently recommended.

☽ in ♏ makes the native courageous, firm, blunt, but sensitive to kindness. He cannot bear other people meddling in his affairs.

Affliction makes passionate, sensuous, partial, vindictive.

Illnesses of the bladder, dropsy, affections of the uro-genital organs, kidney diseases, hernia, palpitations of the heart (□ ♌), throat troubles (☍ ♉).

☽ in ♐. Generally speaking the disposition is that of one who perpetually seeks for what is more and better and therefore talks and argues with every one he comes across.

The inner life is usually very sensitive and characterised by a continual desire for knowledge which cannot be silenced until every question is answered.

The will for what is good is very sincere — almost *too* sincere. That is to say the native speaks so freely about his ideas, ideals and failings that others — if they wish him ill — may use it to his detriment.

His *vitality* is not easily destroyed and every lesson is thankfully taken to heart. Life in the open, journeys and voyages, sport and physical exercise have a great attraction and are pursued with zest. His love for nature is very strong, and he has a pleasant comradeship with all kinds of animals — especially horses and dogs. —

☽ in ♐ makes the native optimistic, jovial, fond of movement. The study of "New Thought", religion and law attract him.

Affliction makes him self-indulgent, unsteady, changeable, inclined to tell tales out of school.

Sciatica, weak hips and thighs, broken limbs through accidents. Weak lungs, asthma, consumption (☍ ♊). Affections of the nervous system. Intestinal disorders, chronic constipation (□ ♍).

☽ in ♑ renders the feelings strong and steadfast and produces reliability. This ☽-position hinders, however, the expression of the feelings, so that those who are loved, will often remain ignorant of it. ♄ is the ruler of ♑ and where this cold, limiting planet influences the sensitiveness of the ☽ a certain distrust arises, a reserve that fears to express itself lest another might profit by some weakness shown. The basis of the disposition is melancholy and pessimistic.

This position gives something *fatherly* to the feelings of attachment, for as a father loves and cares for his child more and better than appears, so in every relation of friendship or love there will enter an element of tender devotion, seldom fully recognised by others.

♑ gives the native a thirst for moral and social advancement and consequently makes him diligent in proportion as this tends to further success and promotion. Added to this desire for higher and better things is a fairly great sensitiveness to outer decorum which must be kept pure, since otherwise wrong things will easily be done, if on the surface they appear to be right.

☽ in ♑ inclines the native to anticipate the wishes of those in a higher station, to ride the high horse and to dress oneself in borrowed plumage.

The *Goat* on his solitary climbing tours is the exact emblem of this self-sufficient seeker for the highest summits of human knowledge; without much interest in the work of others nor great joy of life. — The "tail" of this zodiacal sign points to additional capacities, although these are very rarely shown.

Affliction makes him gloomy, discontented, more or less stingy for fear of poverty, selfish.

Inflammation of the joints, articular rheumatism, lack of synovial fluid. Dyspepsia (☍ ♋). Constipation, eczema, nettle-rash. Weak kidneys, too much acid in the urine (□ ♎).

☽ in ♒. Feeling is humane, sincere; imagination and intuition very well developed. ♒ gives the native a great desire to bring *new ideas* to mankind and equally strong conviction of being able to do so. Whereas ♏ feels related to others through *"falling in the same way"*, ♒ sees the unity through *"rising in the same way"*. Thoughts and feelings from all sides are assimilated and spread to the benefit and development of humanity. But the differences in human nature he should take into account, and before a plan is carried out, the native should seriously consider whether the people concerned will benefit by it or not. Therefore it would be well for him to learn to look at every question from different aspects; for although ♒ has an extremely clearcut view of people and things, yet he is apt to imagine the conquering of others by his own logical way of thinking somewhat too easy. In that way difficulties are likely to arise where nothing but sympathy and helpfulness were intended. Tolerance, acknowledgement of others' good intentions — however defectively expressed — should as much as possible be cultivated.

To the outer world an attitude of indifference is often adopted which induces many to think that life's difficulties do not count for much. The native has a constant desire for intercourse with many and different people, contact with all kinds of divergent courses of thought.

From every side much sympathy and readiness to help will usually be experienced, so much so that enterprises often succeed without much personal share in them. Failure to keep *promises* is frequent, promises are thoughtlessly made and things are often done superficially.

This position of the moon gives a great sense of humour, which manifests especially in intimate and domestic circles. Certain people will often be made the butt of rather sharp ironical remarks, which may lead to trouble.

Affliction makes the native eccentric, chaotic, inclined to upset things.

Anaemia, general weakness, fainting fits, swoons, dropsy of the ankles owing to an affection of the heart ($\mathcal{8}\ \Omega$). — Varicose veins, blood poisoning, ulcers, nervousness hysteria.

$\mathcal{D}$ in $\mathcal{H}$. The native has a great liking for things *romantic, peculiar,* and *sentimental.* He should be warned against exaggerating his feelings and laying too much stress on what seems to be mysterious. Too much day-dreaming, too much living in phantasies should be avoided; sound knowledge of occult science may, however, bring about much good.

He should guard against too great and too sudden a despondency when attempts fail, and against consequent discouragement which might cause the loss of all pleasure in the work, also against the "self-pity" which so easily follows.

Moods of the surroundings are soon sensed and have a great influence on the native's own condition. Passive contact will very easily be made with an other world, but it is not advisable to be often open for such transcendental activities; the inclination to day-dreaming and contemplation should rather be transmuted into a calm, cheerful, well-aimed love of work. Optimistic philosophical literature will effect much good in this direction.

The first requisites of a happy, contented life are much recreation and movement in nature, not to be too much alone, but rather to seek the company of fine, sympathetic people.

Affliction makes for doubt, laziness, self-indulgence, the native is easily led astray, a willing tool for stronger natures.

Feet sensitive to cold, humidity; corns, thickening of the big toe; constitutionally very receptive to contagion; venereal diseases; tendency to alcoholism and the use of narcotics; lax tissues. Weak lungs, consumption. Diseases of the bowels ($\mathcal{8}\ \mathfrak{M}$).

Mercury ($\mathcal{Q}$) in the Twelve Signs.

$\mathcal{Q}$ in Υ makes the intellect keen, quick at repartee, and inventive, acute, which, especially in correspondence, at times may lead to irony and sarcasm.

A person with this position is a keen observer, intelligent and has a fertile mind; he has quick and clear conceptions which make him alert and ready for battle when discussion or argument arise.

Affliction makes rash, thoughtless, restless, subject to exaggeration. Fear and overstrain of thought should then be avoided, quiet, concentrated thought practised.

Inharmonious aspects may also lead to stammering, especially in childhood. But seeing that this is merely a nervous trait, it will disappear as self-control increases.

Nervous headaches, neuralgia, dizziness, insomnia owing to overexertion, dullness, eye defect.

☿ in ♉ gives a good memory, although on the other hand learning does not come easily and quickly. Some outstanding opinions, *hobbies,* are usual, which become rather more and not less pronounced, if met by opposition. When they are opposed quietly and logically, they will however prove not unreasonably vehement. Otherwise ☿ in ♉ makes the native patient, reserved, steady going, obedient, and gives love of art; judgment is guided by feeling.

When *afflicted* the person concerned should beware of becoming stubborn, inflexible, wilful and stingy.

There is a tendency to stammer (when in a passion), difficulty with swallowing; a child with this position often has convulsions when cutting teeth. Further hoarseness, croup, sore throat, nervous deafness, disturbances in the genital and urinary organs (☿ ♏).

☿ in ♊ gives a keen, acute intellect, able to *distinguish* and *compare* clearly; not content with abstractions, but fond of realities. This position makes the native versatile, fond of novelties, witty, fitted for commerce. ☿ here is in its element and — if not afflicted — produces great clarity, logical insight and quick comprehension.

Affliction makes the native superficial, shallow, sly and gives changeable thoughts; honesty should be practised as much as possible.

Gout and nervous pain in shoulders, arms and hands; asthma, bronchitis, pleurisy, intercostal neuralgia, nervous pain in the hips (♐). Breathing should be regularly practised, speaking and singing be done moderately.

☿ in ♋ gives a very retentive memory and a *summarising* view of things. *Silence* and *devotion* are the cause of success in work and career, but a weakness for praise and flattery often plays too great a part in behaviour. ☿ in ♋ makes the native inventive, inquisitive, diligent, economical and tactful, but at the same time gives some inclination to gloom which is less desirable. Interest is felt in the study of antique.

Affliction makes the native continually crave for new emotions, makes him curious and opiniated, leads to troubles in intercourse and brings financial disappointments.

Flatulency, spasms of the stomach, nervous affection of the stomach through anxiety or sorrow. The use of alcohol is very bad. A healthy imagination should be cultivated and exaggerated anxiety avoided.

☿ in ♌. The intellect is clear and pure, the style imaginative and rational. Speeches, talks, oral and written expressions having a definite aim or tendency, will succeed best and will have the desired result. ♌ makes for *broad conceptions* and noble ideals and ☿ gives a pleasant manner of presenting them. A certain *autocracy* in matters of intellect or spirit cannot be denied; contradiction or illogical arguments are always attacked, censured, and if possible made ridiculous. But sentence should not be passed too quickly! ☿ in ♌ makes the native frank, kind-hearted, sympathetic, capable of organising, inclined to take the lead and order others, to work with great schemes, but ignore details.

Affliction renders him passionate, whimsical, speculative.

Nervous palpitations of the heart, convulsions, fainting fits, swoons, backache, brain fatigue; beware of too great exertion, of sitting bent forward at study.

☿ in ♍ makes the native practical, apt to admonish, capable, fond of scientific research and of clear and logical judgment; reserved. This is a position for a student, a naturalist, who prefers to occupy himself with the careful, systematic investigations of small creatures or objects.

When *afflicted* the native will be irritable, cavilling, inclined to set to work at many things at a time and to make light of things which are really serious.

Sensitive bowels, stomachache, colic, diarrhoea, constipation, nervous weakness, nausea, shortwindedness, itching of the nose. Too much thinking should be avoided and regular habits are particularly recommended.

☿ in ♎ gives a correct intuitive view of various matters, including articles of commerce: *well-balanced thoughts* for making plans, the gift of comparison, knowledge of goods. It will prove profitable to work in cooperation, to buy in association, to study and repeat with others. ☿ in ♎ makes the native thoughtful, kind, humane; eloquent and more or less refined in intercourse, whilst he also loves and has a talent for music and art.

Affliction however renders him unbalanced, and arouses dishonest tendencies. His best work is done in combination with and under the guidance of a sympathetic person, because otherwise some of the things wich should be done will neither be begun, nor finished.

Affections of the kidneys, anuria, obstruction in the uretic tubes, nephritis, lumbago, dizzines, nervous headaches (☿ ♈), eye troubles (☿ ♈). It is bad to stand or study too long at a stretch.

☿ in ♏ gives a well developed, *penetrating* intellect. The native naturally takes great interest in all that is *hidden, mysterious* and *peculiar,* and no pains will be spared to get to know more of the mysteries surrounding human life. During school years most work will be done in natural history, cosmography etc. whereas in later life there will probably be much aptitude for the study of medicine (doctor, surgeon, nurse). Great power of

64

concentration and clear logical conceptions enable the native with the aid of a few observed facts to diagnose correctly.

Very likely there may have been sexual experiences in early youth which do not leave a pleasant recollection. It will therefore be very good to try and find an equivalent experience in some form of *New Thought* or other. ☿ in ♏ makes the native resourceful, gives much insight, and a great attraction on the one hand to the study of occultism, and on the other to mechanical pursuits for which he has much capacity.

Affliction makes sly, mysterious, sharp in remarks and admonitions, impudent, bold, querulous and apt to take things badly, obstinate, sceptical and sarcastic.

Pain in bladder and genitals, very sensitive genitals, sexual troubles, deafness, stammering, hoarseness (☿ ♉). Anxiety and fear and absent mindedness should be overcome.

☿ in ♐ renders the native quick and apt to say things which strike home and make for enmity. What is felt to be true is expressed to everybody and defended without any regard for the requirements of good breeding (especially with a ☿-♂ aspect). Otherwise this position makes him thoughtful, prophetic, earnest and religious. The problems of life are contemplated and advice to seekers is readily given. In social life an inferior position will be more suitable than a responsible post. The desire to go out into the world is very strong, also the wish to gather knowledge and express own thoughts to those who are willing to listen. Being a most earnest thinker, ♐ often feels superior in his surroundings, and does not therefore usually feel at home with idle chatter and gossip. ☿ in ♐ moreover makes the native fond of justice, religion and philosophy, freedom of thought and speech, also of travelling.

Affliction gives little perseverance, makes him rash, dissolute, changeable, given to caustic expression, both in speech and writing; dishonest and inclined to *sophism*.

Weakness of hips and thighs, sciatica, paralysis, nervousness, nervous cough, asthma, pleurisy (☿ ♊). This positon warns against too much study and too great a strain on the mind.

☿ in ♑. The planet of the concrete mind in the particularly concrete sign ♑ makes for a clear and logical faculty of thought. Conclusions are only based upon *palpable facts* and in every study the greatest possible objectivity is displayed. In this way very practical results are easily obtained and also understood by others, but much time will be required for this, because in this position ☿ loses some of his quick, intuitive activity. He will *not* learn *quickly*, but *thoroughly*. ☿ in ♑ further renders the native orderly, systematic, economical and diplomatic; it gives concentration of thought, reserve, dexterity and ambition.

Affliction makes him suspicious and melancholy, stingy rather than economical, jealous, spiteful, sly.

Rheumatism in the knees, gout, skin diseases, itching of the skin, intestinal troubles through anxiety and fear, costiveness, nervous indigestion, flatulence, backache.

☿ in ♒ greatly strengthens the mental and intellectual faculties. The mind is very active, original and at times shows some glimpse of genius. Memory is particularly good and if sufficiently and regularly trained, might even recall facts and conditions of former lives. This position gives the desire for a large circle of cultured and intellectual acquaintances; only in intercourse with the other sex it will be somewhat difficult to draw the line between purely mental understanding and personal attachment. And yet this is desirable for the development of moral consciousness and social position. Otherwise this position is favourable for the study of human character, and produces an agreeable talker, able to put forward new ideas in society. ☿ in ♒ makes the native intuitive, independent, idealistic, a lover of art, sociable, inclining to abstract thought; astrological study attracts, as also spiritualistic and telepathic research.

Affliction makes him inclined to philosophize vaguely "ins Blaue hinein," renders unfaithful, critical; easily leads to slander and "sponging".

General nervous disorder, neuralgia, bad circulation of the blood, impure blood, twinging and smarting pain in the whole body, hysteria, impotence to walk, varicose veins, neuralgia of the heart, palpitations of the heart. Such a person should not give way to phantasies of fear, but use his reason to control them.

☿ in ♓. The planet of the reasoning mind is somewhat strange in ♓ and therefore causes a continual conflict between *logic* and the *"assurance of feeling"*. Things are often sensed as perfectly certain, for which no reasonable explanation can be given. This is usually caused by excessive mobility of thought and too little *"pure" reason*. Moreover the native's great openness to others' ideas often causes confusion. For that reason he has very little ability for purely intellectual discussion, although the fitness of others in this respect is much appreciated. ☿ in ♓ makes the native psychic, mediumistic, kind, good-natured; inclines to mysticism and makes him sensitive to harmony and beauty.

Affliction leads to absent mindedness, disposes to worry, gloom, despondency, listnessness, superficiality.

Sensitive feet (also to cold and damp), cramp and gout in the feet, phthisis (□ ♊), general weakness and limpness, deafness. The feet should be kept dry and warm; the brain free from anxiety and excessive exertion.

Venus (♀) in the Twelve Signs.

♀ in ♈ gives the native warm sympathy and makes him fond of articles of peculiar beauty. This position gives a great taste for modern art and interest for new connections though never going beyond certain limits, for by nature ♀ is averse to all exaggeration and extremes.

Affliction makes the native impulsive, hasty, easily falling in love at first sight, passionate, prodigal, whimsical. He has a great desire for change and craves things adventurous and romantic.

Catching cold, catarrh in the head with formation of mucus, disease of the lachrymal glands, eczema. The use of cosmetica should be avoided.

♀ in ♉ gives a *very strong love-nature,* makes the native steadfast in attachment, kind and pleasant in intercourse, faithful in marriage, which brings financial improvement, fond of good manners, etiquette and respectability.

Affliction makes him a spendthrift, sometimes lazy, dull.

A weak throat, slavering, thrush, inflammation of the throat, tumours in the neck, inclined to have mumps, pain in the backpart of the head, goitre. The throat should be protected from cold and humidity.

♀ in ♊ gives a happy combination of *feeling for beauty* and *capacity for self-expression;* makes the native highly respected by his intimates, and gives many acquaintances among artists, intellectuals and much travelled people. All this has a· favourable influence on the "making of name" in the world. ♀ in ♊ however makes the native's affections somewhat *changeable* which may sometimes lead to more than one connection. Further does this position give a liking for pleasant social outings, and also confers a melodious voice and a refined mind.

Affliction makes him changeable, superficial, fickle; and leads to difficulties in correspondence and in matters of love ("je prends mon bien où je le trouve") often two loves at the same time. The interference of relatives in personal matters may be expected, because they are apt to regard the native as somewhat irresponsible.

Bad respiration owing to unsuitable clothing, impure blood, dropsy, warts, bredsore. The blood should be kept pure and too thin clothing should be avoided.

♀ in ♋. This nature is very clinging and *needs affection.* ♀ makes the receptivity to moods and impressions, characteristic of ♋, manifest chiefly in intercourse with those who are favourable disposed, moods of loved people are particularly clearly sensed and their characters understood. ♀ in ♋ denotes very strong feeling of love, for *children* or for those who are looked upon as such. Then the cherishing, nurturing, motherly nature becomes prominent; time and money being willingly spent to give them pleasure. But the native should be warned not to wish for gratitude or attachment in return; for children often regard what is given to them as their *right*, and not as a particularly great kindness or favour. And ill-humour because of this easily spoils the joy of giving. *True love* is a bad bookkeeper; it gives without counting how much it may receive in exchange.

Moreover ♀ in ♋ makes the feelings go out to people of maturer age and (or) more experience, so that with such a position the mate is nearly always older or has experienced far more than the native. There will be a great, almost exaggerated sensitiveness in love affairs, so that small troubles are felt more intensely than necessary, whereas on the other hand the slightest kindness may bring about the greatest emotion.

♀ in ♋ makes the native sensible of intimate domesticity, gives a fertile imagination, makes him devoted and often mediumistic.

Affliction gives changeable feelings. More steadiness and self-reliance should be striven for, otherwise disappointment will be frequent.

Stomachcatarrh, enlargement of the stomach, relaxed muscles of the stomach, stomach tumours, indigestion, nausea, sickness, vomitting, enlargement of the breast, irregularity in the periods. Sugar should be very sparingly taken.

♀ in ♌ gives warm love aspirations, makes the native tenderhearted, faithful in attachment, loyal, promises a happy married life. His love nature is *magnamimous* and *noble,* more or less inclined to *idealise,* averse to mean thoughts. Full confidence is given and when abused, generous forgiveness follows upon honest repentance.

When *afflicted* the native is inclined to speculate, fond of pleasures and of going out.

Palpitations of the heart, enlargement of the heart, illnesses of the arteries, swoons, tendency to affections of the spinal cord, backache. The native should beware of wearing scanty clothing, of sacrificing health to fashion.

♀ in ♍. Feelings of morality, love and beauty will be of rather a *classical kind,* quiet and well-balanced. It remains however uncertain whether they are able to lead to the personal sacrifices which will undoubtedly be required. This will depend on the degree of self-abnegation already reached (♄ ♓). ♀ in ♍ makes the native cool, often averse to marriage or this position may lead to *platonic love.* Chemistry, hygiene and the science of nutrition are favourite fields of study.

When *afflicted* there is a tendency to cherish affection for inferiors, either physical or psychical.

Weak bowels, peristaltics, diarrhoea, tape worm, in childhood worms. Wrong nutrition e.g. much eating of sweets, immoderate use of potatoes and farinaceous food should be avoided; the diet should be carefully composed.

♀ in ♎ gives a love of art which may be greatly developed. There is a great tendency to collect articles of art, usually more than towards actual creation. The emotions are peaceful, harmonious. This position is favourable to friendship and cooperation, propitiates a rise in social position and makes the native idealistic, popular. ♀ in ♎ denotes a happy mariage, social success, gives taste and liking for music.

Affliction causes competition, disappointment in marriage.

Diabetes, poisoning through absorption into the blood of urine-ingredients, uraemid, eczema, a dry skin often covered with sores, thirst, brick-red precipitation in the urine, urates, uric acid salts, polyuria (secretion abnormally increased). Too much sugar and other dainties should be avoided.

♀ in ♏ makes for much selfcontrol and gives helpfulness, practicality, idealism, an inclination to go through fire and water for beloved people. If however the affection is not mutual or even rendered ridiculous, then the native soon retires and does not show outwardly what is in his mind, though his feelings remain the same.

Afflictions make him sensual, rash, imprudent, passionate in sexual desires, intriguing, jealous, fond of luxury. There is great danger of seduction, and likelihood of being cheated. Especially in youth there is a tendency to an extravagant way of living, so he will be well-advised to be careful in his choice of friends, to avoid undesirable connections, and also any sensation of jealousy and curiosity. Restraint of passion through sublimation of the sexual force is desirable. Breathing gymnastics and simular exercises — done moderately — may be suitable.

Propensity to venereal diseases, women's complaints, hernia, throat illnesses (♌ ♉) Intemperance in food and sex-life, and all other excesses should be avoided.

♀ in ♐ makes the native sensitive to *transitory feelings,* but at the same time also to *high ideals* of humanity and justice. Short-lived attachments, mostly idealised or unreasonable, keep the spirit charmed, although at the same time a very strong desire for lasting, harmonious love is present. Much good taste and *"savoir vivre"* is found, also much active optimism and liberal sympathy. Further ♀ in ♐ makes the native generous, pious, philanthropic, gives love of music and other arts, makes him fond of nature and of out-door life, also of *travelling.* His marriage will probably be financially favourable.

Affliction renders him romantic, superficial, given to flirting.

Sciatica, tumours in hips and thighs, bronchial and pulmonary affections (♌ II). Too much sport will do harm in the long run.

♀ in ♑. ♀ is not favourably posited in ♑, especially if no helpful aspects are indicated. In matters of love there is much faithfulness, great earnestness and steadfastness, but there is usually something (difference of age, insight or something similar) that gradually, almost imperceptibly causes *estrangement* and this will be very much hindering expression in the world. The affections will however be of a more harmonious and lasting nature, in proportion as the feelings are less concentrated and jealousy and mistrust are avoided. The relation to inferiors is usually very good, but sometimes they withdraw in the midst of their task to go somewhere else where they have pleasanter or easier work. ♀ in ♑ makes the native prudent, faithful, chaste and is conducive to social prosperity. Marriage is regarded in a matter-of-fact way and rather often postponed; there is much attraction for older people.

Affliction makes the native gloomy, changeable, jealous of honour and respect.

Affections of the knees, propensity to gout in the limbs, — bursitis praepatellaris (inflammation of a mucous membrane), stomach disturbances (δ $\mathfrak{S}$), sickness, vomitting (δ $\mathfrak{S}$), skin diseases. The native should be on his guard against skin specifics and hair washes.

♀ in ♒ makes the feelings theoretically more universal than personal. The love nature inclines more to romanticism, to the *ideal;* platonic attachments are however less the ideal than marriage, provided a special conception of it obtains. Where these ideas clash with current notions and the public opinion, the native's own opinion is not modified. Generally this position indicates extraordinarily strong convictions which enable to defy many conventional ideas and to strive after a love which is on a higher plane than ordinary. ♀ in ♒ renders popular, faithful, chaste, friendly in love relations. Independent, fond of freedom. Intuitively truth will be rightly distinguished from appearances.

When *afflicted* there is danger of false friends, slander.

Anaemia, diseases of the blood, hysteria, heart affections, swollen veins, varicose veins, swollen ankles.

♀ in ♓. This is the sign of sacrifice, of penitence, and therefore feelings of love here reach their *highest expression.* The flesh must be crucified, before the Spirit of Wisdom and Love can be lifted up to heaven. This accounts for his great attraction to those who are weaker than he, to the poor and needy; also for his warm feelings of humanity, although this sympathy or affection will often be abused. ♀ in ♓ makes the native pitiful, loving, ready to help, gives love for social work, for example rescue work and the raising of the lower classes. This position of ♀ makes the native fond of *music,* of ritual and ceremonies.

Affliction makes him emotional, whimsical and inclines to intemperance.

Sensitive feet, |corns, calosities, chilblains, gout, gonorrhoea, tumours, abdominal swellings (δ ♍).

Mars (♂) in the Twelve Signs.

♂ in ♈. Here Mars is in its element and gives the native the whole of its energy, will-power and courage. For him to approve of some question is equivalent to defending and propagating it. He likes to fight in the van for that which is sympathetic and one may often find that "veni, vidi, vici" comes true for him. ♂ in ♈ renders pushing, energetic and dauntless, positive and enthusiastic; but it is obvious that in his zeal a man with this position will at times trample on other people's most precious principles. This does not prevent him from going on even though every one should be against him.

When *afflicted* the native is restless, impatient, choleric, violent, adventurous, imprudent.

Twinging pain in the head, insomnia, congestion of the brain, brainfever, haemorrhage of the brain, delirium, sunstroke, inflammation of the eyes, wounds in the head or face, bleeding of the kidneys ($8 \triangleq$), ringworm ☐ γ). Too impulsive, rash actions should be prevented as much as possible by selfcontrol. The use of exclusively vegetarian food is recommended especially when afflicted.

♂ in ♉ gives perseverance, renders resolute, positive and persistent; the person with this position will be a great worker who is always at it. Sharply defined applied art, etching, wood-carving, crafts, but probably most of all *sculpture* and *architecture* come to expression with ♂ in ♉. This position moreover makes the native liberal.

Affliction renders obstinate, headstrong, difficult to manage, vindictive, reckless, wasteful.

Affections of the throat, boils, rheumatism in the neck-muscles, goitre, adenoids, swollen tonsils, polyps, diphtherea, nasal catarrh, bleeding of the nose, mumps, venereal sores, excessive functioning of the sex-organs (8 ♏), caustic urine. The vocal organs must not be forced.

♂ in ♊ makes the native very observant, able rapidly to survey the whole (but not the detail of a question or thing) and gives a witty, clear way of transmitting impressions to others. He is sometimes sarcastic, more or less caustic and satirical in remarks or admonitions, very fond of friendly disputes and verbal sham fights; acquaintances are often made fun of. This sometimes drives friends away or even makes enemies of them, although this consequence was by no means intended. As a rule pride hinders further reconcilement. ♂ in ♊ renders intelligent and quick at speech, vigilant, active, above-board, honest, studious, inventive, mechanically capable.

Affliction makes the native critical, ironical, leads him to *flitter away energy,* makes him inconstant, whimsical, imprudent, *quick at repartee,* cynical, sneering.

Tendency to haemorrhage of the lungs, pneumonia, bronchitis, coughs, cuts, neuralgia, inflammation of the nerves; fractures and wounds of arms, hands, collarbone and shoulder. Fractures of the thigh-bone (8 ♐). Gall diarrhoea (☐ ♍). The chest should be kept warmly covered, and the blood kept pure.

♂ in ♋. When this fiery, active planet is placed in the imaginative watery sign ♋, the activity will manifest more in the *imagination* than in *reality.* The native has a great urge to achieve big deeds which will astonish the world, but all that ends in either *grandly conceived plans* or a *fantastically exaggerated* story of an insignificant occurrence. (Peer Gynt.)

♋'s feeling for domestic life is usually too strong (if ♂ does not receive very many strengthening aspects) for the native to set out into the world martially, but the domestic circle and friends will often be treated to all kinds of reproaches, lessons and remarks that usually cause estrangement or rupture. A person with this position is very fond of his *personal freedom* but at the same time is inclined of his own accord to assist others with advice and deed. *Compulsion* arouses *passive protest.*

Affliction renders irritable, revolutionary, disobedient, blustering, careless. They should be warned against infections, especially women ought to beware of it, particularly at childbirth.

A dry stomach cough, bleeding of the stomach (melaena), vomitting of blood (haematemesis), heartburn, eructatra, dyspepsia, a tendency to take too much liquor, accidents through fire, illnesses of the gall, vomitting of gall, typhoid fever — miscarriage.

♂ in ♌ enhances the energy, and makes for the resolute carrying through of a plan, once conceived and clearly pictured in the mind. This position renders the native somewhat irritable, bellicose and provocative; but this does not usually give offence, because others feel the good intention behind the action. Moreover Leo's loyal nature is sufficient warrant. It will however be wise for the native to work at his own improvement and progress with the greatest possible devotion, and endeavour to discover the bright side of everything. The temperament is rather vehement and thoughtless, but with some training and an earnest will for good may be transmuted into an invaluable force, although a little difficult whilst developing it is an indication of a strong personal life. ♂ in ♌ makes the native enthusiastic, active, zealous and sincere, independent, bold, fond of a responsible position, fiery, loving, frank.

Affliction makes him choleric, *hot-tempered,* fond of taking risks, irascible, exacting; disappointments may be expected through excessive impulsiveness and haste in love affairs.

Affections of the heart, pericarditis, endocarditis, enlargement of the heart, palpitations of the heart, aneurysma of the veins, rheumatism of the muscles of the back, oppression, apoplexy, fainting fits, swoons, sunstroke, malaria, nettle-rash (herpes zoster) inflammation of the throat (□ ♉). Passion should be sublimated as much as possible.

♂ in ♍ gives a sharply analytical, active intellect, always on the lookout to discover things which may be profitably used against people holding different opinions, who will therefore often be defeated. But apart from this combativeness, there exists a great love for every kind of study. Perseverance in the dull parts of it makes the native fit to act practically and resolutely, also strategically able to put his "men" in the choicest places. ♂ in ♍ renders the native quick to understand, yet cautious, diplomatic, scientific, matter-of-fact, practical in distributing work, a *capable worker.*

Affliction makes the native critical, sly, irritable, worrying, discontented, irascible to dependents, and often causes intemperate appetite.

Peritonitis, hernia peritonea, appendicitis, enteritis, hernia, disturbed liver, typhus, diarrhoea, dysentery, worms in childhood. This position makes the native receptive to contagious diseases; the right diet should always be strictly followed.

♂ in ♎ produces an enthusiastic partner, one who prefers to cooperate and does his work best in cooperation. A person with this position is very sensible of love and kindness and very easily suggests to himself the advisability of sharing another party's feelings once affection has been shown or assumed to exist. So long as sympathy has not turned into ($\triangle$) antipathy, it is found difficult to say anything unkind to people or to refuse them.

Affliction renders the native passionate, inconstant, jealous, whimsical, bad-tempered, argumentative, tyrannical, unfaithful; what others say influences him too quickly.

Kidney trouble, inflammation of the pelvis (pyelitis), nephritis, bleeding of the kidneys, fevers because of inflammation of the kidneys, headache (δ Υ), sunstroke, lumbago. Should beware of infection.

δ in $\mathfrak{m}$. The energy, the pushing force which Mars gives through the sign $\mathfrak{m}$, which at the same time rules δ, should not be *restrained* but *guided into the right direction* in order really to reach something. Otherwise this force which can at most be driven back temporarily all the same manifests itself and finally may even turn against itself, like the "scorpion" which kills itself with its own sting. Appropriate use of physical faculties should be decided on by common sense and reason. All actions should be *controlled from within;* rash speech or writing usually has unpleasant consequences. δ in $\mathfrak{m}$ makes the native courageous, energetic, strong, positive, *ingenious,* autocratic, *undaunted,* once an aim has been set it will be reached whatever the cost.

Affliction makes him selfish, blunt, bitter, caustic, passionate, extravagant, querulous.

Piles (haemorrhoids), fistula, bladder-diseases, irregular functioning of the sex organs, premature births, inflammation and festering of the sex organs, hernia inguinalis, caustic urine. Diabetes, appendicitis, nose and throat diseases (δ $\forall$). Should be warned against infection, immorality. Hygiene of the sex organs is advisable.

δ in $\nearrow$ gives the courage to send one's own ideas out into the world. From a harmonious aspect to $\mathfrak{A}$, the ruler of Sagittarius, it may be assumed that matters relating to self-acquired religious knowledge, will be attentively listened to in small unorthodox circles. If however $\mathcal{Q}$ is Retrograde, the knowledge will not be mastered *completely,* the attitude will be too mental, and the person concerned will be inclined to *trifle away* his energy. δ in $\nearrow$ renders bold, open, enthusiastic, argumentative, just, thrifty, fond of travelling and sports.

Affliction makes the native *contrary,* fractious, sharp, arrogant, foolhardy; inclined to inconsistency. This position warns against inconsidered actions.

Sciatica, inflammation of the hip joint (coxitis), fracture of the thigh-bone, sores on hips and thighs. Cough, pneumonia, bronchitis, consumption (δ $\amalg$), boils, typhoid.

δ in ζ gives to the *will power* a *solid basis,* in addition to patience and perseverance. Discouragement at drawbacks cannot long suppress the native's energy and again and again new attempts are made to get on.

He should guard against having too many irons in the fire, because this makes for failure, entailing a bad influence on the nervous system. ♂ in ♐ makes the native dignified, gives a sense of responsibility, ambition, and enthusiasm; makes him courageous, patient, persistent, active, more respected than loved.

When *afflicted:* rash, impulsive, stubborn, over-valuing himself, more feared than respected, vindictive. A person with this affliction should guard against falls.

Affections of the knees, inflammation of the knee joint (gonitis), gout of the knee, podagra, rheumatic fever, inflammation of the mucous membrane on the kneecap, nettle rash, chicken-pox, small-pox, measles, scabies, dysentery, jaundice, ulcers in the abdomen.

♂ in ♒ indicates success in life through the native's own merits and activity, through the spreading of new or newly revived ideas in literature or philosophy. Business as well as marriage will greatly improve his financial and social conditions, although no *regular* rise may be observable. He has a great love of work in order to be independent, and this increases in proportion as more difficulties or opposition arise. It is advisable for the native not to fly in a passion or become impatient when opinions differ; but he should try as calmly as possible to comprehend the various views.

Affliction renders bolshevistic, revolutionary, contrary, bombastic, foolhardy, difficult in intercourse, makes for great difference of opinion, makes fractious, blunt, and gives *speculative inclinations.*

A propensity to nervousness. Fracture of lower leg, fever, overheated blood, sores on the legs, infection of the blood, skin-eruptions, rash palpitations of the heart, fainting fits, eye diseases. The blood should be kept pure and the native should be careful of infection and contagion.

♂ in ♓ weakens the will and makes it difficult for the native when necessary to put a check upon himself. This position often leads him to feel himself misunderstood, especially under the paternal roof. Under very extraordinary circumstances a love relation will be entered into of which acquaintances will remain ignorant, or know very little. ♂ in ♓ gives a liking for diplomacy and secret leadership of enterprises.

Affliction causes an inclination towards excess in the use of alcoholic liquors, illicit love-relations, doubt and consequent financial loss. Such a person feels himself badlytreated, and is apt to be unreliable and self-indulgent.

Painful feet, bunions, corns, accidents to the feet, perspiring feet (hyperhidrosis), deformed feet, tumours, complaints of the respiration organs, consumption (□ ♊), inflammation of the intestives, diarrhoea (☍ ♍). Temperance should be practised and the use of alcoholic drink be limited as much as possible.

74

Jupiter (♃) in the Twelve Signs.

♃ in ♈ gives a liking for travel, *movement in the open air,* and amusement. As the native emanates vital force, this position is particularly suited for such work as raising the sick, suffering and poor. Further this position makes the native generous, dignified, honest, frank, really willing to do pioneer's work socially. Such a person might arouse those in trouble and anxiety to face life again with fresh courage.

Affliction renders ill-tempered, unbalanced, impatient and inclines to rash, impulsive actions.

Diabetes, congestion of the brain, dizziness, fainting fits, sleepiness, sores on the upper jaw. The blood should be kept pure, and much movement in the open air is desirable.

♃ in ♉ makes the native kind, *sympathetic,* loving, *liberal,* philanthropic, a good steward, fond of etiquette, decorum, ceremonies. The good things of the earth are enjoyed, and it is a pleasure also to allow others to profit by them.

Affliction renders inclined to excessive expenditure; fond of bombastic show, a Lucullus.

Fullbloodedness, nose bleeding, nasal catarrh, apoplexy, inflammation of the throat, sores on the lower jaw, boils. Greediness should not be indulged in.

♃ in ♊. This position makes the native resourceful and kind; excellent in witty conversation, humorous, and optimistically inclined. Others will be given advice in a winning way and a helping hand is everywhere readily offered. Under this influence we find the "happy-go-lucky" people, who thirst for change and are extremely fond of travelling.

Affliction makes them critical as regards religion; improvident, lighthearted, reckless. Intemperance in diet and insufficient clothing are very harmful.

Congestion of the lungs, bleeding of the lungs, apoplexy of the lungs. Blood-diseases, fattening of the liver, pleurisy, rheumatism of hips and thighs (☍ ♐).

♃ in ♋ makes the native very sensitive and desirous of remaining friends with everybody, which renders him fit to be a mediator. But he likes to find his endeavours *valued*—both ideally and actually—, and if this is not the case a certain despondency takes possession of him. ♃ in ♋ produces love of domestic snugness, but also of travelling, provided too much discomfort is not involved. This position of ♃ makes devoted, courteous, mystical; much inclined to saint-worship. The nature is idealistic, imaginative and fond of art, and at the same time gives a good financial, economical view of things.

Affliction causes an inclination towards *greediness,* a certain excess in food which in later years may bring about unpleasant consequences. There is also a chance of apoplexy if self-control fails.

Enlargement of the stomach, diabetes, gout, rheumatism, stomach and kidney complaints, flatulency, indigestion, dyspepsia, dropsy, disorders of the liver, jaundice, pimples and skin-diseases ($8 \: \gamma$), scurvy. The blood should be kept pure.

♃ in ♌ makes for a jovial, hearty and easy manner, it also gives a great inclination to pleasures, luxury and social intercourse especially out of doors. The native should be warned against exaggeration and intemperance in this respect, because both health and position in life might be seriously injured by them. Just a rare and exquisite artistic performance, or exhibition, a quiet "tea" in refined intellectual society now and then, influence him far more favourably than the wilful hunt for less real pleasures and rowdy joviality with superficial acquaintances. His innate sense of honesty and righteousness should never be overshadowed or diminished by a desire for *popularity and fame;* and a beautiful external should only be respected and praised when the *inner* worth is an acknowledged certainty. ♃ in ♌ renders just, noble, loyal, compassionate, self-reliant, courageous, gives a great sense of self-esteem and also love of ceremony and appearances.

When *afflicted:* ostentatious, sensuous, extravagant, fond of pleasure and speculative. It is desirable to keep control of feeling and not to make light of its weak spots; for an afflicted ♃ always gives an inclination to imagine one's own character more beautiful than it really is, since ♌ likes to see himself in as favourable a light as possible.

Fattening of the heart, bad functioning of the valves of the heart, palpitations of the heart, irregular circulation of the blood, apoplexy, pleurisy, swollen ankles ($8 \: \approx$).

♃ in ♍. Religious feelings will probably be too much exposed to inner criticism to be characterized as definitely "religious". The difficulties are principally with regard to the recognition of divine justice, election etc. This may lead to reckless and recalcitrant moods. A person with this position has a sharp eye in choosing helpers, dependents etc., so that often more will be gained by leading others than by working oneself. ♃ in ♍ makes the native methodical and prudent, tactful, apt at investigating, pedagogic, practical, fit for business and dealing with inferiors. He is greatly interested in everything that is generally useful.

Affliction makes him careless and lazy, cynical, critical about others, egoistic, distrustful, unlucky. This position of ♃ warns against excessive appetite and taking too much sugar.

Affections of the liver, enlargement of the liver, fattening of the liver, liver abscess, jaundice, weakening of the intestines, impaired digestion, abscess in the intestines, dropsy of the stomach as a sympton of liver disease, consumption ($\square \: \Pi$).

♃ in ♎ gives a great openness to humane ideas and aesthetic-philosophical ideals, which when consistently applied of themselves overcome all conflicting suggestions. And this is certainly of benefit both to personal development and to the artistic and social position of the native. ♃ in ♎ makes him conscientious and naturally philanthropic, kind-hearted, sympathetic, sociable in intercourse, and therefore very popular. There is great feeling for art, for mysticism and religion. This position is propitious for marriage and comradeship.

Affliction causes psychic depression, self-indulgence, and disappointment in partnership etc.

Inadequate activity of the kidneys, fatty degeneration of the kidneys, kidney abscesses, tumours in the kidney, diabetes, braincongestion (8 ♈), dizziness, unconsciousness, coma in cases of diabetes and kidney disease, skin-diseases ($\square$ ♐) arising from diminished kidney activity; disturbances of blood-circulation, pleurisy.

♃ in ♏ gives great liking for jurisprudence—a taste in which the native's gifts of eloquence and subtlety are a great advantage. This position gives much self-confidence, makes him dignified, enthusiastic for noble aims, resourceful and practical in finding means whereby to realise these ideals and therefore an important worker.

Affliction gives wrong opinions, leads to uncontrolled passions, renders sensual, proud and greedy. The taking of much rich food is very harmful.

Abscesses in the sex organs, spasmodic passing of urine, phlegmy discharge in the urine, dropsy, apoplexy, piles, fistula, skin-eruptions.

♃ in ♐. This position gives a great preference for outdoor life, for the beauty of nature and a *childlike careless* existence. Life in a big town is only valued in so far as it gives an opportunity for more intense living with regard to things artistic, scientific and social. A person with this position insists on reaching equitable social conditions, the *living wage;* he feels socially; sane ideas regarding economics and society are cherished. Further ♃ in ♐ is favourable to intellect, makes the native witty and spiritual, philanthropic, generous, tolerant, forgiving, devoted.

Affliction makes him passionately fond of *sport,* of *betting;* bombastic, extravagant, full of sectarianism.

Rheumatism and gout, bleeding of the lungs (8 ♊).

♃ in ♑. This position is suitable for a public authority; and if the person concerned is not capable of reaching that in his own small circle he will behave as if he were. This position gives fitness for practical work, for taking the lead in organisation, makes the native self-reliant, accurate, reliable and economical. His way of thinking is somewhat conventional, but resourceful in promoting the success of an enterprise; the native always remains true to his principles.

Affliction makes him ambitious, stingy with an eye to the main chance, and gives an excessively dainty appetite.

Fatty degeneration of the liver, sluggish circulation, impaired digestion (8 ♋). Eczema and other kinds of skin diseases, jaundice. One should be careful to keep the blood pure.

♃ in ♒. Favourable to all enterprises along social, educational and philosophical lines, when the native will always be able to rely on the support of friends. He is inclined to and has a talent for public occupations and *social* work, for ♃ in ♒ renders philanthropic, liberal, independent, a social reformer. Further this position gives tact in business, makes the native optimistic, inspired, original and able to set others to work and to control them.

When *afflicted:* restless, indecisive, revolutionary, lazy and unreliable.

Fullbloodedness, impure blood, tendency to a bad leg from childbirth, swollen ankles; when there is heart's disease, dropsy usually begins in the legs. (♌ 8 ♒), apoplexy, palpitations of the heart (8 ♌).

♃ in ♓ makes the native kindly, communicative, philantropic. This position is favourable to intercourse with the sick and poor, to whom practical aid and moral advice are willingly given. *Devotion* and some feeling for art are found and great store is set on luxury in the home. ♓ renders rather mediumistic, but if in the horoscope e.g. the sign ♍ be strongly placed, it will give sufficient discrimination to prevent the native from yielding to it passively which would have a harmful effect on the nervous system and health in general. ♃ in ♓ makes him also practically idealistic, hospitable, charitable.

When *afflicted:* doubting, cowardly, self-indulgent.

A tendency to swollen feet and perspiring feet, enlargement of the liver, anæmia, dropsy, tumours, sick bowels, jaundice.

Saturn (♄) in the Twelve Signs.

♄ in ♈ strengthens the will to *continue* with perseverance that which has once been begun. The feeling of having done what ought to be done gives satisfaction; but during the activity itself the cheerfulness and love, so desirable for success, are lacking. ♄ in ♈ enables the native to lead others and to make plans for them, although sometimes he will behave like a *tyrant*. Patience and tolerance should be practised. Once these virtues are assimilated, they become a great stimulant which leads to better social position. ♄ in ♈ renders self-reliant, tactful, gives organising power; renders diligent, patient, persevering; but the native is critical and takes severe measures against sluggishness.

When *afflicted:* self-willed, *discontent,* gloomy, vindictive, grudging, *jealous,* with sharp and arrogant criticism.

Bad teeth, catarrhal affections in the head, rheumatic headaches, cold in the head, anæmia of the brain, fainting fits, deafness, swoons, stomach disorders (□ ♋) and kidney diseases (♌ ♎). The native should be careful when caught in heavy rain and drenched, not to keep his wet things on.

♄ in ♉ denotes a strong spirit *conscious of its purpose* which may work slowly, but at any rate surely and steadily, and does not easily give up what has once been found. ♄ in ♉ makes the native careful, economical, quiet, silent. He usually possesses more than one would suppose both materially and spiritually.

When *afflicted:* stubborn, opiniated, conservative, lazy; sometimes subject to fits of violent passion.

Chronic affections of the throat; inflammation of the throat, consumption of the throat, nasal catarrh, loss of voice, diphtheria, croup, whooping cough, mumps, deafness, bad gums and bad teeth. The native should beware of catching cold in throat and neck.

♄ in ♊ makes the native accurate, orderly and desirous of intellectual development. But since the nature of ♄ is opposed to that of ♊ this position should usually be regarded as an affliction, at least if no very good aspects better the position.

Affliction makes him irritable, prone to *worry,* and supposes no easy childhood, *much inclination* to study, but *little opportunity* for it. This position causes also weakness of the lungs, especially if the ☉ is ♌ or ☐ ♄. It also points to unfavourable circumstances and early death of relatives, probably of the same complaint. With a careful mode of living and a cheerful mental disposition, the manifestations of this lung-weakness may be limited to a minimum, but the slightest carelessness entails indisposition of an acute nature. The native is advised never to overstrain himself but to rest at fixed times and read good books, on no account sensational and exciting literature.

Acute pneumonia, bronchitis, asthma, phthisis, nervous trembling of hands and arms, dislocation of arm or shoulder, tendency to rheumatic pain in shoulders, arm and hands, general weakness, jaundice, sciatica (♌ ♐), bad digestion (☐ ♍). Perfect cleanliness of body and clothes, and breathing exercises are recommended.

♄ in ♋. The native has a certain *selfconceit,* is apt to be wrapped up in his own convictions and endeavours, without believing in the validity of other opinions, which will be attacked, sneered at, or at most regarded pitifully. His own mistakes are not easily acknowledged and even less easily corrected. Consequently, he asserts himself vehemently when admonished. So that investigation and correction which really ought to have been effected from within, have to come from without. When ♄ is posited in the retentive sign ♋, rather an exaggerated care of money may be anticipated, a degree of economy which often pretends to be wise. In marriage affairs this position brings delay or disappointment. ♄ in ♋ gives a talent for valuation, inclines to moderation, selfcontrol, economy, frugality, religiousness.

Affliction makes the native sulky, sombre, discontented, pessimistic, easily irritated. Disappointment in business and profession will be experienced. This position points to a weak or diseased stomach. Therefore care should be taken to ensure regularity in the consumption of food. A diet should be observed, much meat and spices are bad, although the native will be very fond of them. At any rate it is desirable for him either not to eat too much or too luxuriously and to masticate his food well (fletcherise).

Affections of the stomach, stomach abscess, cancer, bad assimilation, impaired digestion, lack of appetite, sickness, anaemia, cancer of the breast, jaundice, gall-stones.

♄ in ♌ makes the native diplomatic, tactful, silent, selfcontrolled, and gives a sense of responsibility ("Noblesse oblige"). When harmoniously aspected a person with this position may be tolerant, but will nevertheless have a strong inner conviction that his own opinions are better than others, however good the latter may be. This *feeling of superiority* manifests itself in a certain condescending kindness, seemingly preoccupied. All kinds of etiquette are strictly preserved, *"honour" takes precedence of personal feeling.*

When *afflicted* this position makes the native naturally inclined to be jealous and to conceal his feelings. A certain haughtiness then manifests which does not easily confess worsted and would rather bear anything than have to acknowledge that something had not been well organised or that he had been very unfortunate. Excessive physical exertion should be avoided. He should strive for a cheerful, trustful attitude to life.

Weak action of the heart, faints, swoons, calcification of the blood vessels, weak back, propensity to spinal curvature, liver disease, jaundice, gout.

♄ in ♍ makes the native very *accurate in administration,* economical in managing his own or other people's property, and extremely observant of details. This position inclines him to withdraw to his own work with the conviction that, after all, others cannot be trusted; he is also apt to be hard on others—chiefly dependents—who work less accurately and therefore he is prone to alienate them. That is why one or more harmonious aspects here are very desirable. A △ aspect e.g. with ☿ is a good influence and indicates that in all these matters common sense plays an important part. Then there will be little likelihood of economy trying to outdo wisdom or of the native's dwelling on details to such an extent as to lose sight of the important fundamental ideas. ♄ in ♍ gives a good many hobbies, renders schoolmasterlike, orderly and temperate.

Affliction makes him shy, melancholy, inclines to imaginary illnesses, disappointment in the profession, unpleasantness with older people. This position often causes critical words, discontent with one's own social position, and urges continually to hard work in order to do better. Anxiety, fear and gloomy moods should so far as possible give place to a trustful and confident attitude to life.

Sluggish liver, intestinal catarrh, consumption of the abdomen, appendicitis, bad assimilation, costiveness, colic. This position hinders growth in childhood.

ħ in ♎ gives artistic and intellectual inclinations and indicates many more or less intimate relations with the other sex. These relations are not always quite happy and pleasant; misunderstanding, illness or death sometimes put an unexpected end to all illusions and bring a sudden longing for solitude and seclusion. The native's own development depends to a great extent on these relations and their effect; so it will prove of great importance for him not to be easy-going in this respect, but to examine himself earnestly, exercise control of his feelings and beware of being mastered by them. ħ in ♎ makes the native devoted, just, a faithful husband or wife, and is favourable to partnership, especially with older people.

When *afflicted:* apt to take things ill, envious; great difficulties will arise in cooperation and partnership.

Bright's disease, calculus in the kidneys, colic of the kidneys, anuria, impure blood (with nephritis dropsy usually begins in the face, ♈ is opposite ♎) sterility, headache (☍ ♈) toothache, lumbago. This position indicates that the organism is not strong. It is advisable to keep the region of the loins warm by wearing wool.

ħ in ♏ denotes an intense *sence of justice* and much *moral courage.* Added to this a strong will to penetrate into the unknown and unseen powers of the universe, an intense longing to know *"the law"* and apply it. All forms of occultism exercise an extraordinary attraction and many ways will be tried by which to gain occult powers. But care and avoidance of all haste are urgently recommended. Knowledge of these powers will come of its own accord when the lower nature has been conquered and the spiritual side more developed. A very prejudicial influence results sooner or later in the physical body, when this knowledge is gained by forced practices, before the latter is sufficiently controlled, to master the activity produced by the spirit.

Rather unpleasant things are likely to occur in intercourse with acquaintances and the inmates of the home, alienation seems not impossible, although probably there will be a single individual who — possibly unseen by the world — is a great loving support and refuge. ħ in ♏ increases the will-power, gives presence of mind, makes the native careful, prudent, persevering, reserved.

Affliction renders him critical, exacting, a *sham authority,* proud, egoistic, narrow-minded, fretting.

Bladder, catarrh, stone, retarted menstruation, sterility, rupture, costiveness, haemorrhoids, fistula, cariosity of the nasal bone, nasal-catarrh, hoarseness, affections of the throat (☍ ♉), gout, lameness. One should be careful not to catch cold and also not to yield to wantonness.

ħ in ♐ makes the serious thinker with an investigating mind who wants to be charitable, philanthropic and just. People with this position are willing to sacrifice themselves for their ideal (especially if the 12th house plays a part in it); they do not spare any pains or effort to try and reach what they consider to be good and helpful.

Affliction renders insincere, dishonest, cynical, sarcastic, egoistic.

Rheumatism in the muscles of the thigh, gout, illnesses of the hip, dislocation of the hip, bronchitis and tuberculosis (♉ ♊). When afflicted to ♂ or ♅, ♄ in ♐ may cause paralysis, partial or complete, manifesting mostly in the hips and legs. So one should beware of excessive exertion.

♄ in ♑ makes for *persevering* and *concentrated activity,* serious endeavour for betterment spiritual as well as physical; but it also causes the native to care more for his own advantage than is expedient. The thought should always be borne in mind that the individual really gains far more by working for the *community* than by working exclusively for *himself.* For harmonious interchange of thought and cooperation of *all* is far more powerful than the most energetic plodding of an *isolated* individual. A harmonious aspect gives as much respect for other people's ideas and possessions as is desired for oneself. At times however, it would be better were this strong sense of "mine and thine" less prominent — particularly with regard to the minute pigeonholing natural to ♑, as it is a drawback and often hinders cooperation and sympathy. ♄ in ♑ makes the native reserved, faithful, persevering, diplomatic.

When *afflicted:* gloomy, dissatisfied, prejudiced, sly, deceitful.

Rheumatism of the joints, weak knees, gall-stone, dyspepsia, constipation, skin-diseases, crysipelas, eczema, headaches, fevers. Flannel should be worn in order to prevent catching cold.

♄ in ♒. This position indicates "limited ideals", is favourable for the knowledge of humanity, makes the native philanthropic, friendly, distinct and decided in speech, reliable and steadfast.

A certain degree of practical idealism will be found; a person with this position is convinced that not *much* can be done for humanity, but he has an open eye for that small amount of help which can be effected and will consequently give his entire power and devotion to it.

Affliction renders sly, subtle, not always reliable.

Weak and sprained ankles, club-foot, bad circulation of the blood, heart-diseases, varicose veins, calcification of the bloodvessels, consumption of the marrow, sclerosis, spinal curvature, affections of the eye. It is well to be careful to have warm feet and not to overexert oneself, especially not the eyes.

♄ in ♓ makes the native fond of peace and quiet, economical and tolerant, and apt to be greatly valued by many people. Work in solitude is most pleasant and best. This aspect is very suitable to a leading position in a house for people who—of their own accord or otherwise—live out of the world.

When *afflicted* we see an ill-used individual, compelled by circumstances to stay much at home, and kept in the background, such a person is critical, irritable, melancholy.

There is great likelihood of catching cold through wet and cold feet resulting in gout. The native should be warned against the use of all spirits. He should see that the situation of the house is dry and the bedroom on the sunny side. It is advisable to take much fruit and preferably vegetarian food. Corns, bunions, sensitive feet, rickets, scrofula, consumption (□ ♏).

Uranus (♅) in the Twelve Signs [1].

♅ in ♈ (1845—1851) makes the native impulsive, independent, original, an "enlightened mind", energetic and inventive.

When *afflicted:* blunt, sulky, abrupt, irritable, fond of change; this position often leads to sudden alienation from those surrounding him.

Facial cramp, paralysis of the facial nerves, spasmodic headaches, meningitis. A person with this position should beware of too great exertion and should not exact too much of his eyes.

♅ in ♉ (1851—1858) makes the native tenacious, persevering, intuitive, inclines to the *social application of religious convictions* (erecting orphanages and penitentiaries etc.)

Affliction makes him stubborn, *distrustful,* jealous, restless. Large gains and sudden failures may be expected.

Trouble with the vocal chords, lock-jaw, abnormal growths have been observed with this position. Straining the voice should be avoided.

♅ in ♊ (1858—1865) gives an interest in *occult literature,* makes the native resourceful, pushing, and indicates very original ideas, bold phantasies on an abstract basis; propagation of all kinds of new and hitherto unknown theories. Under flashes of inspiration remarkable things may be said and written: sometimes unusually much correspondence will be got through and at other times letters will remain a long time unanswered.

Affliction makes him eccentric, troublesome, foolish.

Asthma, cramp in arms and shoulders, writer's cramp, a dry cough. This position renders excessively strenuous study inadvisable.

♅ in ♋ (1865—1872) gives an *original imagination.* In childhood it manifests as a preference for *fairy tales* and later on as a special talent for oneself inventing and telling new "fairy tales". There is a great interest in old objects and the stories connected with them; further for all kinds of symbols and their meanings and finally for all occult sciences. ♅ in ♋ renders psychic, but also very sensitive, almost *over-sensitive* in personal matters, so that alienation may often arise in consequence of misunderstanding.

---

[1] These descriptions are only valid if ♅ is strongly posited in a horoscope, e.g. when in the Ascendant, in the 8th, 9th, 10th or 11th House; when particularly strongly aspected to other planets; or through a predominant position of the sign ♒.

When *afflicted:* nervous, irritable; sudden changes in domestic circumstances are likely to occur.

Cancer of the stomach, cramps of the stomach, dry stomach cough, flatulency, anæmia, neurasthenia. A bath should never be taken directly after a meal.

♅ in ♌ (1872—1878) makes resolute, severe, strong, self-assertive, in society however entertaining and sociable; and gives original flashes.

When *afflicted:* revolutionary, impatient, passionate, inconstant; strange love-affairs, strong antipathies and sympathies, a great inclination to *adventurous pleasures.*

Heart cramp, palpitations of the heart. There is some likelihood of collisions and falls.

♅ in ♍ (1878—1885) gives original ideas concerning art, especially the *teaching* of art, and about social life in general, makes somewhat cynical about the views of other people, so that the native may really be as dogmatic and stiffnecked about his own theories as about the old-fashioned notions of which he disapproves or at which he sneers. There is a taste for *bohemian* life, but preferably in more refined directions; poverty and slovenliness are abhorred. This position makes the mind clear, resourceful and very practical in applying the principle: *division of work.* Scientific tendencies and a delicate intuition give also mystical and metaphysical capacities and attract to occultism, astrology and similar studies.

Affliction renders peevish, irritable, sharp, melancholy, always contrary. This position usually leads to great difficulties in intercourse with dependents, especially through the tendency to give oneself away; it is therefore better as much as possible to do everything oneself.

Nervous affections, also intestinal cramps and flatulency occur with this position.

♅ in ♎ (1885—1891) denotes artistic talents, at times even genius and extraordinary spiritual faculties. A △ aspect to the ☽ presupposes that inwardly the native longs for and strives after harmonious reciprocal relations with his environment, whereas a harmonious aspect from ♒ or ♐ makes great *popularity* possible. ♅ in ♎ makes original, independent, intuitive, gives a lively fancy.

Affliction renders hasty, bad-tempered, eccentric, anarchistic, unfaithful, leads to peculiar relations, sometimes followed by sudden disagreeable complications. An inharmonious aspect of ♂ gives a somewhat challenging attitude to people of other opinions, causing conflicts and trouble. An inharmonious aspect of ♄ points to wrong judgment and opposition on the part of older and more conventional people, but when this aspect is weak, the latter can easily be overcome by a tactful attitude of give and take. For obstinacy and selfwill are not best fitted for the propagation of new ideas, however good and noble they in themselves may be.

Crick in the back, cramp in the muscles and sudden headaches.

♅ in ♏ (1891—1897) gives a keen and critical mental faculty, great inclination to psychological research, occultism and metaphysics. With a little regular practice much may be reached in this direction. It is good that acknowledged dogmas are *not thoughtlessly accepted*. This will undoubtedly be a factor making greatly for success so long as convention is not repudiated without substituting something new, something *better*. ♅ in ♏ makes the native original, powerful, resolute, persevering, determined, inquisitive but reserved, gives great power of concentration and metaphysical views; problems of life after death attract much.

Affliction leads to perversity, makes the native passionate and often causes sudden death. Social life as it now is, will often be sneered at and opposed wherever possible. A wanton, bohemian way of living attracts most, and for that matter is in some degree best fitted for this character and its peculiarities. ♅'s ideas however demand great *selfcontrol* and very much *"wisdom of the heart"* in order to secure more success than conservative views. It is therefore advisable to gain these virtues fully before one propagates world-reform. Truly, the greatest revolutions take place *inwardly* and not outwardly.

When ♅ in ♏ is afflicted there is danger of mental and physical (especially sexual) disturbances through an immoderate life and thoughtless waste of energy. If ♅ is Retrograde there is a chance of *superstition,* preference for wearing a talisman and similar things for the purpose of obtaining fulfilment of wishes or protection against accidents. Too much is sought *without* which must be found *within* oneself. This is a position for those who by dint of seeking, come to suffer and by suffering attain understanding and through understanding *practical construction.*

Bladder-cramp, tendency to miscarriages. Temperance in all things should be striven after.

♅ in ♐ (1897—1904). Very peculiar conceptions in spiritual, moral and physical *education*. But since these demand great moral power and complete self-control, it will be advisable to delay their execution until these have been attained. ♅ in ♐ makes the native reforming, philosophical, idealistic, intuitive, imaginative; prophetic and interested in all new ideas, new theories and hypotheses, especially in *theosophical* directions. Dreams are often an announcement of coming events.

Affliction renders the native adventurous, peculiar, revolutionary, self-willed, but changeable, so that he cannot be relied upon. There is danger of unpleasant experiences through careless or reckless behaviour. Strange dreams and hallucinations sometimes occur which will however stop, if no notice is taken of them. These constellations are apt to bring into contact with the occult, but the native should be warned against experimenting, because the distinction "white" or "black" is easily lost — and the consequence of their loss cannot be averted.

Cramps in hips and thighs, likelihood of accidents at sport.

♅ in ♐ (1904—1912) gives a scrutinizing, clear view of business, interest in electro-technics and psychology. Hidden powers in nature and in man's inmost being are accurately investigated in order to be able to render them subservient to material and spiritual progress, both in his intimate circle and in wider ones. The fixed earthiness of ♐ acquires higher aspect, which transmutes the joyless drudgery which so often occurs under this sign, into a joyful and practical working for the community. ♅ in ♐ gives much love of work, makes serious, persevering; there is a strong sense of *responsibility,* although such a person will always seem more or less peculiar to his parents and dependents.

When *afflicted* this position gives great ups and downs, and a peculiarly wilful, revolutionary, quarrelsome and masterful disposition.

Deformity of the knees occur pretty often, also accidents to the legs.

♅ in ♒ (1912—1919) makes the native original, intuitive, spontaneous, humane, unselfish, causes unusual experiences. With strong harmonious aspects there is every probability of purely, simply and cheerfully living out ♅'s ideals of brotherhood and love of mankind.

Affliction renders him adventurous, eccentric, narrow-minded, self-willed, fond of dressing peculiarly.

Hysteria, nervous affections, cramp in ankles and the calf of the leg. The mind and the nervous system should be well controlled. With unfavourable directions there is much likelihood of accidents.

♅ in ♓ (1919—1926) gives occult powers; a tendency to introspection and self-examination through which much knowledge and power of sacrifice may be attained.

Affliction makes misunderstood, mediumistic, superficial, absent-minded, fearful.

Cramp in feet and toes, perspiring feet. The native should not drink much at meals, and be careful in intercourse with people who are eccentric and not quite sincere.

Neptune (♆) in the Signs [1]).

♆ in ♈ (1861—1874). Indicates new religious and philosophical ideas propagated with much zeal and ardour, also a strong desire to lift humanity to a higher level. This position makes the native humane, religious and diligent; idealistic convictions are propagated energetically and enthusiastically.

Affliction renders him revolutionary, anarchistic, fanatic.

Myopia, affections of the brains, absence of mind. Inclination to self-accusation; exaggerated ideas and false conceptions should be fought against.

---

[1]) These descriptions are only valid when ♆ is strongly posited in the horoscope e.g. by its positions in the Asc. 9th, 10th, 11th or 12th House; when particularly strongly aspected to other planets or through a predominant position of the sign ♓.

♅ in ♉ (1874—1887). A great liking for what is beautiful and uplifting in nature. A △ aspect with ☿ even enables the native to give fairly good descriptions of these things in *prose* or *poetry*. In the region of music some very pronounced opinions will come to the fore; the native's ear is probably *not quite accurate* and definitely melodious music will be more appreciated than a number of vague chords or sounds. This position augurs much good from the systematic training of thought in the right direction. At first it will probably not be very easy to keep the thought fixed on one abstract idea for five minutes at a stretch, but after uninterrupted practice, signs of progress will manifest themselves. ♅ in ♉ gives great sense of beauty, makes kind and sociable. His trend of thought is naturalistic, philosophical or mystical.

An *affliction* renders sensual, passionate, greedy.

Under an inharmonious direction inflammation of the throat occurs fairly often. The eyes should be saved.

♅ in ♊ (1887—1901) gives *unusual phantasies:* this position occurs with an inspired author. ♅ tends to genius, inclines to study spiritualism; renders profetic, poetic. One of the brothers or sisters often has a very unusual life.

Affliction makes the native absent-minded, chaotic, dreamy, restless, subtle. Such a person should not indulge in fantastic conceptions, but so far as possible should keep his thoughts along definite lines.

Tuberculosis occurs fairly often with this position. Too tight a mode of dressing also over-slimness should be avoided.

♅ in ♋ (1901—1915) renders psychic, sensitive, devoted, *sympathetic,* many-sided, affectionate.

When *afflicted:* melancholy, egoistic, self-indulgent.
The mind is very *open to impressions* and is easily influenced by distrustful or despondent thoughts. The native should above all learn to keep free and by seriously comparing his own existence with that of others, find out whether his life really is so difficult, so hard to bear. He should look at those who possess less, not more, so that the feeling of gratitude for his own abundance give birth to the desire to share these treasures with others and to help them as much as possible.

The native should abstain from all narcotics and alcoholic drinks.

♅ in ♌ (1915—1929). This position makes the native sympathetic, *sociable, kind-hearted, gentle.*

Affliction renders self-indulgent, sensual, cowardly, whimsical, unreliable.

Weak action of the heart often occurs under this position of ♅. The taking of narcotics is very bad for the heart.

♅ in ♒ (1834—1847). This position indicates an altruistic, idealistic philanthropist with utopian ideas.

Affliction leads to very exaggerated ideas and nervous affections. The phantasy should be kept pure and every inclination to day-dreaming should be combated.

♅ in ♓ (1847—1861). This position develops *psychic faculties* and makes the native compassionate, modest, reserved.

Affliction renders him *mediumistic*. The desire for narcotics and alcoholic drinks should not be indulged in. He should be on his guard against coming into contact with impure relations. A person with this position should take care not to allow himself to float on sensual feelings.

X

The Planets in the Twelve Houses.

The Sun (☉) in the Twelve Houses.

☉ in 1. When well aspected: good health in general; *full of vitality,* great recuperative power. This position of the Sun is favourable to the native's sense of worth, renders him optimistic, courageous, confident of success and of his ability constantly to master the difficulties of life. This position inclines to take the *lead* in everything—in as far as others do not oppose this openly. His manner is dictatorial and demands respect.

Affliction weakens the vitality, the native is apt to try to support himself on externals and to do things from lack of assurance, of which later on he repents.

☉ in 2. This position of the Sun, strengthened by good aspects denotes favourable material prospects, and that the financial situation in general does not cause anxiety. The native seems to have a particular talent for acquiring and making use of money both for himself and for those in his care. Money is spent fairly freely, preferably on amusement and comfort and in the society of friends.

An affliction of ♃ warns the native not to start financial transactions before he has made thorough enquiries. He should endeavour to obtain clearer insight into these matters so that he should not be dazzled and deceived by fancied prospects of financial prosperity.

An affliction of ♂ renders him impudent, impatient and pushing, and causes unexpected losses, and failure of speculations.

☉ in 3 gives a cheerful mind and a lively, investigating spirit inclined to reform society and education and the discovering of new methods by which to reach these aims. The native's aspiration lies in the direction of pedagogics, he greatly desires to *spread knowledge,* and to acquaint others with what he himself has lately learned, and to come into contact with noble personalities in order mutually to gain and give spiritual support and power.

A △ aspect indicates a busy *correspondence* about those subjects with serious friends and relatives who respect his ideas.

An *afflicted* ☉ in 3 is a sign of much trouble and misunderstanding in intercourse with relations, colleagues etc.

☉ in 4. It is difficult for one who has this position of the ☉ to feel at home and comfortable anywhere. Inner *restlessness* and *doubt* often spoil things which otherwise might have been beautiful; *especially in youth* when the greatest demands are made. In the course of years however many difficulties with parents will find a solution through a more comprehending sympathy. *Old age* is apt to be quiet and *"sunny";* the fruits of seed sown in a difficult youth will be gathered which will in a great measure compensate the native for all the old unhappiness and anxiety in his "own home".

If the Sun makes strong harmonious aspects it indicates the obtaining of a fixed source of income usually out of the inheritance of one of the parents.

When *afflicted* the native has not enough energy to increase his own capital, but merely passively awaits the coming of his inheritance.

☉ in 5. *Speculation*—to which this position inclines—is only partially advisable, because as a rule the native cannot await the right moment for it. Risky enterprises are best undertaken in company with others—reliable people—, the initiative being taken by the person who has ☉ in 5 in his nativity. Further this position denotes a particularly great inclination for *social life* and more or less luxurious pleasures; but also for an intensified inner life.

The ☉ in the "house of the children" often causes the fire (♌) of passion to scorch fruit before it is fully grown; likewise this position of the ☉ in 5 usually leads to childless marriage, or a child will not be born until after many years of married life.

☉ in 6. A certain *fastidious pride*—a proverb says: pigs should not be too dainty if they are to be fattened—hangs like a cloud over the ☉ and diminishes its vital force. This renders the native subject to disease and as his recuperative power is small, chronic disorders will often result. *Be more cheerful* is good advice! In that case joy of life and power may be given to those who are really ill; then the Sun will begin to shine in the "House of the Sick".

☉ in 6 *afflicted* denotes continual opposition and jealousy of superiors whenever financial matters are thriving, and a disparaging doubt on their part whether lasting prosperity may be expected. Inferiors also do not cooperate, think too much of themselves and of their own advantage.

☉ in 7. Marriage will add to the financial prosperity but the household will need much through its desire for luxury, comfort and pleasure. When *afflicted* rivals, both•male and female, will cause domestic trouble, and jealousy will create a danger of rupture and separation.

☉ in 7 also points to a somewhat *selfish, authoritative* attitude in marriage; if this does not entail domestic quarrels it will be owing to the cheery, pleasant character of the partner who will try to make the house *sunny* in every respect. To outsiders the couple with this position hide their feelings under a certain formal courtesy which might be taken for indifference.

If there is a ☉-affliction and one partner will not give in to the other, if there is no compromise, the sun will leave married life and partnerships will fail through egoism of the partners.

☉ in 8 indicates that the native manages or possesses the life-interest of somebody's money or goods to which he adds by his own personal endeavour. Similarly a material or spiritual inheritance will make it easy to obtain a position in the world. This position inclines to trust a higher power. Great expectations are cherished of hitherto uncertain sources of income, which sometimes are lived on too soon. When *harmoniously aspected* the future of which one dreams and the capital one counts on, are of a solid nature.

On the other hand, when *afflicted* death will prevent their receipt. Often the promising life-work of a gifted child will be nipped in the bud; the possessions of the partner are squandered and run through.

☉ in 9, the house of consciousness in the widest sense of the word, gives *broad views, high ideals,* and *noble ambitions* and also a great desire to solve the riddle of life. As a matter of course we shall find an inclination to the study of comparative religions and jurisprudence. Many and various reflections as to the how and why of things occupy the mind; in every direction *intellectual satisfaction* is sought after and intolerance of other ideas is very rarely met with. Great reverence of truth exists and consequently an abhorrence of lies; from childhood an untrue saying will be keenly felt and condemned.

Plans of going to live abroad will be considered, business with foreign relations are very attactive, so is aviation.

An afflicted ☉ in 9 makes for fanatics, enthusiasts, people with a confused mind, in which one thought almost unconsciously dominates.

☉ in 10. This is a token of *success* and of gaining an honourable, independent position in society. The mind tends to clear, logical trends of thought; peaceful constructive philosophy, based on self-observed facts.

There is much talent for occupying a leading position, the more so, because the individuality, great ability, willpower and passionate love for work (when the aspects of ♃, ♄ and ♂ are good) are an example to dependents or pupils, compelling them to imitate.

An *affliction* of ♃ will at times reduce the strong, self-conscious manner to a certain arrogant pride, less favourable to gaining the affections of those lower in rank.

On the other hand a △ aspect with ♅ opens the possibility of great popularity when one is on more brotherly, equal footing with them. One will truly gain far more love and confidence by sincere pleasant cooperation than by behaving in a selfsufficient, commanding manner.

⊙ in 11 is very favourable to intercourse with others and all that is planned with or by them. This position of the Sun indicates many connections with *prominent, eminent people* who by their personal influence are able to add much to the general success of their acquaintances. Through these connections the native's own *popularity* is considerably augmented, and many enterprises will succeed which otherwise would have had but faint chance of success. Cultured surroundings, good manners and somewhat conventional formalities are greatly appreciated, although the native himself — often on purpose — sometimes infringes on them.

⊙ in 12 gives an interest in *occultism* and *mysticism* in opposition to the religious convictions learned in childhood and therefore easily leads to alienation from the family. The latter will constantly disapprove of them and oppose them strongly especially during minority. But as these peculiar feelings are such an integral part of the character, that opposition is apt to bring about the contrary of the result aimed at.

⊙ in 12 makes it difficult for the native to be understood and appreciated; *lack of concentration and real insight* hinders the harmonious development of talent, so that a great deal of confusion arises. Instead of being a radiating vital force, ambitious for good, and with a *selfconscious feeling of superiority,* the ⊙'s influence manifests here simply as a great *desire for self-preservation,* both spiritual and physical.

A 12th house type should try to become inwardly more self-confident and train himself in wider loving trust in his fellow-men; *by unfolding the good in oneself, the good in others can always be reached.* The way of development is: there is no teacher like experience. Many a time the native opposes in vain and then he is inclined to give in altogether and to serious doubt whether life will ever bring him satisfaction. The less these moods are indulged in the better.

This position further indicates independence of earthly wealth and luxury; the native prefers to work in solitude leaving the material side to others. Much help may be derived from calm, regular meditation on health and strength, unimpeachable purity of thought, and the power to regulate these non-material circumstances according to his own higher conceptions.

The study of astrology especially, will give much satisfaction, because it is able to reveal something of the connection between the individual and the universe.

The Moon (☽) in the Twelve Houses.

☽ in 1. The Moon rising makes the native *very sensitive* and gives *much imagination.* We see here a restless nature, always longing for change of surroundings and field of activity, driven forward by a hankering after new emotions, liking to move in congenial society.

When *afflicted* many indispositions occur which are more or less of a psychical nature.

☽ in 2 indicates that the finances are as changeable as the nature of the ☽ itself. The earning of money will be most successful in *business with the general public,* but carelessness and inconstancy cause unexpected disappointments. Usually however, friends will be found who in case of need lend a helping hand.

☽ in 2 *afflicted* is not a sign of favourable financial circumstances. Excessive liberality and confidence in unworthy people are the cause of loss and ill-luck. Standing surety, inheritances, in short all financial connections with other people will bring disadvantage rather than advantage.

☽ in 3 gives a strong, noble optimism which will prove to be a great support in life and which enables the native to overcome more difficulties than the average man is usually able to do. His innate common sense and sense of responsibility are combined with a certain sense of humour much appreciated by friends and acquaintances. This ☽-position makes him very studious, extremely fit for *tuition* and indicates a great love for small journeys, for repeated changes in every department of life. The desire for new experiences, new knowledge is very strong. A region which the native has traversed in all directions, people who have been for a long time in his neighbourhood, occupations which must be done many times in succession all annoy and weary him.

When *afflicted* by ♂, ♅ or ♆, journeys decided upon are sometimes prevented at the last moment, or accidents happen on the way.

☽ in 4 points to changing circumstances in life and changes of abode; further to a lively imagination, a sensitive nature and great attachment to parents and relatives.

When *afflicted* the position is not favourable to relations with the parents or their mutual relation.

The native's education will suffer because of this and all through later life the lack of pleasant recollections of one's youth will be felt and manifest in a certain despondency, a premature ripeness which even in youth takes away much that is childlike.—Later on this results in lack of compassion, and excessive interest in his own affairs and circumstances.

Financial loss through theft and deceit, probably by most unlikely people, may occur with this ☽-position.

☽ in 5 denotes occupations which bring into contact with the public and gives the necessary talent for them without entailing any loss of personal originality. The life will probably be connected in some respect with the needs or *education of children;* at any rate others will be urged to interest in this department and to assist in moulding a new generation more healthy and better developed.

When *afflicted* a person with this ☽ position should in order to avoid disappointment, consider well before giving his affection to people.

As a rule ☽ in 6 has a less favourable effect on the state of health.

As this position renders extremely susceptible to psychic and magnetic influences, it is most desirable to keep the native's surroundings and sphere of thought "healthy", to see that *"spiritual ventilation"* is maintained. Cheering natural-philosophical literature will doubtless have a favourable influence. Development of *inner power* is essential to the reasonable application of physical capacities. *Diet* plays a large part in preventing or curing illnesses; much fluid is taken.

When *afflicted* dependents will be too critically examined; too many unreasonable admonitions are given and too much is demanded of others, which one can not achieve oneself. So as a rule the domestic staff does not stay long. All this has an unfavourable influence on the nervous system, and on the state of health in general.

☽ in 7 makes the native particularly fit to move in society—of very opposite kinds, at one time formal and aristocratic, at another artistical and bohemian.

This position renders somewhat fastidious and undecided in the choice of a partner in life. When well aspected, in many respects the marriage will be happy, but the partner will in spite of his (her) great charm think much of having his (her) personal notions and feelings shared and will therefore cause many changing moods.

When *afflicted* especially by ♂ or ♅ much tact will be wanted to prevent rash separations and alienations.

☽ in 8 gives a quiet, resigned attitude with regard to death and life beyond. The problem of *Reincarnation* will probably be answered in the affirmative and this causes a clear and conscious trust in the necessity and purpose of death. When harmoniously aspected to ♆ or ♃, personal contact with the spirit-world can also be obtained, especially if watery signs are represented.

Literature and knowledge about these subjects will prove attractive and strengthening, but are seldom accepted by the native's friends.

This position denotes also a strong belief in the *psychic value of art and music* and their effect on those who come into contact with them. The world of *dreams* will also provide a favourite region of research. Occasional hallucinations which occur are not conducive to real and regular spiritual activity, consequently they should as much as possible be balanced by practical healthy thoughts and occupations.

When *afflicted* this position causes the loss of female companions in life; but a harmonious aspect, especially to ♀, renders possible a love surpassing earthly love, which will also manifest favourably when physical separation occurs.

Well aspected this position promises gain from partnership and testators, when afflicted the reverse.

☽ in 9 makes the mind extremely receptive and gives much imagination. Through its changeability the ☽ enables the native by means of reflection and contemplation to study various subjects of a religious, ethical or artistic nature. Such study is based not so much upon actual research as upon an *astral sensing* of the deeper significance of things. Although personally very free ideas are cherished, simple orthodox ideas and unreasoned devotion are always much apprecitated—provided these feelings are *sincere*.

☽ in 9 presupposes a great liking for travelling, preferably in a quite extraordinary way to very peculiar regions, a tendency which will probably manifest early in life as a great admiration for books like those of Jules Verne.

☽ in 10 through the changing nature of the ☽, indicates many changes in the profession and outward life. Further many connections with the public and with women. On the whole the profession will not be taken very seriously, the *private life* being of far greater concern. Yet this position gives more success and appreciation than might be expected. The consequence is apt to be that, considering the effect of relatively slight exertion, the native feels less and less incentive to really serious and devoted work. And this is of course a great pity for all that might have been reached with a little more trouble.

☽ in 11 indicates social intercourse with *many acquaintances* who upon the whole are well-to-do and exercise a great influence upon the outer life of the person concerned. An *inharmonious* aspect here has an unfavourable effect and too often brings the love-element too often into relations which were originally merely friendly; the consequence of this may be intrigues, especially of feminine acquaintances, which may seriously injure the native's reputation.

A △ aspect, especially of the ☉ or ♃ denotes the possibility of a glorious victory, through the exercise of a noble, dignified self-control.

☽ in 12 makes the native very sensitive to people's opinion and easily hurt by an unkind and unappreciative word. At times this may turn into a certain *unsociability*, never however of long duration, because his love of life and desire for harmonious society is too strong to allow him to seclude himself entirely. The feelings have always a flavour of "having been kept in the background" and therefore a somewhat *self-pitying* attitude results. By practising *contentment* inner powers—latent faculty—will best be able to develop harmoniously. This makes it also possible to apply practically in daily life what has been learned in solitude or through suffering.

Good aspects give a great inclination to psychic, occult and theological studies and towards the search for *synthesis*.

Inharmonious aspects however make the native changeable, *restless*, just like the sea, which exercises a particularly strong charm over him.

Mercury (☿) in the Twelve Houses.

☿ in 1. The planet of intellect and discrimination in the 1st house increases the restlessness, changeability and critical spirit, especially pronounced in a characteristic of youth. This type is *eloquent*, often quick at repartee and humorous, a jolly fellow amusing others.

When favourably aspected the mind is more acceptive to the charm and wisdom of myths, sagas, legends and fairy tales—the deeper and occult meaning of which is very purely sensed—than to exact-scientific study. Memory is upon the whole fairly strong.

When *afflicted* the native is not always reliable. Remember, ☿ is the God of merchants and thieves. A person with an afflicted ☿ in 1 likes to make others ridiculous and to laugh at them.

☿ in 2 promises much profit through administrative, commercial or organising work. The intellect is versatile, the way of thinking logical, the love of exact knowledge very great. When well aspected the ☿'s virtues such as intelligence, observation, inventiveness and adaptability will best be developed in a sphere of commerce and industry.

When *afflicted* superficiality arises, unreliability, opiniatedness, which require much patience from superiors or educators.

☿ in 3 denotes a pleasant—although somewhat superficial—understanding with relatives and acquaintances. In their troubles and difficulties the latter always find a willing ear and good advice. Great *popularity* both in a personal and in a business sense results in *widely-spread connections* and very extensive correspondence. The native's style of writing is characterised by systematic explanation, his description being sometimes apt to wander, but always carefully exact with very suggestive, clear indication of detail. Speeches etc. are put together very easily and well and usually provoke admiration and praise from the auditors. This position of ☿ arouses a great interest in *education,* private lessons especially prove very attractive in which pupils are encouraged to think for themselves.

He who has ☿ afflicted in 3 will do well to learn to concentrate his thoughts and should practise meditation.

☿ in 4. Well aspected this position gives a certain commercial spirit; the superintendance of the native's own property, usually large inherited estates, will be profitable.

Commercial relations in other continents will also bring advantage; a new area of sale and new commercial goods will be found where others do not expect anything. Here the proverb holds true "the eye of the master makes the horse thrive".

When *afflicted* no peace can be found anywhere, the person concerned moves hither and thither without being able to find what he seeks; and all kinds of difficulties in the domestic circle may be expected to arise from this cause.

☿ in 5 makes the native fond of agreeable, intimate, but merely *friendly,* intercourse with the other sex and gives much love for and interest in the education of children. Much sought after as a witty talker.

When *afflicted* this position renders superficial, rambling from one subject to another, inconstant in love-affairs and subject to alienation from the children owing to lack of interest. Thoughtlessness and recklessness may lead to loss through speculation. Greater seriousness, deliberation and penetration should be cultivated. The world is sometimes looked upon as a hurlyburly.

☿ in 6 gives a logical clear mind, especially capable of making mechanical calculations, accurate application of formulae and drawing up balance sheets. Conversation is subtle, entertaining and pleasant, but when *afflicted* this position makes for conceit and the native is apt to allow many a white lie to slip into his stories. This constellation also indicates that liver and intestines generally are sensitive to infection and to over-spiced food.

☿ in 7 makes one suppose that relations with intelligent people are most sought; the helpmeet will also be intelligent. In marriage a cheerful spirit usually prevails, more spiritual than sensual.

When *afflicted* differences of opinion will occur in ethical, religious or social matters, which will be much discussed; education and morals are also favourite topics. *"La critique est aisée"* is true here, but it would be a pity for the attacker himself, as well as his object, if his criticism were to overlook things which are really beautiful and instructive. That is why it is well for the native to accustom himself more to *listen* and *appreciate* than to attack and demolish. And especially when subjects are concerned for a skirmish of personal judgment.

☿ in 8 makes the light of practical mind and reason shine on what is unknown, intellect striving to penetrate the secrets of invisible worlds. Problems regarding *reincarnation, psycho-analysis* etc. are always studied industriously and with much interest. Details about death and the life beyond are very absorbing and in them a correct intuition is often shown.

When *afflicted* insight will be marred by rashness or selfwill. This position of ☿ makes the native very keen to have the last word in disputes or debates in which he usually succeeds. In leisure hours hunting for old books and for sagas, fairy tales, old stories, and also for scientific and philosophical disquisitions is much enjoyed.

☿ in 9 gives much penetration and the *faculty of speedily finding* the connection between various subjects which is so useful in abstract study.

There is a danger that an excessively adaptable mind may get to know too many *contradictory* ideas, resulting in doubt and indecision. Much trouble and unpleasantness may be caused by promises being made too readily, which are not easily fulfilled. The first necessity for the nature is to acquire concentration and system in thought. His intuition should not be allowed to degenerate into a vague impartiality concerning divergent ideas. The "mobility" of ☿ must never turn into "restlessness", unable to find contentment and tending to make him go from one place to another—and not find rest anywhere. St. Augustine probably meant this type when he wrote *"Our soul is restless till it finds its rest in thee, o God."*

☿ in 10 gives ability to do unexpected jobs: practical organising of work and a talent for putting into practice *a great deal of acquired know-ledge*. Too much repetition should however be avoided, and compulsion from outside weakens both energy and zeal. This position inclines the native to have more than one profession at a time, to enter into relations with many people and to „deal" in various things. When ♊ or ♐ is in M.C. a journalistic career is most probable.

When *afflicted,* especially by ♂ or ♅, there will be likelihood of many rash and unfortunate changes of profession: *a jack of all trades and master of none.*

☿ in 11. Position and attitude in society will be closely connected with acquaintances, relations and other ties. Some friendship of a particular character among prominent and well developed people will be most important, not only for the native's career, but also for the growth of his character. Otherwise this position gives great *organising talent,* clear views on various matters and circumstances which results in a suitable and correct conduct. Interest is taken in commercial matters and *literature.*

When *afflicted* this position renders cynical, apt to sneer at one's own feelings and those of other people.

☿ in 12. ☿ in the house of self-communion and seclusion points to the fact that the circumstances do not help in a social sense; when well aspected however, much will be reached in the higher development of the Ego. In the spiritual "struggle for life", the native should count only on his own strength, guided by superphysical inspiration. As this is the house of self-examination and self-understanding, a more contemplative aspect of ☿ is here seen. A △ aspect acts very favourably, giving a fine intuition, and a special aptitude for synthesis. After some practice *meditation* will come easily and is an excellent means of progress.

Work will be best done in solitude, concentration of the thought not being possible in a busy or hurried atmosphere. Here intuition must guide intellect and when the former is sufficiently valued with a sincere desire to reach truth, without hurrying or forcing the process, then much which is dark will be made clear.

Retrograde position and afflictions arouse an attitude of *doubt,* which shrinks from every decision on the mental plane. It is only with difficulty that logical reasoning finds solutions to the riddles set by the afflicting planet. One of the senses is often defective.

A harmonious environment, regular occupation, in short *as little excitement as possible* are advisable.

Venus (♀) in the Twelve Houses.

♀ in 1. Generally speaking this position is favourable to the acquisition of friendship and affection, to the development of musical and artistic talents and gives a personal charm that strikes many. Very probably love will play a great part in life. Though really deep feelings of the kind are present, there is a great tendency to flirt—especially when *afflicted*—which entails consequences that were not really intended. And this may give rise to trouble and disappointment. It is advisable for the native to act more thoughtfully, consciously and with greater reserve in these matters, to try to get at other people's feelings and not put *his own self* so much in the foreground. *Love is not a matter of honour, it is a matter of feeling,* in which the partner's happiness is of the greatest importance.

♀ in 2 indicates favourable financial circumstances through social activities and contact with others. Well aspected this position gives a great devoted love for the profession which gives satisfaction both spiritually and materially. When entering into a legal union material interests will be ignored, while fairly high demands are made on the outer and inner make up of the future partner whether of business or marriage.

♀ in 3. This position of ♀ has a very favourable influence mentally; *good taste* and a *sense of proportion* are combined with *practical insight*; beauty of proportion is more valued than works of decorative detail. Further this position has a particularly favourable effect upon the intellect which therefore becomes very refined and greatly appreciates all that embellishes and uplifts social life, music, art, literature etc. A △ with ♨ or ♇ points to original ideas in this direction, successfully applied. Affliction of ♄ in 11 causes opposition of friends and relations or fear of such opposition, which may be equally bad for the nerves. If the ruler of the 3rd house [1]) is favourably posited with regard to ♀, there will be extraordinary ease in talking and writing, which greatly facilitates intercourse with others.

But since, when *afflicted,* the boundary line between friendship and love in intercourse with the other sex cannot always be easily drawn, it is advisable for the native to exercise self-control in order to prevent unpleasant entanglements.

♀ in 4 is favourable to domestic affairs, childhood is upon the whole *agreeable* and *fortunate,* and the relations between the parents and the native are very pleasant. This of course influences the whole life favourably; "old age" will be characteristically full of many precious memories.

When *afflicted* difficulties and disappointments in love affairs will occur; but though comparatively little return of affection is received, the native's feelings regarding his object remain constant.

♀ in 5 inclines the native to be somewhat self-indulgent, and to act on impulse. Most attention is preferably given to what is agreeable, charming, artistic and mysterious (speculative). There is a lack of true love of work, of *tackling* things, although much time and trouble are given to, let us say fancy work e.g. organising 'sales of work', making artistic articles for sale with a charitable purpose, Christmas distributions to the children of the poor etc. It should always be borne in mind that from all those occupations the person concerned ought himself to *learn* and the mind should gain by them, otherwise they are sure to bring disappointment at some time notwithstanding the good intentions with which things were begun.

Relations of love and friendship rest upon a more or less earnest-idealistic basis. When well-aspected this position denotes a marriage blessed with many and dear children.

When *afflicted* this position renders the native naturally amourous, reckless, speculative.

♀ in 6 denotes *good health* in so far as no excessive demands are

---

[1]) i.e. the ruler of the sign on the cusp of the 3rd house.

made on the body, but it also presupposes that *when* once illness masters it, it will probably be of long duration or return repeatedly. In that case sunshine, air and light are the best remedies. The throat (♀ is the ruler of ♉, the throat) is the weak point of the constitution.

Favourably aspected the relations between employer and employed will be pleasant, irrespective whether the native belongs to the former class or to the latter.

♀ in 7 points to the fact that love, affection, partnership will influence life very greatly.

The native's feelings are strong and faithful, *sincere* and *devoted;* meanness is much despised. The object of affection is made much of, the partner admired and respected.

If ♀ is afflicted there will be difficulties and disappointments in the above-mentioned matters, resulting in a withdrawal of feeling. This is however not the way to enrich and intensify one's inner life; for that purpose our love has to increase, to grow wider and more pure from selfish motives. As a rule whatever is hardest for us is precisely that which is best for us. Thus in this case when the native draws back too soon having experienced disappointment, the lesson of life will be: *to give oneself for the weal of others, to open oneself to their sorrows,* to give generously and plentifully, without caring for gratitude or enquiring whether the others are sufficiently pleased with what we have done or said. If we can do that, sacrifice ourselves in love for others—not only for another who is especially dear to us—then this will enrich us inwardly to such an extent that the unkindness or ingratitude of others cannot in the least affect our feeling.

♀ in 8. Great likelihood of a rich wife or husband or partner. Speculation with, or insecure investment of, this money should however be avoided, since as a rule these end in disappointment and consequently do not improve the relations involved.

This position denotes feelings of love of a more *universal* than personal character and renders the native receptive for deep pure affections. It requires however much inner moral strength to keep the feelings pure and natural and excessive analysis and experiment with them should be avoided. Friendship and love will very likely require more of the partner than is given in exchange and more than is desirable or possible for the person concerned. Great interest is taken in psychical research, symbolism, and esoteric conceptions of religion, theosophy and occultism, enlightened by which search will be made for the *great unity underlying all things*—the relation existing between all creatures. For the same reason a favourable attitude obtains towards experiments in spiritualism and telepathy.

♀ in 8 *inharmoniously aspected* gives difficulties with regard to legacies etc.; hallucinations, a very deceptive kind of phantasms, which arise from a supposed communion with one or more persons in the spirit world. It is better for the native not to concern himself too much with these questions in order to prevent excessive strain of the nervous system. Moreover it is desirable to be careful of the bloodcirculation and regular functioning of the kidneys.

♀ in 9 gives a clear imagination. Combinations and conclusions are also easily made. This position of ♀ makes the native sympathetic, ready to help, very much esteemed for philanthropic and religious work. Travelling gives great pleasure.

When afflicted excessive demands will be made with regard to social success, so that often dissatisfaction, disappointment and isolation or intractability result, according to the nature of the afflicting planet.

♀ in 10. The profession will in some way be connected with things which *embellish* life or make it more *pleasant* and will on the whole be lucrative. Only strength to persevere, to finish what has been begun, will sometimes be lacking when no aspects are formed.

This position further denotes a great desire for contact with others, connections with *cultured* or *artistic* circles. And the career will be favourably influenced by these.

When inharmoniously aspected it will not be easy to find the exact direction in life and various disappointments will precede lasting happiness. When, however, at last the right choice has been made (e.g. during a fortunate direction or transit) it will cause much progress both spiritually and socially.

♀ in 11. This being the house of *friends* and in general of wider inter-course with people, it is very comprehensible that the wish for *universal brotherhood and peace should* be prominent. Intercourse with others occupies an important place in the native's life. Friends and acquaintances will generally be people of culture and taste — although this condition is not so pre-eminent, as it is with ♀ in 10 — of noble, though somewhat conserv-ative feelings. The ♀ nature usually feels at home in well-bred, well-to-do surroundings and does not easily disregard etiquette and courtesy, not even in intimate relations or friendships of long standing.

♀ in 11 gives the probability of much assistance and *"luck"* in all enterprises; many unsought for opportunities of showing acquired knowledge and capacities facilitate attainment of the native's aim.

When *afflicted* obstructions will be caused by *jealousy* or *partiality.* Others will often try to profit by a certain degree of good-nature and condescension and exploit their "friend".

♀ in 12 forms a "difficult point" in a horoscope; as ♀ symbolises feeling for art and love, it may be expected that in the 12th house, the house of limitation, this will be very strange and disproportioned. The native's personal self with its less good qualities is too much involved for it to obtain really harmonious expression.

Extraordinary and *mysterious* cases captivate the mind; the more *unusual* and sensational the more they are studied and cultivated with the consequence, that they influence the whole nature. Only when very favourably aspected, ♀ in 12 may be an indication of one who does good in silence.

The native should endeavour to purify his feelings from *selfishness, jealousy* and *blind desire* (when afflicted by ♂); to control and guide them by a *sense of responsibility* and *serious work* (when afflicted by ♄) and to sublimate them to the level of a pure and lofty humanity (when afflicted by ♅).

Mars (♂) in the Twelve Houses.

♂ in 1 gives a fiery, energetic manner, self-conscious love of enterprise and tireless activity. The native has a deep abhorrence of all that is not *frank, fair* and *honest.* Strict justice is the highest ideal which he strives for as much as possible and endeavours to practise. He should cultivate self-control, because it is the factor most needed for success.

♂ in 2 warns the native against haste, partiality or excessive love of *speculation* in business and actions. Not enough benefit is derived from favourable circumstances owing to premature interference.

When *inharmoniously aspected* money will be lost by investing it in good faith in attractive enterprises or by spending it recklessly in other ways.

A great energy and untiring love of work enable the native to overcome failure and loss so splendidly that in the end his development shows constant progress.

♂ in 3. A strong *sense of independence* and *some egoism* are always prominent. But an *idealistic spirit* is evident, which sees beauty everywhere in nature and enjoys it to the full. The native has also a great trust in the power of good in the end overcoming evil. In writing letters ♂ makes the style bold and firm; the native expresses his opinions with determination and enthusiasm, although not always quite logically.

♂ in 3 *afflicted* indicates continual conflicts between the higher and lower nature. Especially in childhood this gives rise to rash, ill-considered actions of which the native repents later. A sharp way of expressing himself often leads to unpleasant relations with his environment. There is a great danger that energy will be squandered or used for wrong actions. In youth much rebelliousness against authority and generally accepted rules will manifest; when travelling, recklessness may easily cause accidents.

♂ in 4. ♂ the planet of action in the house of "home" and parental surroundings, indicates that quite early the desire arises to leave the parental roof and go out into the wide world.

When *afflicted* it is probable that the home will be the scene of many *"rows"* due mostly to the passionate and rather masterful manner which ♂ engenders. In this way the wish to escape originates, which may manifest as an impulsive running away from home. This does not prevent that much store is set on intimate domesticity and when abroad the attractions of the same home which once was so willingly left will often be a favourite topic of conversation.

If however, as well as an affliction, a good aspect of ♂ prevails, there is some hope that in the end good results may be reached — probably one of the parents (most likely the mother) will be favourably disposed towards the native's ideas, and at the end of life he will be able to look back with satisfaction upon the work accomplished.

♂ in 5 indicates great *"pluck"* in starting enterprises and carrying out plans, and gives quick insight into new possibilities; a good understanding may however be seriously threatened by an excessively rash, uncontrolled and masterful manner in word and action. If the native acts tactfully and with insight, a profitable career may be made, especially in industrial matters with big companies or public works.

As this house also gives indications with regard to children we may conclude from this position of ♂—especially if afflicted—that grief and trouble will probably be caused—directly or indirectly—by one of the children. Finally this position warns the native against excessive impulsiveness and changeability in feelings of love and in the use of sexual force.

♂ in 6 has an unfavourable influence upon health. Cuts, attacks of fever, inflammations occur fairly frequently, especially with inharmonious (progressive) directions.

The principal causes of illness are *impurity of the blood* and irregular action of the heart. When diseases occur the safest and best means of recovery will be by electric treatment, massage, light treatment and similar methods. Specifics and medicins are unnecessary and not effective. Work in the open air, pure non-stimulating food, regular, simple life are the best remedies. As every physical indisposition has its mental counterpart—or cause—it is desirable for the native as much as possible to create a *pure,* humane, calm, appreciative atmosphere, to think less of himself and to keep his eyes open to the merits of others, especially of inferiors; not to jeer at them, but to try to understand them. In general intercourse with domestics will not be pleasant especially if one has to contend with un-willingness or impudence. On the other hand nowhere do modest people meet with greater appreciation and sincere sympathy than here.

♂ in 7 is a token of much passionate affection but at the same time of much strife and opposition, particularly with those for whom the most affection is cherished. The feelings are extremely vulnerable and when once—though it may be only in imagination and not in reality—the feelings are hurt, the attitude becomes combative, irritable, sarcastic and quasi-indifferent, which usually makes matters worse.

If well aspected everything will soon be smoothed over again, but if *afflicted* the breach which was at first imaginary becomes real to the grief of both parties concerned. It is therefore advisable to think as little as possible of oneself and to try and imagine the other's feelings. This is of course a difficult lesson for passionate ♂, the more so as the native's choleric character may result in some degree of rancour and revengefulness. Much *love,* real *self-less* love will be necessary to mollify the influence of ♂. And not until then will the "fire" no longer scorch, but warm beneficently.

♂ in 8 points to increase of property through the partner or through legacies and inheritance. This ♂-position also symbolises strong feelings and a great deal of vitality in the senses. When harmoniously aspected, especially by ♀ or ♃ the love-ideal will prove to be too pure to be spoiled by martial desires, and satisfaction on a lower plane will not easily be sought, when higher regions have not been attained.

This position gives enthusiasm for *spiritual* research. But it is well to remember that in this department scientific study and reflection are essential in order that the native may gain reasonable insight into the possibility of appearances from the unseen worlds, and thus prevent harmful consequences resulting from psychic experiences.

♂ in 9 symbolises desire for *many-sided action,* for continual *instruction* and *precept.* ♂ in this place makes the native enthusiastic for everything affecting head and heart, especially for discussion and propaganda along religious-occult lines.

If inharmoniously aspected this position often gives a feeling of *being bound,* of being unable to reach as much as is wished; the consequence is a certain whimsical attitude and dissatisfaction with oneself. The native often supposes that he will be able to act more freely abroad, away from home, but once there, he finds the opposition is greater than ever.

It is difficult for him to keep a tolerant attitude towards the opinions of those who differ from him and he has a great desire to interfere immediately where injustice is done. This may occasion a somewhat nervous, *fanatical* state of mind. All this brings about a very pronounced attitude to life which shows itself in many ways — theoretically as well as practically and attracts much attention. Great intellectuality and philosophical insight may be found here and many radical improvements may be brought about in many regions of life, if the mind can manage to keep free of all *exaggeration, self-interest* and similar ignoble influences. It will be best not to have too many irons in the fire, but quietly to do the nearest duty with the conviction that indirectly this will contribute to the attainment of the desired aim.

♂ in 10. Great *energy for progress,* love of enterprise and also much love of work, which will always be based on *strong and lofty ideals,* sustained by a firm belief in the possibility of reaching them and their helpful influence on society. And it is this sense of Truth, this faith, this love of work which embody the greatest possibilities of development. The calling chosen will be one in which a *resolute manner* is desirable and where ability to use sharp-edged tools is needed e.g. that of a surgeon, medical man, officer. This position gives love of fame and honour.

When ♂ makes few aspects it is wise to strengthen its influence consciously by guarding against pessimistic or weakening feelings and by opening oneself wide to new thoughts, the healthy joy of life and love of action.

When afflicted a revolutionary nature manifests, which opposes all restraint, hot-headed. If the native succeeds in guiding the unbalanced energy of ♂ into good directions — e.g. by work that is largely constructive — sorrow, trouble, anxiety and disappointment will in the long run *result in such good things* that could perhaps never have been obtained had the course of life been easy.

♂ in 11 indicates friends who are rather hot-headed, so that differences of opinion will occur fairly often. They are however frank and courteous, so that as a rule a solution will soon be found and the thunderstorm will prove to have purified the air.

Because the 11th house symbolises also the fulfilment of desires and wishes, this ♂ position intimates that everything depends on the native's *own energy* and personal will-power. It is not only outer work, but especially that which is done within which will bring victory. Not to be dejected by disappointments, but to investigate their causes; if need be, not to fear to blame one's own egoism or thoughtlessness and then to try and take the lesson to heart — that is the path to victory!

♂ in 12 is a very precarious position which especially in childhood may cause a great deal of trouble. The feelings are vehement and intense and as they usually are long repressed they are apt upon occasion to burst out all the stronger. From a child the native likes to lord it over others; lack of appreciation wounds him deeply and he reacts to it by falling into capricious silence. His feelings are apt to predominate over his mind and this may greatly injure his "capital", that which is within, as well as outward.

It will, however, be possible for the native with relatively little difficulty to form such a noble and strong ideal of love that it completely dominates physical emotions. Thus in every region to which his enthusiasm is drawn, equilibrium of feeling and reason must be sought. *"There can be no enthusiasm where there is less spirit than passion"* is a saying which is very apposite here — which should be taken especially to heart. By means of frank and impartial discussion and philosophic calm many a bad mood may be transmuted into cheerful diligence.

Jupiter (♃) in the Twelve Houses.

♃ in 1 gives a certain *optimism in all enterprise*. When everything has been done according to the natives perception and capacity, with confidence and faith the decision will be left to a higher power.

If — when *afflicted* — expectations are frustrated or if others try to lay too much stress on the possibility of disappointment, a sharp outburst is apt to follow suddenly or a quasi-indifferent silence sometimes completely disconcerts the outsider. In that case health is not so good as it should be.

♃ in 2 gives great confidence in financial prosperity and indicates a peaceful existence so far as concerns pecuniary matters, inasmuch as there will not be any speculations in big companies or untrustworthy institutions (Monte Carlo), things to which this position tends, ♃ being fond of luxury and comfort, society and recreation. In intercourse with others a light jocular and jovial manner often manifests, a comrade-like frankness which — when *afflicted* — is apt to be taken wrongly and misunderstood. This may lead to situations which, although not originally intended, in the end cannot easily be avoided; in the end much may be reached by showing less indulgence to others and doing more to encourage one's own pure ideas. This is the feeling, the wish to remain as much as possible on good terms with every one which is a hindrance and prevents the worthier friendship of better situated or nobler people.

♃ in 3 enhances the inner vitality and brings the native into contact with favourable, helpful influences. Philosophic and pedagogic subjects are contemplated. New ideas will be much discussed with friends and relations, orally or through correspondence.

When *afflicted* although some *idealism* will be evident in all that he utters, the native is *unpractical* in daily life and only few will share his views from beginning to end.

He likes to travel especially when locomotion is rapid. This is the very reason why care should be taken, for — when afflicted — the likelihood that accidents happen is fairly great and his whole life may be ruined in consequences of some careless act.

♃ in 4 presupposes that the parents were well-to-do, even wealthy and that education began in a grand style. This position makes the relation to parents, and atmosphere in the domestic circle especially hearty and benevolent. It gives a *deep, inner support,* a *spiritual prop* which again and again helps the native to overcome all difficulties. Such a person will meet with much cooperation and respect in his native place.

When *afflicted* it will be better for him to settle *somewhere else* where one is less known, in order that he may at least feel more free. But it will be difficult for him to find lasting prosperity, because he takes things too lightly and cannot cut his coat according to his cloth. This leads to thoughtless and frivolous expenditure, which may result in danger of bankruptcy.

♃ in 5 denotes much sociability and satisfaction through children. The native likes to associate with children in a large family. This position makes him fond of physical pleasures and indicates a knack of speculating.

When *afflicted* there is a tendency to go in for gambling and lotteries, also a dislike of work and no heart for the care demanded by children. Through *recklessness* and ignorance his best chances will pass unused; trusting to his knowledge and the necessary good luck he will fail to notice opportunities for development and progress until too late or not at all.

♃ in 6. This position makes it likely that the native will be richly endowed with ♃'s gifts of cheerfulness, popularity, health etc. — but his watchword should be *help!* Even a strongly harmonious aspect is unable to manifest fully, unless the native does what he can to help. All good impulses, kindheartedness, sympathy, charity, unselfishness, and love of work must be utilised and strengthened, so that they may take the place of less favourable tendencies. His deep confidence in God's goodness should grow, the thoughts being always permeated with that idea, then the words illness and weakness will disappear of their own accord and the inner joy will overcome the desire for lower, unreal pleasures. Good consequences will soon follow if this lesson is learned willingly; if however the helping hand is scorned, the native has no alternative but to learn the lesson in the hard school of experience. This position makes him open to new ideas and tolerant of ancient wisdom, but at the same time gives a propensity towards self-conceit.

The disorders which arise when ♃ in 6 is *afflicted* will be psychic rather than organic and this not so much owing to organic weakness as to the reaction of nervous strain. The native should above all acquire peace and inner harmony — for without these, recovery is impossible. Difficulties with inferiors or pupils will also occur through the native being exacting — sometimes unfair.

♃ in 7. Religious, social and moral ideas are very pure, and prominent. Thus placed ♃ usually is a sign of pleasant reciprocity between the native and the world; and especially of a happy mariage. This will probably rise to a *higher level* than is the case with most marriages, husband (wife) will be inspired with the same ideals as the native, so that both inwardly and outwardly much happiness may result.

Many pleasant, intimate connections, which, although not always visible to others, are lasting, will have a very helpful influence on the native's spiritual life.

Afflictions render marriage troubled through callousness, pride, self-will, wastefulness, in fact conflict between the higher and lower nature according to the planet aspecting inharmoniously. The date for the wedding is often postponed, possibly even put off altogether, owing to doubt as to the partner's trustworthiness. When and if in the end the couple are married, much trouble will be caused by the partner's laziness and egoism.

> We starve each other for love's caress;
> We *take,* but we do not *give;*
> It seems so easy some soul to bless,
> But we dole the love grudgingly, less and less
> Till 't is bitter and hard to live.

♃ in 8 gives a *hopeful confidence* in the path of life including the *beyond,* inclines to believe in Providence, in a great, good Power guiding and regulating everything purposefully and bringing everything to a good end, if only we listen to the voice of our conscience and act accordingly. But is should never be forgotten that earthly daily life and ordinary things all have a claim on us which cannot with impunity be neglected. This position indicates clear dreams, a lively imagination and an interest in occult teachings.

Afflictions make the native sceptical about these things — he can only believe what he himself has experienced.

♃ in 8 gives a possibily of inheritance, legacies, money through insurance etc., but an inharmonious aspect causes much trouble, mainly legal difficulties in really getting them into one's possession. Relations will probably try to interfere through jealousy or selfishness. Too good a trust is not advisable in suchlike questions.

♃ in 9 has an *exceptionally favourable influence on the entire horoscope*. The 9th house is most congenial to ♃ which in this position renders the native extraordinarily fitted for religious and philosophical contemplation, jurisprudence and pedagogy. A △ aspect gives him great interest in each new point arising from the study of these subjects, and screens him from narrowminded self-conceit; also makes him studious, and gives a liking for teaching.

♃ deepens and ennobles the mind and gives zeal for logical argument. That is why this position of ♃ enables a speaker to contact and charm his audience; thus a missionary can make his ideas acceptable to an undeveloped population, or an educator will improve and strengthen his pupils' characters. This kind of work always gives satisfaction and has a benificent effect on the whole nature. The native's faith is not of a common kind and does not fall into grooves, but is based on a fervent and somewhat mystical conviction. His religious beliefs, of whatever kind they may be, are always founded on christianity, the idea of *Providence* and the *Redeemer*.

Upon the whole the native's mode of thought is broad, peaceful, tolerant, manifesting chiefly when opinions and ideas are expounded. Here ♃ gives a strong feeling of justice and fairness; and when a legal career is chosen, it is chiefly the desire to help the weak and outcast that prompts the native. His maxim is rather to *educate for good action* than to *punish for evil done*.

A journey will give great pleasure and contribute to the expansion of consciousness.

> "Beyond the meadows the hills I see,
> Where the noises of traffic cease,
> And I follow a voice that calleth to me
> From the hilltop regions of peace."

Afflicted ♃ here makes the native *arrogant* and inclined to live *above his station;* there is even a possibility that he may lose his credit. When travelling he will fairly often make mistakes, such as using a time-table that is out of date or getting into a wrong train etc.

♃ in 10. There is every likelihood that the native's occupations or situations will harmonise with his inclinations and temperament, and therefore give him every satisfaction. And if perhaps in the horoscope an afflicted ♄ makes him disposed to worry about material things, the presence of ♃ will remind him that ideal victories have also value which may be greater.

Here ♃ gives great ease in intercourse with other people and a keen sense of humour. The native has a great sense of responsibility and justice but also a certain partiality for outward show, as well as for public recognition and esteem.

Further this position strengthens vitality, especially when there is sufficient movement in the open air, sun-baths etc. Listening to good music may also have a physically helpful influence. This position makes the native very fit to be a calm, benevolent guide of younger people, not excessively strict, but clinging to definite principles "suaviter in modo, fortiter in re".

His love and attachment are very great especially to his own children, and also relatives, although an affliction is sure to cause a passing conflict. He should ever bear in mind that though his own ideas may be excellent, as a rule youth has other views. And our task is to seek to understand these and to guide them aright. His inner feelings of religious brotherhood and humanity are stronger than they appear on the surface to be. He likes to help with advice and action, but the latter only when it has been proved that assistance will be really useful and is really necessary.

When *afflicted* ♃ does not point to a strong position in social life. There is a possibility of slander which might harm the native's good character. This position therefore requires great prudence in all personal matters, actions and sayings. Reckless action may have fatal consequences, with regard both to health and finances. Intercourse with relatives will probably cause much unpleasantness through mutual misunderstanding. With regard to subordinates trouble may also be expected and this gives a possibility of a change of fortune and loss of credit.

♃ in 11 denotes many connections with older people, of great influence, experience and good position in life; who are much in contact with the public. Acquaintances are sought among *superiors* rather than *inferiors,* because in that way a more rapid social progress may be expected. Once he has reached a high position, the native willingly exerts his influence to help others on. Therefore he is very fit for a leading position in a big society or institution where young and unskilled people are trained to greater capacity.

♃ in 11, the house of friends emphasizes the *ideal of brotherhood* in society and also in religion. When *afflicted* the native should keep his own possessions and those of other people well apart; should never force upon another what his own mind takes to be true, and never take away from another what is of value to that person. For these things tend to estrange rather than to reconcile; only love and tact can in the end lead to the goal.

♃ in 12. When ♃ in the 12th house is harmoniously aspected at birth confidence that everything will come right will enable the native to surmount the troubles which may arise. This position promises much from *social work* connected with hospitals and institutions for nervous disorders. He should be warned not to be upset by possible lack of cooperation and appreciation. Fortunately, ♃'s confidence helps him greatly, but it would be more of a support if the native were to reason logically about it, because ♃'s ideas are not always founded on practical insight.

Once he truly realises that a *good action* must always have a *good effect,* visible or invisible, he will continue to work in that direction with more constant devotion and when discouragement comes, it will perforce give way to an indomitable, and purposeful strength of mind which nothing can destroy or daunt.

Affliction leads to enemies and opposition physical as well as moral, attacks by orthodox theologians — but also opposition from the native's own self! He has indeed some difficulty in living according to his own higher-sensed ideals and in defending them against others. This position renders somewhat indolent, careless, counting on support from other people.

Saturn (♄) in the Twelve Houses.

♄ in 1 lays his oppressive hand specially upon *outer appearance and manner;* if however it is harmoniously posited the native's will to be serious will not degenerate into pessimism. This position of ♄ gives the native something 'oldish' in appearance and demeanour and little inclination to form quick attachments. Everything that he takes in hand requires a good deal of patience and perseverance and if no assistance comes through ♂, things will often be given up through lack of these qualities. The result is that only the unpleasantness of work and not its satisfaction will be experienced, which in other respects also affects the native's love of work unfavourably. He should endeavour to do work for its own sake, rather than for any profit which may accrue.

The native works much and strenuously; holidays for which others may perhaps occasionally be envied, would indeed soon lose their attraction. Even in childhood work will occupy an important place in his life, owing to unfavourable circumstances, and later on he is apt to exact much in this respect from others also, which often causes conflicts. He is not usually in the mood for careless, light-hearted merriment; *"work and be watchful"* is his maxim.

The native only works willingly for others, if through it his *own greater capacities* come to light — hence also his love of *teaching.* Upon the whole his attitude towards strangers is cool, reserved or somewhat forcedly kind; his attitude towards life seems to say "we are not going to expect much, then it is likely to give us more than we anticipate".

This position often causes fits of despondency and distrust. When harmoniously aspected much help may come from a pure, strong, sincere friendship with an eminent man or woman, when the better saturnine qualities, such as sence of duty, reliability, perseverance and self-control become more evident and pronounced. Then, too, more rigorous and lucid self-examination will lead to an increase of love, compassion and for-giveness and thought be less exclusively fixed on his own self.

The tendency to pay more attention to *bad* than to *good luck* should be resisted so far as possible since this prevents the native from beginning a plan or attacking a new task and thus makes a happy solution altogether impossible. ♄ in the ascendant does not make him sanguine; renders him distrustful regarding the possibility of reaching a position, renders him at war with himself and causes him to feel that he is misunderstood and too little appreciated.

Opinions and feelings about people and things are pronouncedly "pro" or "con", although as much as possible this will be hidden.

Domestic circumstances — especially in childhood — are by no means rosy; the native should also be careful of health.

ħ in 2. Financially much anxiety and difficulty will often be met, of which the world remains ignorant. But much may be changed for the better by dint of great diligence, insight and reflection.

When *afflicted* by ♂ the financial situation will not improve until the distrustful economy of ħ is transmuted into a sensible and energetic manner towards things connected with money. An affliction of ☿ requires great care in the choice of servants (dependents). If the affliction is caused by ♃ or ♅, almost worthless articles will be bought fairly frequently in the belief that the native has made a real bargain; it is a case of "economy deceiving wisdom", and who acts thus is compelled to a large expenditure when even small expenses were grudged.

ħ in 3 brings earnest, deep and pure thoughts, concentration, honesty and justice. The superficial "airy" side of the 3rd house (♊ house) is restrained by ħ's stern sense of duty, whilst his restless uncertaintly becomes something more determined. The mind likes to be absorbed in mathematics, mechanics and similar subjects which call for *more action* and *less talk* than languages.

ħ in 3 — when *afflicted* — easily causes frequent unpunctuality. Circumstances however, will indicate the serious necessity of always being in time (ħ symbolises *Time)* and of not postponing what must be done. A person with this ħ-position is usually the youngest child or the only one, and often does not harmonise with the mother, gives her much disappointment during the first year of life and the whole education. In a few instances we have found that a child with this position was of the opposite sex to that desired before birth.

ħ in 4 makes the native careful, economical; anxious about his *old age* and therefore always endeavouring to increase the likelihood of lasting prosperity. Especially when *afflicted* the native is probably too much concentrated upon his own gain and advantage; he would do well to consider whether in the end the individual does not really benefit more virtually by the progress of the *community* than by augmenting his *own* means — may be to the detriment of that community — in order that in his old age he may become a miser or a hermit.

Here the management of money is in good hands, the native is also suited to being at the head of some institution or family. In his own parental home however, less pleasant things will occur to which probably is due the circumstance that to a great extent this character has to develop by itself. The father will probably be the "master of the house" in the fullest sense of the word and exact obedience not easy to fulfil. This will be especially evident in the choice of a calling and also in discussions about religion, etc. Yet time will prove that much might be learned from the father and that inwardly there is possibly greater agreement than was supposed in youth.

At the age of adolescence there will often be a gradual alienation from the parents. No wonder that the native seeks from others what could not be found at home. Difficulties will arise through oversensitiveness, but yet one individual will probably be found to brighten his solitude by understanding and a cheerful attitude. And such a friend will be loved, made much of, adored in a way seldom seen.

It is also possible that illness or early death of one of the parents darkens his childhood.

He will probably harmonise particularly well with the mother which — in a man — is conducive to reverence for the entire sex. The parents will possibly often have differences of opinion about the education of their child. The tie with the mother will be particularly intimate and peaceful, though an inner strength emanates from the father which arouses respect.

It is possible that the greatest progress, both spiritually and socially, may be expected *in a foreign country* and his native place will play but a small part in his development.

ℏ in 5 is favourable to the *investment of money* — and *careful speculation* — in trustworthy concerns, mortgages, the conclusion of a reliable life insurance through "care" for the children etc. We find here a serious educator of a limited number of children who will probably be neither very healthy nor strong.

When *afflicted* adversity in enterprises may be expected, the fruit of labour will be shriveling before it is ripe; with women miscarriages occur.

ℏ in 6. A serious, business-like, accurate manner will demand respect and obedience from inferiors, without need of much talk. ℏ *afflicted* however makes the native fearful, melancholy, listless, not very popular with employers and clients. Such a person has a hard life.

Health is poor and most of his diseases are chronic. Much trouble is caused by cold feet, rheumatism and *costiveness*. Diseases of the heart occur through overexertion. If an illness is epidemic, it will soon attack the native and last longer than with others; and an affliction from the 12th house makes deafness probable.

All this arises principally from the afore-mentioned feelings of fear and distrust which, as it were, *attract all ailments*. The native should endeavour to attain and so far as possible to keep in a cheerful and contented frame of mind, also take fewer drugs etc. His diet should be pure and simple, the blood-circulation increased through much physical exercise — (a sedentary life should be avoided) and his mind strengthened by beneficent New Thought literature. *A healthy spirit creates a healthy body!*

ℏ in 7. An indication of many hindrances and troubles in intercourse with intimate acquaintances. A ⚸-aspect presupposes that again and again a pleasant understanding will come to a sudden end, while no possibility seems to exist of later conciliation or renewal. Disappointment in an ideal causes a lasting feeling of distrust and suspicion through which many possible openings for valuable relations of friendship pass by unnoticed and unused.

ℏ here somewhat hinders married life. For various reasons the wedding will more than once be postponed. *Affliction* renders it very difficult for the native to find the right person or to enter into a close relationship with him. If, however, love of another enables the native to conquer the egoism natural to Saturn by the magnanimity of soul also characteristic of ♄, the tie will be *more pure* and *strong* and able to render others happier than might at first be expected. ♄ is exalted in ♎, and this is ♎'s house. With favourable directions an older partner who is practically inclined will be the one chosen.

For a person with a similar ♄ position nothing is so bad as to sit idle and talk about himself and his own feelings, emotions and thoughts. We, humans, must *act*, act according to the best of our knowledge, and if we are not willing to do so, others will do it for us and by means of us — which puts us years back. *We can always do more than we think we can, if only we try honestly!*

♄ in 8 makes the native prudent with the partner's capital. If ♄ is afflicted, it makes him listless, indifferent and this will also mean the loss of the money which has been put in by the partner.

♄ here inclines to *melancholy,* which although perhaps not strong enough to prevail in a horoscope otherwise harmonious, nevertheless causes many an unpleasant mood. These gloomy fits usually arise from *financial anxieties* which frustrate many grand plans. The best thing to do is not to allow oneself to become dejected by circumstances, but without grumbling to do what can be done.

> If you *can*not do what you *wish* to do
> You should *be willing* to do cheerfully and
> Faithfully what you *can* do.

For this only can make up for what has already been spoilt, and helps to improve future conditions.

Thoughts about the Beyond will crowd in at definite times and remain with the native for some time. The end of life will not come until after much reflection and opportunity to prepare for it.

♄ in 9. This indicates the native's *wish to rule* with the understanding, however, that he will constantly strive for the benefit of those ruled — if need be sacrificing his own happiness. This is the type of the father of whom it is said that he *chastises with tears in his eyes.*

Experience has taught us that people with ♄ in the 9th house are usually *restrained* in the first stage of their self-governing development by their father whose views on finances are not in harmony with the direction adopted.

Therefore ♄ in 9 symbolises opposition, continuous impediments and *distrustful pessimism,* manifesting at each new enterprise. All this orginates chiefly with the father who, though well meaning and without personal prejudice, cannot sympathise with modern theories and tries again and again to deny or condemn them. In this way conflicts continually arise which, though sometimes secret, make themselves deeply felt.

In the long run however — *when favourably aspected* — the native's own will, although possibly in a circuitous way, will conquer and good results will be obtained through his purified and tested tendencies. The father's interest and confidence will however not be won easily. Owing to the lack of encouragement from this quarter, much energy will be applied although to the onlooker the *result* will usually appear to be less than could have been achieved with the same amount of zeal and expenditure of energy had the cooperation of the environment been available. This position of ♄ teaches the native *to stand on his own feet,* in his own way transmuting his capabilities into deeds.

The native has a great disposition to travel, especially abroad, when he prefers to visit the most inhospitable and remote regions, difficult of access. This holds good also in spiritual affairs: the most difficult problems attracting him most.

♄ in 9 requires especially a good use of time so that the native's many aspirations do not come to grief through the dissipation of interest, since he is always in danger of being greatly interested in so many things that in the end he achieves nothing.

♄ in 10 gives opposition and perseverance in the profession as well as ambition which aims very high. *Affliction* seriously demands great self-control and tact in all connections with the outer world, because otherwise a public collapse may occur at the moment of the greatest fame (Napoleon I). Notwithstanding all the native's good qualities, perseverance, love of work and self-confidence, the feelings of *modesty* and *responsibility* should always be prominent and he should never undertake any enterprise which is beyond his control.

In affliction discontent, dissatisfaction with the native's own being and position arise.

In general, even when this constellation is not unfavourably aspected, it is apt to cause great whimsicality and *bad temper.* The native should fight the inclination *to concentrate, when opposed, wholly upon himself* — for this is sure at some time or other to manifest physically as some ♄-disease.

Further this position indicates a great love for public, responsible offices, preferably abroad, and makes the native very sensitive to signs of reverence or respect from outsiders. ♄ *afflicted* hinders its fulfilment.

♄ in 11 indicates many connections with well-to-do and intellectual people and great help from them if their views and ideas are respected. True friends will be rare and they will usually reside at a considerable distance, so that the feelings are only expressed by correspondence or very restricted intercourse.

The native's attitude to his contemporaries and to those younger than he, is characterised by a peculiar *"fatherliness"* which however may grow into schoolmasterliness, into a tendency to meddle, which causes irritation in others. It is therefore well for him only to give advice when asked and even then as reservedly as possible. There are only few people able to understand and appreciate all the ways of this character; as a rule he is admired from a distance — which for that matter flatters the person concerned — or his masterful air and unreasonable fits of passion give offence; people are also suspicious about his spells of despondency and reserve. To many the native will give the impression of being eccentric; only those who have much experience of life and knowledge of human nature will prove to be true friends.

The effect of ♄ when well aspected is a talent for organising, directing, making plans and carrying them out practically. There is however a tendency to intolerance towards those who cherish other opinions or show opposition.

This position indicates many disappointments, difficulties in intercourse with others, because this character's queer tendencies are often misunderstood by others. They will often exploit him and cut him when they have no more need of him.

♄ in 12 gives a difficulty in distinguishing friends from foes, because the latter usually keep in the background and do not let much escape them. This position makes the native's manner somewhat reserved, especially in the society of strangers. In the midst of the greatest sociability a sense of isolation and misunderstanding sometimes manifests, overshadowing all other impressions.

This position symbolises lack of confidence, the *thought of fear* which causes many enterprises to fail and spoils many beautiful moods for feelings. It is, therefore, desirable for him always to cultivate thoughts of hope and trust, to strive along the line of religion and philosophy to attain that inner peace which leaves no room for disturbing or evil thoughts.

This position brings the native into contact with *work in hospitals and prisons.*

Uranus (♅) in the Twelve Houses.

♅ in 1. The planet of new ideas makes the native's appearance and manner original, bright and lively and gives a special liking for abstract study, occultism and modern lines in science and art. Little store is set on convention and the usual ideas of the surroundings.

Placed here ♅ strengthens what is the peculiar and particularly characteristic side of the native and indicates very *original theories* and *methods of working* which he applies successfully. He is especially interested in education in the widest sense of the word, the formation and development of strong characters. Also philosophy and religion, physics and metaphysics, electrotechnics and mechanics. His mind is always seeking to extend the field of its activity and does not shrink from difficult problems especially if he is able to suppose that really valuable results will accrue. The chief difficulty is the gift of — the *absolute surrender* of — *himself,* through which the link is made between the single individual and the world around him. So long as this has not been reached a certain isolation and unrest will always be felt, in spite of great inner spiritual wealth.

When *afflicted* this position often causes a sudden disturbance in the contact with others (especially with more eminent people), a misunderstanding of the native's attempts and desires for progress, an intense and vehement craving for something that cannot be reached and so forth.

Feeling needs to be better controlled and guided by the true self in order to prevent troubles, sudden separations and alienations.

This position indicates occasional blunt behaviour, sudden impulses, shortlived exaggerated dread of illness, induced by insignificant occurences or symptons.

♅ in 2 indicates sudden, unforeseen circumstances in monetary matters, varying income, many *ups and downs*. This position gives little probability of a regular fixed income, but when very well aspected or with good progressive directions, some "windfalls" may be expected, especially through marriage, partnership, good employees who are well and sensibly managed. Further good money may be earned by work which is not really in harmony with the ideals cherished; work of a more practical-businesslike nature which suits the taste of the public. But the native's innate originality will usually add something special to this.

Warning should be given against *speculation,* for any small gain is apt to be followed by much larger loss. Antique, curiosa or similar uncommon things will play a part in financial affairs.

This position gives the character a great desire for *independence* and great obstinacy which will be very difficult to overcome. Once an idea has got a firm hold of the man it will be maintained with calm assurance and imperturbable perseverance. This leads to enterprises the result of which cannot be clearly foreseen, since they are founded on some invention.

♅ in 3. Humanity and *social idealism* will be prominent both in thought and discussion and quite early a great desire will manifest to make the ideas of community and humanity better known. Very uncommon conceptions are held with regard to faith, morality and education. The native stands aloof from convention and also dislikes etiquette and "ignores Mrs. Grundy". But a person with this position should consider it his duty to show conventionalists that extraneus laws are here superfluous since control is from within!

Further does this position indicate an extraordinary talent for occult and metaphysical study in which surprising results may be achieved and great intuition and imagination.

When *afflicted* ♅ denotes here inconstancy and great eccentricity and causes sudden alienation from brothers, sisters and neighbours. Very peculiar adventures may be expected when travelling — pretty often accidents also, especially if ♅ is in a mutable sign.

♅ in 4 presupposes no agreeable childhood. The native's character is not well understood by the parents, his tastes and tendencies and shyness wrongly interpreted. A definite feeling for domesticity is lacking, though he desires to mix with many and all kinds of people. Quite early in life parents and the whole of the near environment will be in despair about the queer child and doubt his ever getting right.

Owing to his many sudden crazes and whims the native is very rarely fit to found an establishment or home of his own. He is much more inclined and fit to live in a larger community of like-minded people than in a small family-circle.

♅ in 5 warns the native against extravagances in love affairs; against too free an intercourse with the other sex, and all sorts of reckless enterprises and excessive dissipation. ♅'s sudden uncommon impulses should not be thoughtlessly carried out; they require self-restraint and self-knowledge to bring about the good results which they of course intend. This position gives clear intuition, so that with a certain amount of concentration important spiritual discoveries may be expected. ♅ is here favourably posited for various enterprises in which *new inventions* are implied and applied, especially in the fields of physics and chemistry, probably also in occultism and metaphysics. The native's mind is very active, and fertile in this direction and at times shows genius; nor does he lack the strength of will and perseverance to reach his aim. He likes to acquaint other people with his own — often very *utopian* — social views. Although a harmoniously aspected ♅ may for himself have reached clear and true vision, a practical ordinary man will regard his views as "music of the future" never to be realised.

When *afflicted* all kinds of unexpected hindrances arise, so that plans cannot be carried out; with women miscarriages occur, and the children themselves will often meet with accidents or suffer from rare diseases.

♅ in 6 gives to the native's way of working and living a great measure of originality and inventiveness, an intense abhorrence of banality and convention and strong craving to be able to live his own life in accordance with his own views and habits.

This position gives the admiration and friendship of people who are the exact contrary and who hope to gain in wit by this connection. This involves of course a possibility of the native's being spoiled especially by those who are lower in evolution. If however he is able to retain his innate ingenuousness and honesty, a cheering, inspiring influence will emanate from this character.

♅ in 6 *afflicted* makes the native unreasonable, nervous, at times vehemently passionate. Sudden *fancies* of *fear* or *delusive ideas* rob him of both his courage and love of work. Afflictions may lead to very eccentric ideas and actions. Such a person has great difficulty in keeping to the work that ought to be done and again and again is quite unexpectedly diverted so that his subordinates receive all kinds of confusing injunctions. If the person concerned is a subordinate himself, nothing will ever be delivered in time or rightly.

♅ indicates here peculiar ailments, difficult to cure and of a mental nature; so it will be much the best for the native to keep at rest as much as possible and allow his mind to expand until possessed by purity, peace and freedom from care and anxiety. This will by no means be easy to this passionate and hasty temperament, but spiritual welfare is too important to physical health for this advice to be incontinently rejected. Regular work, a simple way of living, avoidance of all stimulants and above all *fixed times of rest* may prevent or compensate very much of the bad influence of ♅. In an advanced stage of disease much help may be derived from massage, electric treatment, radiation and similar methods.

♅ in 7 gives platonic ideas regarding marriage. The native wishes marriage relations to be more idealistic than the reality usually is or than the social relations of the day allow. A person who has this position of ♅ is not easily understood by a partner.

This position often causes jealousy and slander or pharisaical criticism of the ordinary common-place man who cannot follow a ♅ type with his crazes. A divorce followed by a continuance of comradelike intercourse is beyond the comprehension of the "sensuous" man. When there is a difference of opinion or something for which they have gone to law ♅ will lose his case before the earthly judge, but feel fully justified before the Heavenly Judge. But as so little reliance can be placed on ♅'s impulses, it is advisable for the native to keep as much as possible current ideas rather than to walk on thin ice.

♅ presupposes a very large circle of acquaintances. The intimates however will often vary, since great estrangement may arise from trifles and yet again and again comrades are wished for. The native's *own irritability* is usually the cause of difference unless it be a kind of fear that he may not receive as much affection as he is conscious of giving. In this way sometime friends may turn into enemies, an end which might have been avoided. Here the best advice is *'Do well and never mind the consequences'*.

Marriage is often looked upon as too great a limitation and therefore banished from thought.

♅ in 8. Harmoniously placed, this position of ♅ indicates great interest in the problem of heredity, sin, death and penitence. And connected with this also psycho-analysis. There is a likelihood of strange dreams, also of so-called *day dreams*. Things will often happen of which he has already dreamt. Occult faculties are present, but as soon as they are "toyed" with they disappear or revenge themselves in some other way.

The power of suggestion to cure illnesses can also be applied to others but only *if there be no attempt to derive personal profit*.

The 8th house (♏) symbolises the raising of mind above purified matter — generation and regeneration — and ♅ here is strongly posited. Matter must be overcome before the mind can find happiness in the 9th house (the house of philosophy, consciousness and knowledge); for which many voluntary sacrifices or many bitter experiences will be necessary.

Death comes unexpectedly, usually through an accident. It will be well at all times to be prepared for the transition.

When *afflicted* this position leads to sudden, unaccountable difficulties as regards the partner's possessions.

Much unpleasant Karma must be worked off here but there is also great likelihood that when rightly solved important progress in evolution may be made. *Higher insight* is therefore very needful in all occurrences and circumstances. Every action should be directed by a desire for what is good and great confidence in its power. Apparently the most impossible and unexpected situations will occur in this life and cause much amazement and alarm; they dissolve however in as peculiar a manner as that by which they arose, and sometimes prove clearly to have been brought about by the native's own wrong thought images, which purer, clearer conceptions enable him to dispel.

♅ in 9. This "progressive minded" planet is thus placed in the horoscope of a man who makes extensive plans to work in and seeks for an increasingly wider sphere of activity. It is a position for an inventor, a big manufacturer, a resourceful man. We find this position in the case of air-men, successful publishers, the manager of a factory with a world-wide sale.

This position however usually makes people *superstitious,* they are addicted to the carrying of talismans when travelling, (cf. the many mascots for luck on motorcars, flying machines, motor cycles, all of them ♅ vehicles!).

When *afflicted* travelling accidents or the collapse of lofty enterprises are very probable. Great care must be taken of the nerves.

♅ in 10 indicates somewhat peculiar occupations in a *social-ethical* direction. ♅ is the planet of altruism and inspiration, and posited in the house of calling indicates a field of activity whereby the weaker people of the world are protected, educated, and generally supported. Nursing, morally as well as physically, emancipation of women, the relief of the outcasts of society — all these will have his active approval — and in these fields he will meet with success.

It goes without saying that when *afflicted,* this cannot be done without incurring resistance or even ridicule. Sedate respectability and selfish cal-culating reason will be unable to join in the aim of this life and again and again resistance will be felt.

When well aspected the ideals may be expected to be strong enough to hold their own in the midst of much opposition and disapprobation, and in the end the fruits of this difficult but courageous work may be gathered. ♅ placed here gives something original, at times even genius. A lively imagination and peculiar and rather special ideas render the per-sonality very attractive even to those who understand but little of this character. But this fact does not prevent the native from being a "black sheep" for his family and the more old-fashioned of his acquaintances, a being whom in all possible ways they will try to convert. This however will only increase the alienation.

Upon the whole this position is an indication of a *life full of vicissitudes,* which cannot be disregarded. It points to the fact that only after many and various disappointments will people recognise that here is an original talent. ♅ renders intuitive, resourceful, gives magnetic healing power.

♅ in 11. The native will have many connections among *romantic, eccentric or bohemian people,* with whom he busily discusses occultism and art. Joking, courteous, airily social contact with various people, also of the other sex, may be expected. If not quite strongly and harmoniously aspected the affections will have to grow in constancy, although their intentions are pure.

When afflicted, this position gives a probability of very peculiar ex-periences in intercourse with others — relations in between love and friendship, connections entered into suddenly, under romantic circumstances, and broken off equally suddenly.

The native's feelings of sympathy and antipathy are very strong but changeable. Many acquaintances are found among idealistic, original and unconventional people with whom he talks much and enthusiastically and together with whom he devotes himself to the formation of a new human race and the construction of a new world, in which *true brotherhood* reigns and money does not exist. But he should be advised not to set to work too rashly or boldly, because trouble with public authorities and the general public may result.

Undeniably the native has a tendency towards philosophy, and cherishes very high ideals regarding justice and love. He should however be careful not to exaggerate these ideas and not be in too great a haste to proclaim them.

When *afflicted* this position of ♅ makes the native reckless, quickly decided, obstinate and wilful, sometimes passionate and unreasonable, hated or feared by many.

Sometimes a rashness contrary to all better knowledge is evident and he turns a blind eye on all the dangers which may be entailed by a thoughtless action. It is desire, the native's lower nature which must be restrained if he will reach real and lasting happiness; and it may be overcome by emphasizing and increasing his sense of responsibility.

♅ in 12 the house of selfcommunion and isolation, symbolises very clearly all the hidden sorrow, all the sudden and acute distress of disappointment, and the continual, unaccountable fear of accidents which make life so hard for people with this position. If ♅ is retrograde (i. e. apparently going backwards) it indicates that all this exists in *thought* rather than in *reality* and that all these symptons will disappear of their own accord if the native always keeps *pure* his thoughts.

Well aspected ♅ strengthens intuition in a high degree and adds a great mechanical capability to much originality.

He will be interested in the fate of prisoners, and the possible improvement of prisons, also in law and the protection of minors and the lower classes. The native has a great desire to aid and help on his fellowmen, especially those who are weaker and less-developed both spiritually and materially; to bring loftier truth, more intense consciousness and greater joy of life to all in need of these things.

It goes without saying that to this end the native's own self must be completely under control and therefore self-control will have to be cultivated as the foremost necessity.

He is greatly attracted to spiritualism; but he should be warned against thoughtless experiments in this direction, when ♅ in the 12th house is *afflicted* and therefore renders a less favourable effect upon the mind possible. He should then avoid any spiritualist séances, but attribute great value to the sudden suggestions of his Higher Self.

This position gives a love of freedom which often causes more distress than sensible selfrestraint. It is advisable for the native to keep himself on a high spiritual level by means of good *books* and *music* in order to control the lower emotions and impulses, so that his entire mental attitude will become balanced, and a purer and more stable joy of life brighten his path.

Neptune (♆) in the Twelve Houses.

♆ in 1 gives a *kind nature,* although often *dreamy* and *absent-minded* and therefore liable to be rude. This position hinders the development of intellect, but furthers that of the sensitive side. Especially in childhood the native's tendency to wander from a subject will get the better of him, so that he will allow many an opportunity to pass by unused.

He is inclined to float on moods, to be influenced by prejudices and sometimes to wish to do too many things at a time. Putting on one side the thoughts of self will improve his temper as well as health. He should not permit himself too much dreaming about remote ideals, or grumbling at the difficulty of attaining them, or wasting of time with less important matters, but cheerfully and firmly aim at being of service to others — in this way the less pleasant side of ♆ may be overcome by strengthening that which is *good.*

This position gives mediamistic and clairvoyant faculties, but at the same time warns the native against their imprudent use. It will be advisable for him to take his bearings in this field beforehand, and not to risk experiments before his astral and mental bodies are sufficiently strong. No spirits nor narcotics should ever be taken. Good recreation and help in gloomy moments may be found in music — ♆ rising always makes the native musical — and though he may lack ability to perform, he is always able to enjoy other people's playing.

When well aspected ♆ in 1 strengthens the native's love of *nature* and attracts him especially to the *sea.* This position gives the demeanour something *inspired;* life will probably be characterised by peculiar circumstances and extraordinary experiences. It is an open question whether the lesson is learned for which they are intended, or whether only a vague submission results. This will depend on the aspects of ♆. The native should as much as possible maintain his confidence that all things work together for good as well as the assurance that he himself can contribute to that end.

♆ in 2, the house of *finances* by its metaphysical character causes a more certain *indifference* as *to these things;* an instinctive confidence that they will look after themselves. And indeed, money comes in sometimes in the most unexpected way, through strange people or unusual occupations, without the native having exerted himself for it. But there exists also a danger of sudden losses; *prudence* is recommended in business matters. Here a good aspect to ☿ is very useful because this planet, though it gives way to its surroundings possesses too much business-capacity for it to remain unexpressed. A strong ♋ influence will also prevent the native from being "done in" by others.

When *afflicted* not too much should be expected from financial good fortune, legacies etc.; they may suddenly prove to be insignificant, or the native may lose his claim to them through some circumstance or other. Little value is set on money as such; but consideration, and care in this matter are advisable, for obligations towards others must be fulfilled at some time or other.

♆ in 3 gives a taste for *modern art,* especially in the field of *literature.* The native's thoughts often wander and as his fancy is very active, he will sometimes find it difficult to distinguish between memory and imagination.

This position gives mediamistic faculties which had better be avoided so far as writing is concerned, since his relations with his family as well as has own health will suffer by them.

This position of ♆ further denotes a special love for boating and voyages. When *afflicted* the native should be careful. Then also many conflicts may be expected between the personality and the native's environment. Attempts at reconciliation with the majority of his relations or usual environment seem to fail quite unaccountably, the most ordinary things and sayings being wrongly interpreted, thus forming an insurmountable obstacle.

Also when the native attempts in some way or other to come into contact with the public, something will always crop up and intercept it, or else at the exact moment he will lack courage to tackle the thing.

♆ in 4 gives great taste and liking for somewhat *mystical art.* The native will venerate old religious art treasures and precious articles, knowledge of which he likes to collect. At the same time he has a great inclination to imitate old customs as much as possible and to maintain them.

A person with this position likes to dream in harmonious surroundings. His early years are spent with *imaginary* friends. The passing to the Beyond will be in a trance.

When *afflicted* narcotics will be taken and there is a possibility of poisoning.

♆ in 5 gives peculiar thoughts about love; these run in an idealistic direction and the native has even a liking for platonic ideas. In business, enterprises, personal-intimate intercourse there is a singular element of vague speculation and good faith. Wide-spread connections not always well-known, but reliable, as also unexpected changes may be expected here. The children of a person with this position are usually of a dreamy disposition.

An affliction especially with ♂ or ♀, indicates a conflict between the higher and lower nature and points to strange experiences in this respect.

When *afflicted* there is a possibility of loss through deception.

♆ in 6 favours the development of latent psychic faculties. Towards illness and sick people an attitude of will (imagination-Coué) may be adopted which is the starting point of recovery. Intercourse with inferiors is made easy by this position; it renders the native kind-hearted to simple or less developed people — which particularly in those circles may do so much good.

Sharp and exacting as a person with this ♆-position may be to his equals, he is patient to his inferiors and devoted to his betters — these gradations being always directed by his *own feelings* and *not by social relations.*

♆ afflicted in 6 warns the native against eccessive exertion spiritual or physical; his nerves are not overstrong and cannot stand as much as he desires and expects. Trifles may be very irritating to him and sometimes lead to violent nervous outbursts which usually are not understood by his environment.

The honesty of his staff should be tested. And it is also very advisable for the native to control himself continually in thougths, feelings, emotions and to *keep to his own line* in everything; business first and pleasure afterwards should be his rule and he should avoid going into detail again and again. It is advisable for him not to occupy himself too much with occult phenomena and not to dwell too long on inexplicable things. He should keep his mind clear and pure and rather turn his attention to art than to mystical or magic subjects.

♆ in 7 indicates very *lofty, ideal connections of soul*, affections of a platonic nature, friendly relations with artists, mystics etc. things which might effect much that is good and noble, but that — when afflicted — easily turn into a less desirable direction.

The native should demand more of his "intimate" friends. He must not be too indulgent towards them, nor too ready to "sacrifice" himself, since there by he might do violence to his own inner nature. ♆ in 7 inclines him to sacrifice himself, even for those who are not altogether "worthy", so that it will be well for him to cultivate independence of character and ambition in order to be able to control this tendency and to remain himself. Pity or unbounded admiration usually form the basis of love, and the person for whom that love is felt, is probably some one who is physically not quite normal or healthy, or lower in rank or standing or one who possesses very strange talents.

When *afflicted* this position makes indeed high demands on the native's morality. His soul will only be *free,* when it has strength enough to *limit itself* where necessary. In other words the *constraining power of an inner sincerity* should conquer *instinctive tendencies*.

♅ and ♆ are planets to whose vibrations this earth finds it hard to respond — even when they form good aspects. — A crystal bowl is beautiful and precious, but if a child handles it there may be serious results. In order to really profit by their influence, the native's inner nature should be brought into complete concordance with it (the child should learn to realise the value of the bowl), the mind be opened to it; the lower self will then withdraw to the background or disappear altogether. Not until then can these planets exercise their full power and bring utter harmony also into earthly circumstances.

♆ in 8 indicates great sensitivity to *peculiar dreams* of a somewhat prophetic nature, inspirations. The conditions in the Beyond forcibly arouse the native's interest, so that this ♆-position strongly inclines him to *spiritualism*. There is every likelihood of a conscious double life and distinct experiences on the astral plane may be expected. When favourable aspects guard the native against excessive discursiveness he may be able to profit in daily life by the knowledge gained in other worlds.

Yet moderation and carefulness are advisable, because the influence of ♆ always is more or less unreliable. This constellation denotes further a faculty of preventing or curing much suffering, through the diversion of thought from physical to psychic subjects. Music also will have a very beneficent effect on the general disposition.

When *afflicted* the native should be seriously warned against exaggeration in spiritualistic or other research; it will be sensible to adopt a somewhat critical-expectant attitude in these matters, seeing that the phantastical side of this ♆ position tends to go further than is either necessary or useful.

Affliction indicates financial disappointment through a false representation or understanding of the partner's financial situation. From the mother's or the wife's side some financial advantage may come, but this will come to naught through fraud or deceit, if the aspects are inharmonious.

It is very probably that death is caused by an accident, poisoning, suffocation or drowning.

♆ in 9 gives the native a great desire to get to know the world outside his own self, both spiritually and materially. Long and distant journeys are taken, preferably with a view to serious research which may be generally useful. This position makes the philosophical mind somewhat dreamy and vague and inclines the native to meditate on supersensuous and psychic problems. Mystical and occult teachings will give him the greatest satisfaction.

When *afflicted* there is a danger of nervous overstrain at repeated experiments in things spiritualistic; sensitiveness for finer vibrations makes itself too much felt; therefore prudence, and in particular moderation in these things are strongly recommended.

If ♆ is retrograde (apparently moving backward) or afflicted in this house the finer mental operations will manifest little to the physical consciousness. Then there will only be un unaccountable fear of accidents which might happen when travelling.

♆ in 10. As ♆ by its position in this house exercises an influence on the calling and position in the world it will bring peculiar changes and occurrences in these. *Romantic situations, strange intricacies* which, after all, are solved quite simply will again and again occur in life. This position gives also the faculty to reproduce one's experiences in some form of art and to extract teaching from it in order to be able to help another with its result. The native's occupations can certainly not be called common.

The native has *gifts,* which however are not developed with sufficient assiduity or devotion; he has *not enough system,* not enough organizing talent with which to make his own gifts productive. This will cause the outer world to receive an impression of a chaotic indefinite mind without any solid foundation.

There is great sensitivity psychically and astrally and experiences and ideas in this direction can always be traced in the work and behaviour.

When *afflicted* this position may prove dangerous for demonstrating occult powers publicly and even for their excessive cultivation. Great care should always be taken, because otherwise nervous disorders may result.

♆ in 11 indicates peculiar experiences in friendship, much contact with talented, but often deformed or invalid people; singularly *romantic relations* which start with an external trifle and take a strange course.

Taste in the arts tends to the *fantastic, mystical, symbolic.* Music especially has a strong charm. In the invisible world sympathetic relations are sensed, which may be of great support in daily life.

♅ in 12 points to a great deal of serious contemplation in solitude and silence, about all kinds of occult sciences, psychical phenomena etc., in these many new points of view are discovered with which the native likes to acquaint others. This should however be done with great tact, since otherwise unpleasantness may be expected and quite the contrary result achieved to that which was intended. This position presupposes that a tie exists with some one of the *world of spirits* which is favourable to both parties, and much stronger than an ordinary physical friendship. This will probably be a supersensual contact with some beloved dead person who already in this life did much for the native.

A favourable aspect denotes that in the field of religious, occult study and various directions of social work much good may be experienced from this influence of ♅. If the native listens to the Voice of the Silence, good inspirations will come that ennoble action and enhance the happiness of life.

XI

The Part of Fortune (⊕) in the Twelve Houses.

⊕ in 1 gives a certain impulse and even necessity to look for happiness *in the world.* This position strengthens the native's tendency to move much in the world to see and be seen. Not so much because contact with many people brings purely pleasant experiences, but because it is looked upon as a kind of duty, as a means to development and progress.

Inharmonions aspects [1]) make disillusion and disappointment probable owing to excessive and too ready a confidence; they also hinder somewhat his philosophic thought and make it difficult for the native to put his ideas into practice, owing to his oversensitiveness to external things and influences. But he should always try to realise that it is not so much what a man *experiences* that matters, but what he *learns from that experience;* that the greatest possibilities to development are given to the Ego in trial and conflict. And this realisation will be a great support in life.

Happiness will be found in acting independently (1) once he has given up counting on other people's help (7).

⊕ in 2 denotes financial advantage. What the native strives for *without assistance* he will attain sooner and better than with the help of others.

---

[1]) The aspects of the Part of Fortune indicate only a *cooperation* or an *opposition* in reaching happiness along the line denoted by the house in which it is placed; the *nature* of the aspecting planets seems not to be of much account.

Happiness will be found in the quiet certainty of being able to add credit (2) to trustworthy enterprises, whereas all deep investigations or mystic speculations (8) are deemed needless. "Only believe, and all things will drop into your lap".

⊕ in 3 indicates that most satisfaction comes from imbibing and propagating ideas and thoughts; lasting happiness may be found in the immediate environment, among intimate friends or nearest relatives who understand and sympathise. And this is reached by a sensible and tactful give and take; a just impartial judgment on oneself and others. It is never good that one man should have to hide his inner life from an other. What is good in each man is related to all others; so he who develops the good in himself, gets nearer to all his fellow men. This is indeed the right direction for the evolution of a soul with this position.

Happiness will be found in drawing one's own conclusions from heedfully listening to others (3), without wishing in the first place to apprise others of one's own views as if they alone were true (9).

⊕ in 4. Pleasant harmonious domestic surroundings are greatly valued; also artlovers, intellectual, sensitive people, with whom the native can talk confidentially and without clashing, may share his moods and emotions. The good effect of such circumstances is clearly visible in the whole mien, work and general mental attitude and health of the native.

When *afflicted* disappointed affection will usually exercise a very depressing influence on the state of mind and therefore also on health. ⊕ in 4 presupposes that there is a strong, spiritual link with the *parents* and the *home of one's childhood* influencing the whole life for good — also after the parents' death — and this will be especially noticeable in later life.

Happiness will be found in being contented with one's own domestic circumstances, the relations and traditions (4), after having renounced all desire for admiration and reputation (10).

⊕ in 5 gives a great liking for somewhat adventurous enterprises, both materially and ideally. Great value is attributed to meetings both serious and merry. All that is new and promising attracts and interests the native intensely. Thus too the *world of children*. "Every child is a strange and touching riddle." It makes for good relations with children in general and presupposes that intercourse with children will have a favourable influence on the growth of the native's own Self. There is something egoistical in the love of one's own children in the desire that they should act exclusively in accordance with the parents' ideas and continue what the parents have begun. Externally the children will in some way be a credit to them, but when *afflicted* there will be one among them who causes trouble and difficulty in the home through the freedom of his ideas, reckless prodigality etc.

Happiness will be found in autocratic conduct, which exacts as well as gives magnanimously (5), after the native has wholly renounced his tendency to be all things to all men (11).

⊕ in 6. Happiness will have to be earned by *work* and *devotion*, and will depend on self-control. ⊕ in 6 indicates the necessity of taking a thing in one's own hand because otherwise — in spite of much help — little lasting effect will be reached. Once ambition is aroused great things may be achieved. Self-limitation is here the first necessity.

When *afflicted* far less will be reached with one's partners and inferiors than by simply relying on one's own powers. Whenever the others do not understand quickly or clearly enough to execute what is intended, he easily falls into the mood: "I'd rather do it myself". From the financial point of view it will certainly prove more profitable to do everything oneself, because unfitness and dishonesty of dependents will often cause damage or loss.

Happiness will be found in serving many and manifold things (6), a service in which every longing for seclusion and solitude (12) will have to be wholly renounced.

⊕ in 7. The Part of Fortune in the house of union and marriage denotes that most satisfaction will be sought and found in these. An *affliction* presupposes many hindrances and delays, so that the union will only take place at mature age. When *favourably aspected* there is a likelihood of happy companionship, provided that the partner is capable of a very great love, both understanding and unselfish. If such a union is reached, it will doubtless prove to be a very great influence for good on the whole character.

Happiness will at last be found in being absorbed by cooperation, marriage, and partnership (7), after having given up all egoism and desire for priority (1).

⊕ in 8 indicates that reflection on occult subjects will be able to transmute occasional moods of depression into hopeful progress on the difficult path; courage and strength are found for the performance of the earthy task by the recognition of good and invisible powers. In moments of despondency the reading of beautiful, uplifting books or a talk with a serious, honest occultist may achieve wonders. An *inharmonious aspect* denotes that it will not be easy for the native to feel at ease in less favourable financial circumstances. So long as "happiness" is considered to be dependent on material welfare, disappointments along that line will be experienced.

Happiness will be found by doubting the value of the palpable, destroying old fetters and through investigating the hidden side of things (8), after having given up trusting exclusively in the material world (2).

⊕ in 9 shows a thirst for the *expansion of consciousness,* the *widening of the field of vision,* literally as well as figuratively. Much solace for disappointment and aid in difficulties may be found in contemplating God's wisdom and justice. ⊕ in 9 indicates a great desire for philosophical scientific religious research. The problem how best to teach the results to humanity will be the subject of much reflection. The study of the soul is a favourite subject.

Happiness will be found in expansion of the native's own consciousness, in travel and philosophizing (9) once the inclination to imitate other people's plans (3) has been given up.

⊕ in 10 gives a possibility of a fine career and successful work. When inharmoniously aspected difficulties will indeed arise, chiefly through jealousy or distrust of others. In that case more than otherwise, much energy and patience will be required and it depends on the remainder of the horoscope whether the person concerned will be able to fulfil the demands.

The native should find happiness as a self-made man in the world (10) after having renounced all the comforts to be derived from a quiet life at home, among relations, in accordance with family tradition and custom (4).

⊕ in 11 symbolises the longing for both peace of mind and inner peace and for a congenial circle of friends. It is an important indication of profit and advantage being gained through relations of friendship. Where there is some ideal to be realised or aim to be reached, everywhere people will be found willing to help — and one's own actions in matters of general interest usually meet with success. In clubs and unions these people are much thought of and they themselves value these things highly.

When *afflicted* obligations which have arisen in that way will sometimes not seem so pleasant, and in the long run the native's pride tends rather to make him endeavour to free himself from his protectors — which gives rise to *"ingratitude"* of which he is so often accused. It is therefore by far the best for the native to stand as much as he can on his own legs and to accept as little help from others as possible, whenever it is not quite (including morally) disinterested.

Happiness will be found in promoting brotherly relations (11), after having given up all feeling of superiority (5).

⊕ in 12. This house symbolises trial, seclusion, self-examination; and when the Part of Fortune is here, only *serious endeavour towards improvement* will bring happiness. This position brings much trouble and strife, but therefore also a possibility of a great victory. The difficulty lies in being too personal on the one hand and on the other in lack of balance in what is individual. The victory can only be won when the native learns to acknowledge first the smallness of the sphere of his own self, and then the greatness of the Divine Spark smouldering within him. And when that greatness is felt and realised, all small objections will drop away, life will become a blessing to oneself and others instead of a source of care and worry. The native with this position should beware of being too *self-contained,* since this would have a prejudicial influence on his whole disposition. In every case this reserve must not be rooted in some degree of "self-pity" or hopelessness about the attitude of mankind.

When *afflicted* this will not be easy, because some hard lessons must be learned and some important points in the character modified. This position of the Part of Fortune intimates that this can only be reached through introspection, through profound inner recognition of one's own being which is at the same time the key to the heart of all that exists. For the meaning of the 12th house is *to lose oneself in order to find oneself again in every creature of God.* But not till after much strife and difficulty will the true selfsacrifice be reached which does not pride itself upon good work, but does well because it cannot do otherwise — quietly, modestly, unnoticed. *Without humility no riches, without limitation no freedom.*

Happiness will be found in solitude, in oneself (12), after having given up everything one served before (6). "In silence and confidence shall be thy strength".

XII

Aspects of the Planets.

Aspects of the Sun (☉).

☉ ☌ ☽. The *sign* in which this ☌ takes place, is very prominent in the character — and as to the *House* in which this ☌ occurs, everything in life will depend upon the nature of that special house.

If e.g. the ☌ occurs in the 1st house, the native will chiefly think about personal success; if in the 2nd house, capital takes the first place in life, in 10 his attention will be rivetted upon the honour and respect to be gained in the world; in 7 the glory of the partner must illumine the native's own personality; in 11 it is the influential friends — preferably with names which sound fine — whom he mentions with preference in society, etc.

This aspect renders the native very vital, but somewhat one-sided with a tendency to feel ill-used.

"Our soul should have someone it reveres, and for whose sake it guards its inmost being." *(Seneca).*

☉ ✶, △ ☽ indicates good health and great power of curing oneself of occasional indispositions. Inner insight will usually enable the native rightly to invest his capital both spiritually and materially, so that an ascending line in life may be discerned. This aspect makes him an ambitious worker, hearty; it betokens friendship, the native being both willing and able to help in word and deed.

People with a harmonious ☉-☽ aspect know the great secret of how to remain *young* notwithstanding advancing years and grey hair; they know how to retain their enthusiasm by means of poetry, inward life, and love, and how to keep their soul in harmony.

"Whosoever is happy brings happiness to others, and takes it from nobody. Happiness returns to him who has given it."

(Carmen Sylva).

☉ □, ☍ ☽. Under certain circumstances the native is very *undecided* what to do. He finds too a difficulty in keeping an aim steadily before him, also in determining his will, and *in directing himself,* though he strives ambitiously for a line in life. Times of depression often last long and a feeling of loneliness lingers. Excessive excitement and overstrain, pleasant as well as unpleasant, should be avoided. This affliction gives a probability of the nerves not being very strong, which may in the end undermine the whole constitution. Close intercourse with the other sex is usually the cause of rather a late marriage, while even afterwards variable affection is liable to disturb conjugal happiness. Severe restrictions on stern prohibition *from outside* have a bad and irritating effect, therefore the native should strive to acquire *inner* control. As to health, these aspects incline to those indispositions peculiar to the signs in which the affliction occurs.

These aspects incline the native to overesteem himself and to be ambitious.

"*Go out of the sunlight into the shade, to make more room for others.*"
(The Voice of the Silence).

$\odot$ ♂ ☿ [1]). Too a close conjunction (1°—3°) renders the logically thinking intellect not so quick in its action as is desirable. The wished-for results are found, it is true, but often too late. Striking, apt remarks only occur when they have little effect left ("l'esprit de l'escalier"). This may be much improved by cultivating quiet, logical and concentrated thought.

If the distance is at least 5°, this aspect makes the native intelligent, and matter of fact. The mind is particularly fit for and inclined to be absorbed in pure mathematics, definite and abstract problems.

„*Human knowledge is separation, but Divine knowledge is unity.*"
(Dr. A. Besant.)

$\odot$ ♂ ♀ [2]) makes the native fond of *popularity* and superficial pleasures; talent for art may easily be developed. This aspect renders him *courteous,* harmonious and well-adapted for intercourse with people.

„*Love is gold, to give is to receive, to forget oneself is to find oneself.*"
(Weiler.)

$\odot$ ♂ ♂ makes the native courageous, enterprising, energetic, resolute, often impatient, rash, careless, reckless. It will be well to bear in mind that a sensible man does not allow himself to be ruled, as little as he wishes to rule others; everywhere and always *reason* should rule.

The $\odot$ (inner relation of dignity) should remain superior to ♂ (active desire).

„*In order to control the power of a passion one should not try to destroy it but to lead it into another and loftier direction.*"
(Mrs. Wachtmeister.)

$\odot$ *, △ ♂. With these aspects will-power and *desire-nature* are harmonious. The native will form an ideal, strive towards it — and usually

---

[1]) No other aspect can be formed between the $\odot$ and ☿, because ☿ does not move further than 28° from the $\odot$.

With too close a conjunction (1° to 3°) Mercury in called '*scorched*', its good qualities then seem to be destroyed by the Sun's rays.

[2]) As ♀ moves only 48° from the $\odot$, besides the ♂ only a ⋁ aspect can be formed.

also realise it. He has clear view of good opportunities and knows how to make the utmost use of them in order to attain his goal.

These aspects render self-reliant, active and strengthen the health in a great measure.

"*Rely on thyself. Every heart expands under that steel spring.*"
(Emerson).

⊙ □, ☌ ♂. These aspects give all the qualities of a leader, except self-control. But a leader of men must above all be master of *himself* and act thoughtfully and tactfully in everything.

These ♂-afflictions sometimes cause difficulties through thoughtless, spontaneous expressions or remarks, making a foe where it would have been better to have a friend. It is wise to put a guard on one's lips and take more into account the standpoint of others.

These aspects lead to unforeseen desires, render excited, irritable. They give a likelihood of accidents, wounds through burning and cutting, and inflammations through carelessness and recklessness. The recuperative power is however soon able to repair the damage. Very high fever often occurs with this aspect. (Science to-day realises that in itself fever is no illness, but only a means to dispel germs of illness which have entered.)

"*One's will will never be satisfied, even though it receive all for which it wishes. But it is immediately satisfied when one denies oneself something.*"
(Pascal.)

⊙ ☌, ✶, △ ♃ makes the native sunny, cheerful, trustful, jovial, frank, generous. These aspects may be a great help in life; they indicate that nothing has such a favourable influence on the mental attitude and health as study and work; especially *religious-philosophical* study and *responsible* work. For both the capacities are there and much may be reached in both, besides the satisfaction they give. The more beautiful things look with us inwardly, the more beautiful we see everything around us.

"*Out of the consciousness that we are inwardly free and move freely, eternal youth and eternal peace arise.*"
(Schleiermacher.)

⊙ □, ☌ ♃. These aspects render careless, tactless, boastful. The native is inclined to imagine himself better than he is, and even in the greatest prosperity feels himself ill-used and neglected. The constitution may be ruined by excessive use of "the good things of earth". Liver and heart are the weak points here, there is a danger of apoplexy and liver complaint. The best remedy however is: to live simply, naturally; to keep heart and brain fresh and pure and avoid all excessive excitement. It should be remembered that faith is the substance of things hoped for.

"*Does not uprightness mean having the heart directed on high, and does not this lead us to reflection and then to the perception that every good quality builds up and every bad one destroys?*"
(Stainton.)

⊙ ☌, □, ☌ ♄. These aspects make the native prudent, gloomy, apt to take things too seriously but therefore also fit to cooperate with older people. Only cooperation must not lead him to lose his independence. These aspects are not favourable to general prosperity — they indicate unpleasant lawsuits and similar things in connection with legacies, money of partners or associations, — in short it will prove to be difficult to convince others of the native's own rights. He should beware of catching cold and of excessive physical exertion. That part of the body is weak which corresponds to the sign in which ♄ is placed. The native should be careful since it is probable that other members of the family contract similar diseases. Most likely the father will die early.

A healthier and more joyous attitude to life will be created and greater and more intensely vital power communicated to those around him if the native meditates at regular times upon cheerfulness, simplicity and self-denial, endeavouring also to strengthen his confidence in the future and never allowing himself to be ruled by thoughts of possible disappointments. Many capacities may be acquired, if only he strives perseveringly to gain them.

> "Be still, sad heart! and cease repining
> Behind the clouds is the Sun still shining
> In every life some rain must fall
> Some days must be dark and dreary."
> (Longfellow).

☉ ✳, △ ♄. These aspects give a serious, *reliable* foundation, which for the greater part is due to the father for whom great admiration and sympathy will always be felt.

The native is conscientiously self-controlled, has a keen insight into his own faults and shortcomings and having discerned them, he fights against them. He is careful in his speech and actions, while his organizing talent fits him to look after the old and needy and to manage affairs. His thorough work will everywhere be respected.

The native's deep sense of duty, justice and order will be a great support in times of trial, and is not seldom the cause of others finding rest and strength through him. The morality of this character is not rooted in superficial ideas of respectability, but in knowledge of human nature derived from experience, and in love of his fellows. It goes without saying that at times other influences may overshadow the effect of this constellation and that through progressive positions less fine tendencies may come to the fore. When through introspection and meditation the ♄-voice can again be heard, it will of itself suggest the right direction to be taken in life.

"The heavenly hosts fight with him who faithfully performs what he considers to be good and just." (L. Whiting).

☉ ☌ ♅. Special experiences will lead to increased appreciation of metaphysics and occultism. This conjuction renders *constructive, intuitive;* when supported by other favourable aspects a strongly suggestive power will emanate from the native, helping many „weaker brethren".

"If we are willing to open our heart to the voice of the infinite Spirit, we shall become seers and look into the very heart of things." (Trine).

⊙ ✳, △ ♅. This leads to flashes of *genius* and *capacity*, inspiring and stimulating others also to work, which spread a warm and intense joy of life aroud. These aspects render the native what is called *eccentric*, idealistic, attracted to the study of astrology, to occultism. The secrets of nature, electricity, air-craft, wireless interest him greatly.

"*Multiplicity of knowledge is not wisdom, but wisdom is a pure structure of the soul.*"
(Fred. van Eeden).

⊙ ☐, ☍ ♅. A conflict between the ⊙ and the planet of new and peculiar ideas, causes the inner conservative view (⊙) in the native to be in continuous battle with all that is thrown on the market as "new" (♅). Notice is taken of all that, it is true, but chiefly with the desire to be able to reject it or represent it in a ridiculous way. These aspects represent the "tempters", the "seducers", and that is why one cannot be sufficiently on his guard against exaggeration of occult research and the reckless application of knowledge. The results of naturalistic scientific research and the facts of exact science should always be compared seriously with occult teachings in order to arrive at a correct insight.

These constellations bring domestic difficulties, financial cares, sudden and unexpected separations, opposition; they make the native thoughtless and cause ill-luck — and a general feeling of distrust and cynicism. On the other hand he has an inclination to confide in many people and manifold things.

All that cannot be done in *material* life is possible in *spiritual* life. And so soon as one becomes conscious *that he is spirit and lives accordingly*, he will be able to receive more power than anyone who looks on himself as merely material.

"*Prove to me only that the least
Command of God's is God's indeed,
And what injunction shall I need
To pay obedience?*"
(Browning).

⊙ ✳, △ ♆. Unquestionably the Ego wishes for higher things and through earnest self-examination and reflection it is possible to arrive at a decision as to what must be done and what left undone. Much will depend on the degree of "strength" of ♆'s position. This favourable ⊙ influence makes it possible to acquire the desirable qualities through meditation and contemplation. Thus e.g. by regular, repeated, devoted meditation upon the ideas "harmony", "purity", "peace", "wisdom", it is possible for spiritual power to grow so strong that no weaknesses will manifest any more. These aspects render refined, dreamy, communistic in the good sense of the word, humane.

"*The purport and goal of all gnosis is the one-making or union of the little man with the Great Man, of the human soul with the Divine Soul.*"
(Mead).

⊙ ☌, ☐, ☍ ♆. These aspects make the native reserved, secretive, addicted to narcotics, sensuous; they warn him against all kinds of spiritual or other experiments which aim at getting to know something about life after death. It will be of little use or help for him to yield to his interest in this direction and he would therefore do better to guide it into other channels.

"The starting point of love is the sacrifice of that which in us opposes all sacrifice." (Vinet).

Aspects of the Moon (☽).

☽ ♂, *, △ ☿. These aspects make the native keenly observant, quick at repartee, give a practical mind with ready knowledge and a correct insight in people and things.

> "Knowledge is indeed good, but action surpasses it,
> He who knows much well, may fitly be called learned;
> But he who measures his time, and restrains his passions,
> And guides his actions well, he is wise and pious."

This happy union of feeling and intellect gives a lively imagination, much tact and ability to explain things to others.

"Wise is he who knows how to learn from everyone." (The Talmud).

☽ ☐, ☍ ☿. This aspects causes a *conflict between feeling and intellect;* it is difficult to give oneself unreservedly, especially where there is some fear of being ridiculous; the wish to thwart someone as a kind of defense will often arise. For the rest these aspects make the native very intelligent, good at estimating the value; sharp but peevish. He should be warned against doing two or more things at a time since that renders him nervous and ill-tempered. It is advisable for him to allow both body and mind to rest thoroughly at fixed times. This is really of such great importance that he should not overlook it, thinking that the work does not allow of it. By serious, calm and well-balanced work with regular times of recreation, much more will be reached than by nervous, discontented haste without any system. These aspects cause oversensitiveness which often takes a disappointment or a remark much more seriously than is necessary and in this way engenders unnecessary and un-intentional alienations. There is a danger of nervous overstrain, periods in which the mind will not be able to do its duty regularly. If these afflictions occur in *fixed signs,* they will probably be expressted by *fixed ideas,* an exaggerated concentration on one point which only has value when seen as part of a whole. It is therefore good for the native to disentangle himself regularly from subjects which occupy his mind greatly, to leave those things every now and then and engage actively in practical work of an entirely different nature.

"Our thoughts are often our masters. They hinder us sometimes from keeping our attention fixed uninterruptedly on something; they often make us discouraged and may even drive our sleep away."

(Dr. W. H. Denier van der Gon).

☽ ♂, *, △ ♀. These aspects give the native that *considerate kindness* which is so engaging, and meets with response from even the most

hardened grumbler; they make in a high degree both loving and beloved.
"He who loves, sees correctly, because he sees deeper and further than others whose glance is not sharpened by love." (H. Lou.)

☽ □, ☍ ♀ These aspects cause disappointment in friendship, love and marriage. They make the native slovenly and wanton, prodigal and careless and incline to articular rheumatism. These afflictions — especially in ♎ and ♋—symbolise also a certain extravagance, a thoughtless sensuousness which is inclined to be self-indulgent and liable therefore to cause much trouble. Bad blood-circulation, disturbances in the digestion and sex functions are likely to be the consequence.
"He who is not willing to learn from the past, will be punished by the future."

☽ ☌ ♂ makes the native *compulsive,* restless, hasty; ill-tempered, despotic, easily *touchy at mere trifles* (especially in ♍). On the mental plane this aspect gives much enthusiasm and receptivity for new thoughts, suggestions etc. He is however rather lacking in the power to *persevere,* to *retain* sudden flashes of insight and to *work them out,* and must most certainly be strengthened in order to bring about something good. And to this end it is first of all necessary for him to learn to restrain his desires, to make his will subject to that which intuitively will be judged better, in short to *learn to free himself from himself.*
"With great difficulty do you rule matter by matter, when will you learn that spirit is the true master over matter?"

☽ ✶, △ ♂ gives the native great willingness and much energy when he is attracted and believes in the matter concerned; makes him firm and strong in every circumstance that arises, always trying to make the best of things. So soon as we realise the fact that we *can* rise, we *shall* rise. These aspects render industrious, enterprising.

☽ □, ☍ ♂. These aspects make the native prone to exaggerate, hasty, irascible, despotic, they indicate a passionate nature which needs the control of *reason;* otherwise there is great danger of illness. In fixed signs the sense of one's own worth may work very favourably, in cardinal signs the sense of responsibility, especially if in childhood the educators strengthen it; by well-deserved praise and honest appreciation much will be reached. In movable signs such an affliction exacts much patience and self-control. If ♂ and ☽ are in the 2nd and 5th house, the native is reckless in his enterprises, speculations etc. and through that suffers financial loss. Failure in speculation may however stimulate to more serious, effectual work which will meet with better recompense. In this way loss and trouble will urge the native on to wisdom.
"Conquer your own nature, for if you do not teach it to obey you, it will compel you to obey it." (Horace.)

☽ ☌, ✶, △ ♃. These aspects give the faculty of raising oneself to a higher spiritual consciousness which helps to greatly facilitate the sublimation of lower qualities into higher. By it the interest in material matters may be transmuted into an enthusiastic absorption in the cosmic consciousness. This enables the native to feel free of all material anxieties and burdens and to become so joyous and full of the love of life that one might speak of a 'conversion', a 'miraculous cure'. These aspects render hopeful, fortunate, just and upright.

"To make others happy is a sensation one never tires of; one lifts one's soul by it and gets nearer to the Almighty."

(Marie Corelli.)

☽ □, ☍ ♃. Religious ideas lack force and conviction. It is true the mind is often occupied with these things, but the *proofs* although so greatly desired do not seem to be sufficiently valid to make enquirers embrace the teachings. They will often allow *doubt* to arise about what once was valued; things which were cheered to-day, may be abused to-morrow. These aspects render arrogant, fond of outward show, prodigal.

"You must seek it yourself, and find it yourself
In your heart, in the word, in your fate.
Otherwise the whirling winds, oh! Man,
Play with your heart, your faith and your God."

(De Genestet.)

☽ ☌ ♄. This aspect gives *depth* and *power of concentration,* but also often depression. The desire for seclusion should be indulged in as little as possible and also the tendency to feel oneself misunderstood and unappreciated. For this often repels people who, but for that, might have been a very helpful influence in life. The native's attitude of reserve impresses others sometimes as haughtiness and self-conceit, attributes which do not at all tally with this inner ideas. Feeling (☽) should not be exclusive (♄), but the seriousness (♄) should be made sensitive to feeling (☽).

"Discriminate well: the true bearing of the cross is not passive, but active."

(De Bussy).

☽ ⚹, △ ♄ makes the native self-controlled, devoted, faithful and careful, and if sufficiently strengthened (by the constant realisation and development of the *sense of community)* greatly facilitates intercourse with others. A person with this aspect is however somewhat inclined to retire from busy *society life* and feels most at home in his own peaceful surroundings, working harmoniously with joy and devotion.

"If you perform even the humblest part of the work that is allotted to you with zeal and contentment, you will attain perfection."

(Giron.)

☽ □, ☍ ♄. *Conscience,* the acquired *sense of duty* is quite overruled by *rebellious* feelings, especially when disappointments and opposition arise. If, however, the native finds the strength to stand above those emotions instead of allowing himself to be disturbed by them, his inner being will prove to have been considerably enriched. These aspects make him distrustful and reserved, discontented, sombre. The feeling of being ill-treated often dominates; and though in fits of despondency one's own "inferiority" or "unreasonableness" will be admitted, there is always an inner desire for and *expectation* that these things may be contradicted by others. The great difficulty here is: "know thyself". For through the un-balanced state of his feelings, the native has little insight into his own psyche. These aspects denote very changeable moods, a tendency to fear the worst at the slightest drawback and to become over-confident at the least success. Difficulties often arise with both superiors and inferiors through this and also through the great demands made on people and on life. Thus the wish for social independence will grow very strong, but in order really to reach and to maintain his independence, the native must *first* become *inwardly free. Self-examination* and *self-liberation* are the great tasks for this life.

"*We are only hindered by outward things in so far as we mind them.*"
(Thomas à Kempis).

☽ ♂ ♅ makes the native *resourceful,* good at investigating and com-bining, fond of *antiques, ancient wisdom* and gives particular interest for tracing the truth in the various forms of public worship and superstition. Such a person will always act according to the suggestion of his feelings, without minding what people may say. This aspect renders eccentric, impulsive.

"*Whilst the soul is listening to music and comes under the influence thereof, it is unconsciously doing a higher kind of arithmetic, it tunes itself unwittingly.*"
(Leibniz).

☽ ✶, △ ♅ gives special liking for *occult sciences, astrology. spiritualism, theosophy* etc., and also the native's most intimate friends will prove to have ♅ strongly posited in their horoscopes. With those "congenial souls" he will like to talk much and often about all kinds of mystical experiences and experiments. Opportunities will arise of raising the consciousness to a higher plane; inwardly power will be developed which enables him to accept life's difficulties humbly, which renders it easier for him to learn to submit to his position in life. This is no passive submission, but a higher realisation enables him to acquire the insight to perceive that more intense happiness may grow out of limitations both social and physical than could have been gained from a more respected situation in life. These aspects make the native original, resourceful, intuitive with a very lively imagination.

"*Before the soul can see, the harmony within must be attained.*"
(The Voice of the Silence).

☽ □, ☍ ♅. These aspects make the native whimsical, peculiar, romantic, eccentric, and give sudden tendencies to seclusion and self-accusation. They also arouse a taste for being contrary and then when the fit seizes him, the native is apt to defend through thick and thin some opinion of his own or of others, even against his better conviction. This is not opposition to the sense of truth, but should rather be regarded as a *proof of strength,* namely a wish to know how long a certain theory is tenable.

This characteristic indicates that as much liberty as possible should here be given in order that the native strive after his own ideals. When that is done, sufficient will-power and love of work manifest to allow of a good result being reached.

„*A favourable wind does not make a good sailor.*" *(Old proverb).*

☽ ☌ ♅. This conjunction makes the native refined, psychic, inconstant. He will like to day-dream in woods and fields and float on his feelings. This aspect promotes taste and love for the beautiful and also the luxurious. Through this position the personality acquires great attraction for others, especially for those artistically and mystically inclined, while some *telepathic talent* will also be found. In quiet moments when the mind succeeds in liberating itself from material cares, extraordinary visions will loom in the inner mind; i..e *day-dreams.* It will be well worth his while to observe these in detail and fix them in his memory to analyse them and meditate on them; in a symbolic form these dreams contain life's truths. If the knowledge of life embodied in them is *seriously elaborated,* the native will again and again be astonished at the riches life holds, far beyond those he once valued.

"*The secret of optimism is the spirit's endeavour consciously to remain one with the infinite, eternal Spirit in us*".

☽ ✶, △, ♅. Exact study does not come easily, more especially as the native's mind often wanders. He has, however, a special talent for choosing the right people for various work, so that usually more will be reached than might be expected. A certain desire to guide and manage is always very strong, and although this need not show outwardly, yet behind the scenes everything will be regulated according to the native's ideas so that the result is usually the one wished for. Here also in a greater degree than with the ☌, prophetic dreams, symbolic visions with a deep meaning will occur. Occult faculties may be developed. These aspects render imaginative, sympathetic to those in mental affinity.

"*The stronger we make our feeling of unity. the more powerfully something in us is at work, which even without our active help continually works at our union.*" *(Dr. W. H. Denier van der Gon).*

☽ ☐, ☍ ♅ gives vehement criticism of all kinds of "ism's" and modern crazes, though the personal conceptions will be far from being 'ordinary'. Through a vague indecisiveness or indifference or for the sake of an impractical ideal, the chances of progress which present themselves will often pass unused. These aspects make the development of occult faculties possible, but the finances and business relations may be expected to suffer from it.

In ordinary life this influence manifests chiefly as a certain retiring tendency or unusual conception about conditions after death, which will lead to many discussions. There is a great love of music and literature, although in this respect also the native will not share the current taste.

The way to derive benefit from this position is to seek for a combination of *logic* and *intuition.* These aspects render peculair, self-indulgent.

„Life is built up by the sacrifice of the individual to the whole. Each cell in the living body must sacrifice itself for the perfecting of the whole; whenever this is not the case, sickness and death press this lesson home."

Aspects of Mercury (☿).

☿ ☌ ♀. This aspects renders well-bred and gives an eye for what is beautiful in meaning and in form; it presupposes however a love nature so excessively disposed to argue, analyse and theorise that the native cannot expect much happiness or joy from it; and generally makes more practical than ethical.

"To be systematic shows one possesses knowledge of life."
(Dr. J. D. Bierens de Haan).

☿ ☌ ♂. This aspect makes the intellect *active, discriminating,* but renders the native sarcastic and irritable. It gives a great desire to bring about things of practical utility through logically worked-out constructive plans. There is a strong desire to defeat competitors by quick and timely interference and a tendency to sneer at or condemn stragglers.

"One need only grow older to become milder in one's judgment; I see no error committed which I have not also committed." (Goethe).

☿ ⚹ △ ♂. These aspects give a strong, optimistic nature, make the native frank and honest, watchful and resolute.

"To have done whatever had to be done,
To have turned the face of your soul to the sun,
To have made life better and brighter for one,
This is to have lived." (Clifford Harrison).

These aspects give a clear mind and quick judgment able to use good opportunities to increase both spiritual and material possessions.

"The best — nay, the only good man is he who does the work of life with the force of a man of business." (A. Pike).

☿ □, ☍ ♂. *Derision* and *sarcasm* often manifest and at times a kind of satisfaction is found in "nailing" opponents in various ways and in outdoing them; this does not always make a pleasant impression but the intention is seldom bad.

It would be better if the native did not abuse his own talents by attacking those who are worse off; when exhibiting his own knowledge he should be more considerate for the possible ignorance of others. These aspects hinder concentration on mathematical problems; warn him against imprudence when travelling, cycling, riding etc. In particular the opposition of ☿ and ♂ causes the manner to be hasty, sharp, impulsive and bad-tempered. This often leads to things being said and done of which one repents when too late.

"Have patience. All things are difficult before they become easy."
(Persian saying).

☿ ☌, ✶, △ ♃. These aspects make the native philosophical, dignified, *broad-minded* and *tolerant*. They give contentment and prosperity in material and spiritual matters, and willingness to help those who are worse off with word and deed. The mind is active, suited to study — especially law — fluent in correspondence. By inner trust on the one hand and practical application on the other an attitude of life may be reached which makes many things possible of attainment.

"When good thoughts constantly encircle us, the inclination towards good will grow so strong that we can no longer act badly."
(Swami Vivekananda.)

☿ ☐ ☍ ♃. These aspects render the native *sceptical,* and full of doubt, thereby he allows many opportunities to pass unnoticed and does many stupid things simply because he cannot make up his mind to practical actions.

"Not started to-day, not finished to-morrow,
Bides always to-morrow, never reaches to-day."
(Ten Kate.)

The difficulty of a task, the importance of some matter will always be *undervalued,* so that in the end one will be troubled by things which a first one overlooked.

"Appearances blind us, for we take differentiations in matter for differences in everything." *(Dr. W. H. Denier van der Gon.)*

☿ ☌ ♄. This aspect makes the native reflective, melancholy, distrustful, shy. It promotes the *acquisition,* but hinders the *spreading of knowledge;* there is a certain fear of other people's opinion, and therefore a wish for seclusion. A person with this aspect should bear in mind that so long as there still is good to be done and evil to redress, life is of importance and to live is a duty. The higher one's conception of life is, the more one will know by experience the sharp contrast of light and darkness in one's own being.

"Be humble if thou wouldst attain to wisdom, be humbler still, when wisdom thou hast reached." *(Voice of the Silence.)*

☿ ✶, △ ♄. These aspects make the native *methodical, sober,* they strengthen the desire to achieve sound work, give organising talent, and as a result of this, reverence of superiors will be met with. It is sometimes stated that this position of ☿ renders particularly fit for detective, enquiry agent. At any rate details are not overlooked, but as seriously investigated as things which are more prominent.

"True power is exercised in quiet moments." *(Emerson.)*

☿ ☐, ☍ ♄. These aspects render nervous, impatient, easily discouraged, sneering and discontented. When the native does not succeed speedily in a newly-begun venture, he shows a great tendency to *ill-temper* and *sulkiness,* or even to passionate outbursts and vindictiveness, especially towards inferiors, when more is apt to be said than one can answer for. Domestic troubles will probably occur, often caused by the native's bitter criticism and lack of meekness. By preserving his self-reliance and faith in the future the difficulties he has to overcome will not harm him so much as if he retained an attitude of pessimism and isolation.

"A just cause always triumphs, if one believes in it."

(Lamenais.)

☿ ☌ ♅. This renders resourceful, ingenious, witty, but also sudden changes may be expected in thoughts and in the plans to be carried out which easily leads to misunderstanding. Especially in the cardinal signs this ☌ enables the native to influence others through thought, to lead them to change their opinions, to suggest to them thoughts of cheer, trust and health.

"We are spiritual beings, manifesting in a physical body so long as we are in this physical world. In the degree that we become more conscious of this spirituality, the intuitions, powers and forces of the spiritual world become the sources of every thought and action." *(Trine.)*

☿ ⚹, △ ♅. These aspects render independent, progressive-minded, idealistic. The plans and schemes made by one with such an aspect are characterised by genius and a broad conception; to the ordinary every-day man however they are *utopian.* The guidance of life should be left entirely and with perfect trust to the in-dwelling Divine Spirit; then nothing can fail.

"Whosoever desires to find himself in the infinite, should discriminate and then unite. The exclusive occupation of a reasonable man is to survey things which are opposite in order to bring them into agreement with each other." *(Goethe.)*

☿ □, ☍ ♅ indicates very progressive, somewhat risky theories concerning social and moral conditions, which may necessitate changes of occupation or abode. These aspects give great powers of observation, but also render recalcitrant and bellicose. The lesson always is not to *hurry nor to force things.* If there is no need, one should not say what one considers to be true, whenever one knows that some one might be hurt thereby.

"Be gentle and simple and you will conquer your strongest antagonist."

(Melanchton.)

☿ ⚹, △ ♆. These aspects give a *very lively imagination,* a clear faculty of making mental pictures and an extraordinarily *retentive memory,* and render artistic and mystic. A romantic element is present in various relations, especially those with women. The △ aspect of ♆, the higher octavo of ☿ endows the native with special gifts clearly evident in speeches, pamphlets etc. which are drawn up fluently and easily, being characterised by their suggestive style and logical trend of thought. Owing to a common-sense (☿) view of business, he will know instinctively (♆) when to act, to buy in association, how to play his trumps.

These aspects indicate connections with people inclined to occultism, a partiality for metaphysical subjects: astrology, theosophy; speculative thoughts about the beyond once heard from others, will be retold with gusto. This may make an uncommon impression, sometimes even seemingly abnormal. Some will think these ideas strange, but interesting enough to listen to them in a kind spirit, and when later on they reconsider the thoughts then aroused and investigate the matter more deeply, this may lead to the formation or strengthening of ties of friendship.

"There is nothing which spreads such a warm glow over human life as to cherish an ideal." *(Hugenholtz).*

☿ ☌, □, ☍ ♆ gives *a memory which at times functions very badly,* causes the mind to wander sometimes very peculiarly, which may be felt very unconveniently especially if there is a strong umpulse to get on, to make a name in the world. A great many mentally defectives result from this affliction. The intellect is very critical towards religion and though there is more doubt than faith in the inner feelings, the outer form will probably not be publicly attacked.

These aspects indicate that during sleep the native becomes conscious of conditions of life after death; these will again and again cause a certain conflict between the lower (selfish) and the higher (universal) consciousness. ♆ makes fantastic, idealistic, whereas ☿ will remain rather critical in face of these experiences and therefore tries to argue away the worth of metaphysical sensations; the person concerned will be in a high degree unpractical.

"The perfect control of a quality alone constitutes its worth." *(Prentice Mulford).*

Aspects of Venus (♀).

♀ ☌ ♂. This aspect denotes a thirst for peace and love in domestic surroundings, but when ♂ makes more inharmonious aspects, the temperament is too irritable, too impatiently emotional and also too vain to bear misunderstanding and — even only imaginary — ill-treatment, which therefore causes nervous overstrain. If the ♀-influence is stronger this influence may be consciously strengthened by the enjoyment of pure art and through self-denial a strong radiating charity may emanate from the whole being which arouses response and imitation in the surroundings.

"A child never respects a man who loses his equanimity." *(Ouïda).*

♀ ⚹ △ ♂. The native's energy and inner *volition* is of a noble character more *altruistic* than egoistic, and it consequently will guard him against less desirable things which other ♂ aspects might possibly cause. These ♀-♂ aspects denote that love is a great help in the battle of life. Not love in a purely material sense, but in one that is higher, more universal; personal interests will be sacrificed to the general welfare. In this way — by understanding the place of the individual in the universe; and the voluntary sacrifice of the former to the community — it becomes possible for him to raise himself to a higher plane. Then, prompted by pure impulses life will be tackled in a manner that is energetic, thoughtful and right.

> *"Think truly, and thy thoughts*
> *Shall the world's famine feed;*
> *Speak truly, and each word of thine*
> *Shall be a fruitful seed;*
> *Live truly, and thy life shall be*
> *A great und noble creed."*
> *(Horatio Bonar).*

♀ □ ☍ ♂. These aspects render the guidance and control of the feelings difficult; they make the native passionate, kind-hearted but exacting, excessively extravagant, especially to the other sex. The lack of control of these aspects may also lead to financial difficulties, if the 2nd or 8th house have a share in them. A person with this aspect should learn early to bridle his passions, otherwise they will weaken his will-power and make the spirit a slave to matter.

> *"Self-restraint and purity,*
> *The knowledge of noble truths*
> *... This is the greatest blessing."*
> *(Teachings of Buddha).*

♀ ☌, ✶, △ ♃. These aspects give a great inclination to *philanthropic* and *educational* and other so-called *social work*. The native is also interested in music, art, philosophy, literature, in short in everything that contributes to the raising of humanity and makes life more pleasant. He is naturally optimistic, jovial and balanced; his attitude towards others is kindly, magnanimous and tolerant.

> *"People often attribute the idea of happiness to outward things only,*
> *but truth seeks it in the heart, in calm and peace of mind."*
> *(Opzoomer).*

♀ □, ☍ ♃. The native's general conceptions of love and morality are of a very peculiar nature: on one hand very *liberal-minded* and on the other *extremely severe*. At any rate they are usually *different from the opinions commonly held* and form an important trait in the character as it manifests in the world. These aspects indicate opposition and jealousy of friends and acquaintances and much slander and gossip concerning the husband (or wife). They bring difficulties in domestic life and in monetary matters, and cause differences of opinion about things religious with theologians and people of the native's nearest environment. It will therefore be well for him to express his own views as carefully as possible. The character inclines to vanity and flattery.

There is a possibility of kidney disease and diabetes and fattening of the liver.

> *"Too great a boldness and too great a humility are both characteristic*
> *of a very weak character."* *(Spinoza).*

♀ ☌ ♄ gives a tendency to respect and admire all old people and things, but limits a sunny radiation of love; inclines rather to make the native reserved, lacking in courage, not frank either in affection or financial matters; economical. This aspect indicates some unpleasant experiences in youth which probably do not have a favourable influence on the feelings and notions regarding sexual purity. A favourable aspect with ☿ gives the possibility, if the discerning intellect cooperates, of forcibly counteracting those influences; a ⚹ aspect with the ☉ or ♃ also may be a help. The native's chief need is *insight* and he will therefore do well not to yield blindly to every impulse, but to analyse accurately and when he disapproves to reject it immediately.

"We remain piteously below life, if we do not realise that we must be above it."

♀ ⚹, △ ♄. Taste is refined by these aspects; intellectual insight deepened, and morality raised to a higher plane. *Perseverance, sense of responsibility, sense of duty* are plainly expressed and call forth much respect from dependants and adherents. But it is very necessary for the native to cultivate more *joy of life* and to see to it that the work is always done with love and not merely from habit or compulsion, — even though it be inward. — Much will depend here on the attitude of the husband (or wife) and on the marriage in general. What is useful is always combined with that which is pleasant, and it will often happen that occupations originally of a merely recreative character prove to have a very favourable result in a practical sense. These aspects give *sensitiveness to art* and a *balanced mind* which may tone down possible afflictions; they render devoted, economical and faithful.

"Love in its most noble motions aims always at the fulfilment of a law." *(Vinet).*

♀ □, ☍ ♄. These afflictions cause a certain *egoism*, an excessive solicitude for one's own welfare, which with inadequate self-control tends to harden all feeling for others. They necessitate also a special sex hygiene to prevent affections of the throat and skin. Otherwise such an aspect is an indication of ambition and pride, of jealousy also — and consequently some *sarcasm* — which may cause older people or the native's own pessimistic, limiting thoughts to oppose and hinder the carrying out of beautiful ideas or the entering into exalted relations of love. He should therefore keep his own life of feeling and thought as pure as possible!

"Do not wait for extraordinary opportunities, seize ordinary opportunities and make them great." *(Swett Harden.)*

♀ ☌ ♅. This conjunction will cause agreeable, unexpected changes in the position of life by connections with particular people, or by books which suddenly arouse all that was latent in the soul. It renders fit for work in connection with the pleasures and care of others, romantic, and imaginative.

"To love is to penetrate into all hidden things."

♀ ⚹, △ ♅. *Extraordinary gifts of heart and mind* make themselves known sometimes in a surprising way; and even if the material intellect —

e.g. through a weak ☿-position — is not over-active, some sudden, ingenious impulses betray a higher kind of intuition. The unity of individuals will be sensed, the submission of the individual to the community along occult-inspired ways; and the native will give profusely and willingly of his own possessions — spiritual and material. The conceptions of love are also distinguished by a very particular idealism, incomprehensible to most people, though it does rouse *appreciation* or even *admiration*. It chiefly depends on the moral height of the person beloved whether the love will triumph in its fulness, or remain platonic. For admirers of the extraordinary only, we often fail to see the deeper significance, at most an indulgent kindness will be shown. If however ♅ is Retrograde (i. e. going back) it will have to be supported in its effects by a powerful personal will in order to give definite shape to the ideas. These aspects make fond of variety and popularity.

"All beings desire. happiness, therefore be kind to all."

(Mahawamsa).

♀ □, ☍ ♅. Intuition is usually *not pure,* it will therefore be advisable not to rely too much upon it. This applies especially when people and enterprises for others or together with others are concerned. These aspects strengthen the magnetic attraction to the other sex and incline the native to risky speculations and curiosity. They render very attractive and prone to airy flirtations, which, however, will not always be looked upon as such by the other party, so that sudden and unexpected scenes cannot be avoided. These aspects give many strange — *fundamentally idealistic* — ideas about love, friendship, requiring a high degree of self-control and spiritual development if they are not to result in conflict. Very probably some tie will be suddenly broken off. The nature of the two parties will very likely differ to such an extent, that at a special juncture some sacrifice is required or some modification of ideas, which will prove to be too hard. This causes a separation painfully felt by both parties and not easily forgotten. Only by cultivating really high, unselfish feelings of love can ♀ be strengthened here and similar occurrences prevented.

"That which keeps us from, and will for a considerable time continue to keep us from the treasures of the universe is the abominable resignation with which we remain in the disconsolate prison of our senses."

(Maeterlinck).

♀ ☌ ♆. This aspect gives a somewhat *platonic love-nature* and *ascetic inclinations,* chiefly engendered by some notion of the impossibility of being loved sufficiently well. It gives however much artistic and musical feeling.

"On the one hand our love should expand and deepen and on the other pass into the feeling of unity that envelops it at the same time, but is more, since it is the conscious in contrast to the unconscious."

(Dr. W. H. Denier van der Gon).

♀ ✳, △ ♆. The mind possesses capacities which when well-applied may bring about great progress on the metaphysical as well as material plane; whilst every piece of work, every enterprise betokens a strong impulse, a *higher inspiration.* There is much likelihood of a pure, ideal affection, a high-toned, mental tie which may give great value to life. Life's difficulties may be conquered here by a peaceful way of living, with recreation in nature and art (especially music). These aspects enable the psyche to sense things even at a fairly great distance physically.

"Your love should be without bounds, your will heroic, your devotion without any hesitation." (Fred. van Eeden).

♀ □, ☍ ♆. These aspects truly denote a continuous search for the beautiful and good, but it will prove to be very difficult for the native to remain consistent in it, since an exaggerated meekness leads him for the sake of a good understanding, to follow quite another way of thinking and acting than his own inner being would have led him to chose. These aspects of ♆ also easily lead him to fall into some pose which is quite different from the real attitude of his feeling. Voluntarily to give up that pose is exceedingly difficult, especially if the financial conditions are favourable or the person concerned enjoys a certain fame which gives him much opportunity to move in circles where such a thing is *expected* and *stimulated.* There is a certain tendency to the romantic and peculiar, but as this may cause much disappointment and vexation, it is very advisable to set to work in such affairs with great care and keen investigation; better even to avoid them altogether. These aspects make decadent, self-indulgent, sensual.

„Simplicity, purity and uprightness are the qualities which contribute most to the moulding of our character." (Trine).

Aspects of Mars (♂).

♂ ☌ ♃. This aspect augments the native's *vitality,* but also renders him somewhat blustering, boastful, passionate, extravagant, not always honest towards himself nor to others. With this ☌ he is inclined to say more than he knows and does not quite realise what he says. Therefore the art of keeping silent is more necessary here than anywhere else.

"By silence are those recognised who bear God in their hearts." (Tersteegen).

♂ ✶, △ ♃. The native's *ability* to work as well as his *love* of work is very great, so that much may be reached. Right distribution and organisation prevents overstrain and keeps the imagination alert. Although the native is very *idealistic,* he does not lose sight of the *practical side* of life. These aspects give much talent for organisation, great influence on others, and through them financial profit. Enterprises started and conducted for others — also various forms of social work — are usually successful. These aspects render the native fond of liberty and self-reliant.

"To those who believe they are able to conquer, victory is assured." (Emerson).

♂ □, ☍ ♃. These aspects make the native sceptical, atheistic, caring neither for God nor for His Law — "il y a avec le ciel des accomodements!" — indifferent, extravagant. Under this constellation one finds dishonest gamblers, sanguine people who act impulsively and do not take their duties seriously. Those who work with them will therefore also deal with their property in a reckless way; like master, like man!

"Let us be obedient to the law, then from bondage we shall attain liberty." *(Marbach).*

♂ ♂ ♄. This aspect renders fearless, undaunted, able for the sake of an ideal to persevere in difficult enterprises with energy and great strength of will, exacting similar conduct from others. This aspect also makes great demands with regard to humaneness and gentleness, since it has a tendency to make the character somewhat too *hard, headstrong* and *severe.*

"Kindle your fire. — If people do not see it to-day, just let the years pass — then it will shine for every one." *(Eugen Reichel).*

♂ ✶, △ ♄. These aspects enable the native to reach something of real value, to take decisive measures, to hit the nail on the head. In this aspect lies what is fundamental in life i.e. the energy to defy life's storms and to trust in the outcome of the strife and to persevere in the path adopted. "Perseverence conquers" is the device. These aspects promise success after persistent, concentrated work; they render tactful, self-assured.

"Each one of us is born to his own special work in the world, to which he is adapted, more than to any other. It is a high duty of the parent or the instructor, and of the youth himself, watchfully to search for what it in each case is, and eventually to discover it. *(Gladstone).*

♂ ◻, ☍ ♄. The contradiction in the nature of ♄ (concentration and limitation) and of ♂ (daring and energy) accounts for the contradictions in this character: on the one hand serious, diplomatic, discriminating — on the other passionate, aggressive, imprudent. These aspects give sensibility to new impressions and an instinctive hope of success. Through his combination a tendency arises for occult research; originating in curiosity, but ready to approve of it at the slightest proof of its worth or reasonable explanation. At times an excessive depression may manifest, if a well-considered attempt fails. And although the sense of duty or responsibility usually prompts the native to persevere, *yet the inward joy in work has gone* and some stimulus from outside is needed in order to cheer his flagging spirits. These aspects render irritable, passionate, spiteful, bitter and unreasonable. On the whole feeling will be more inclined to initiative and pioneer work than the practical mind admits. Inwardly a certain admiration will be shown for those people who can enjoy life in a way which astonishes all, who always *want* to see the sunny side of everything and evidently do see it, too. But ♄'s cautiousness does not risk limitation.

"We grow much wiser through attempts that fail than through those which succeed. We often get to know how to make a success of something, after we have seen how it should not be done; and he who is never mistaken, will probably never discover anything." *(Ter Haar).*

♂ ☌, □, ☍ ♅. These afflictions make the native active and original, but eccentric and unbalanced, anarchistic-atheistic, ill-tempered, irritable. Although he himself does not know very well what he wants, he is self-willed, rebellious, and fanatically opposed to any compulsion or limitation.

"Every reform at which we aim, ought to start with ourselves."

(Thorbecke.)

♂ ⚹, △ ♅. The native is very receptive to *inspiration,* which benefits both work and ideals. These aspects are found in the case of practical idealists. They render self-reliant, and prone to reform.

"Help nature, and work on with her, and nature will regard thee as one of her creators, and make obeisance."

(The Voice of the Silence.)

♂ ☌, □, ☍ ♆, the "mystical planet" promotes the faculty of the astral body to leave the physical sheath consciously and manifest elsewhere. Inharmonious aspects of ♂ however, warn the native against carelessness or haste in these things and also against applying his capacities with a selfish aim. ♂ symbolises desire, personal energy; where therefore this clashes with the higher ♆ nature unpleasant consequences may be expected. *With complete self-control and purity of thought,* these aspects may bring surprising results. But there is a great possibility of spiritual aberration and nervous overstrain, so it will be important for the native to keep his nerves calm. Further, these aspects cause uncontrolled passion and lead to abuse of energy.

"Not what a man knows, but what he wills decides his worth or worthlessness, his power or impotence, his happiness or unhappiness."

(Lindner.)

♂ ⚹, △ ♆. These aspects enable the native to work out a mystic experience, to carry it out into the world, to demonstrate it. Such a person is able as it were to see the Kingdom of God in the world. These aspects make him artistic, and give a belief in the omnipotence of the good and beautiful, so that he has also great confidence in his fellow-men. This easily leads to disappointment, if the horoscope is not otherwise harmonious.

"In the small degree that unity is already felt and known by us, we should take it as the basis of all our other feeling, thinking and acting, and of all our seeking and striving."

(Dr. W. H. Denier van der Gon.)

Aspects of Jupiter (♃).

♃ ☌, □, ☍ ♄ indicates that there is little probability of *"luck",* and that money must rather be earned by dint of hard work. This position gives the character on the one hand a longing to uplift and ennoble mankind and on the other a cynical resignation in bad social conditions. The lower nature and momentary impulses should be well controlled, otherwise the consequence will be loss of popularity and reputation, of which others will make use. The native should remember never to pose as if some good had already been reached when he is only striving for it — a thing to which an afflicted ♃ easily leads. For instance *confidence should not turn into presumption, sense of justice into partiality, religious feeling into fanaticism.* We shall surely reach that for which we earnestly strive, but if we wish to sell the skin before the bear has been shot, we are sure to go backwards. Theosophically speaking: a person who in a former life allowed many good opportunities to pass unused and abused many gifts, will therefore on all sides in his present life meet with opposition and resistance. Nevertheless — once these difficulties are overcome through unflagging and indomitable energy, confidence in his own inner powers and in the never failing help of good — enormous progress in true humanity will be made and a great step forward taken on the road of evolution. It is advisable to read and study books which teach what great powers are given to man with which to control and improve his character, his feelings, even his circumstances in life.

These aspects cause headaches, disturbances in the functioning of the senses and kidneys. There is also a tendency to calcification of the blood-vessels. A diet is to be recommended.

"At every occurrence in your life do not forget to commune with yourself and to ask of yourself how you can profit by it."   (Epictetus.)

♃ *, △ ♄ gives great likelihood of success if there be sufficient confidence, appreciation and use made of every advantage however small. Here, the uprightness, humanity and ethical-religious idealism of Jupiter and the seriousness, accuracy and watchfulness of Saturn combine into an active capacity for work not easily too highly valued for the welfare of mankind.

"True confidence is characterised by perfectly calm patience."
(Jan Ligthart.)

♃ ☌ ♅. ♅ rouses a higher consciousness and therefore gives special novel ideas, also insight into the connection of seeming contradictions. Great interest will be taken in e.g. astrology, the native will like to read and reflect and talk about this subject, correspondence concerning it will give much satisfaction. ♅ leads to unexpected changes and to new ties of friendship which contribute much to an increase of knowledge. Uncommon experiences will be met with and the solution of many of the problems of life will be found in theosophical and astrological literature. These aspects make devoted and give pure and lofty faith.

"The perfect devotee cannot be harmed by anyone."
(Dr. A. Besant.)

♃ *, △ ♅. A correct outlook on the metaphysical world is rendered possible by these aspects. The will to succeed is strong. These aspects make the native fortunate, enthusiastic; they give great interest in religious and occult studies and excellent educational powers in this direction.

"The more complete a thing is, the more effective it is."
(Spinoza.)

♃ □, ☍ ♅. Here the higher mental faculties sometimes manifest as *genius,* and a remarkable vein of *subtlety,* but these usually come into conflict with public opinion. Much spiritual battle arises from this *sensing of the Truth* and the *impotence to outline it clearly*. These aspects give changeable opinions and render stubborn, refractory.

"If one throws life away, it comes to him in a new form and with a new meaning." *(Light on the Path.)*

♃ ☌, ⚹, △ ♆. ♃, the planet of philosophic confidence favourably connected with ♆ which emits the higher, godlike vibrations, gives a valuable power of 'self-cure'. It is "faith" which "preserves", spirit which dominates matter. These aspects give a liking for being in the open air and for idealistic day-dreaming. The native would like to be a painter, or a poet in order to live more intensely with everything in nature. He prefers to read the writings of mystics and he tries his utmost to live with his own thoughts in the same ideal sphere. These aspects give lofty human conceptions and render contemplative, meditative.

"To those who constantly strive after unity and honour in love, I give the striving after unity of knowledge through which they come to Me." *(Bhagavad Gita.)*

♃ □, ☍ ♆. These aspects denote disappointments and losses *through excessive confidence,* and exaggerated and unreasonable enthusiasm. Mistakes, carelessness, lightheartedness, will often cause anxiety and fear, and may even lead to legal difficulties. A great amount of business knowledge must be acquired before the native can invest or manage money successfully. True insight will only be obtained after serious comparison and investigation, and a great deal of practice.

Orthodox dogmatism attracts little, but dream life and mysticism all the more. These aspects render slow, indifferent for practical life; generally the ideals are more meditated on than commonplace occupation, so that the activities will suffer by it.

"Whenever you have a good intention, do not let the grass grow over it, for speedily the grass will grow over you." *(Laurillard.)*

Aspects of Saturn (♄).

♄ ☌ ♅. This conjunction gives a deep, serious power of thought, renders reserved, diplomatic, fond of knowledge and influence.

"Even in his obscure striving, the good man is well aware of the right way." *(Goethe).*

♄ ⚹, △ ♅. These aspects render *open to new ideas,* and also give true insight into *ancient truths;* they enable the native to concentrate keenly on a thought which asks to be worked out. Probably some new inventions will be made in the field of administration, management, statistics etc. These aspects denote a deep and serious attitude to life, a sensitive conscience and give a faculty to clair-audience.

"Truth is in ourselves, it does not originate in things outside us."

♄ □ ☍ ♅ is favourable for personal achievement, gives flashes of genius at times; but much opposition may be expected, especially from older people. The progressiveness of ♅ in the direction of modern-sociology is to many old-fashioned people an abomination which, on the one hand is apt to provoke obstinacy and on the other spiteful speech. But if rancour and refractoriness are evaded or controlled, such a constellation will purify and redouble energy, and results will be obtained which demand admiration even from former antagonists.

These aspects lead to unusual elaboration of ideas, reversion of the inner attitude to life, conversion.

"Hatred never ceases by hatred, hatred ceases by love, this is the old law." *(Dhammapada.)*

♄ ☌, □, ☍ ♆. The attitude adopted towards occult teachings is somewhat reserved, although this is a consequence rather of education than of the native's own consciousness. In the beginning they are only studied for study's sake, but gradually they will exert a strong influence on life when it is seen that little by little the exact sciences also are proving the occultist's theorems.

Further these aspects give a tendency to melancholy, discontent and jealousy of others engendering unpleasant relations in the environment. In childhood and during education disappointments will arise through the clashing of idealistic ideas with naked reality. Happiness often lies in another direction than that to which inclination draws, and it is rather a question whether the will is strong enough to let go sham pleasures for that which in the long run gives the most intense satisfaction, and to set forth consciously on the path that in one's best moments is acknowledged to be good.

These aspects lead to sentimental crazes, bring unaccountable opposition and adversity, make distrustful, doubtful.

"All disappointment which reaches us from without is the reflexion of uncertainty which is in us." *(Dr. A. Besant.)*

♄ ⚹, △ ♆. Artistic tendencies will be found; they may express themselves somewhat mediumistically or abstractedly. These aspects incline one to allow oneself to be governed by the thoughts of a stronger personality in this or another world. Most will be achieved for the sake of, or at the will of, some one who makes a deep impression or greatly influences thought. Queer dreams or *presentiments* often occur and contain more truth and deeper significance than is surmised; it will be well worth while to analyse and reflect upon them.

"The wise one preserves earnestness as his most precious gem."
(Dhammapada.)

Aspects of Uranus (♅) and Neptune (♆).

♅ ☌, ⚹, △ ♆. If ♅ and ♆ are strongly posited these aspects give deep feelings, great inner assurance. The native likes to dwell in thought in loftier, more poetical regions than earth can offer. Artistic feeling, the

150

feeling for what is purified and beautiful is an important factor in this character and may often — sometimes unconsciously — exercise a great influence for good on his general circumstances. Such an aspect promotes the maintenance of high ideals which is one of the chief conditions of this life. His consciousness may be raised to such a height as to enable him to live in the Universal, Cosmic Consciousness, the "Mind" of the Christian Scientists. With a favourable direction an opportunity will offer itself for the native to be the means of opening the eyes of material science, by the demonstration of a so-called 'miraculous' cure, to laws as yet unknown.

Financial matters will not always be fortunate, although windfalls and a trustful attitude will help to overcome all earthly worries.

"Let the light shine in thyself, so that thou feelest no need for help from outside, nor for the peace that others can give."

(Marcus Aurelius.)

♅ ☐, ☍ ♆. These afflictions cause *a conflict between higher and lower aspirations,* uncertain feelings, mistakes and unaccountable disappointments. They bring quite unexpected modifications of thought and habit. The native's peace of mind is continually menaced by *anxious premonitions,* in a discontented mood all kinds of plans are made which although often very ingenious, had better not be carried out. Thought should be constantly controlled by *truth* and *love.*

"All money and all property which you do not wish to possess in order to give, or of which you do not consider yourself to be the steward, is not in your possession, but has possession over you."   *(Bronswell.)*

How to calculate a Progressive Horoscope.

Conclusions as to the succeeding years of life are drawn from the movements of the planets — including Sun and Moon — in relation to their position in the birth-horoscope.

We can calculate the positions of the planets for any moment *after the birth* and they form what is called the *continued* or *progressed horoscope.*

Astrologers have stated that there are various cycles in our Solar System to which we, human beings, react. Most investigators of astrology recognise that cycle to be the principal one, by which the motion of the planets during *one day is the measure for* the native's *experiences of life during one year,* since this gives the *highest percentage* of correct results.

We shall explain the calculation of progressed positions according to this method.

The motion during the first day after birth denotes life's experiences during the first year; those during the fifth day after birth will indicate life's experiences during the fifth year of life, those of the tenth day after birth denote the experiences of the tenth year of life, etc. The planetary positions for the n-th day after the birth diagrammed show the progressed horoscope for the n-th year of life.

The hour for calculating the progressed horoscope is always the hour of birth.

If therefore we want to calculate the progressed horoscope for the 25th birthday of a person born at 1 p.m., we calculate the horoscope for the 25th day after the date of birth at 1 p.m. which is done in the same way as for a nativity (see. p. 28).

When this progressed diagram is ready we must see what aspects the planets now form compared with their positions in the birth horoscope. In order to distinguish them, in the progressed horoscope these aspects are called *directions.*

In a later chapter we shall deal with the way in which the various directions make themselves felt.

On an average the **Sun** apparently moves one degree per day, therefore in a progressed horoscope one degree in *one year* i.e. 60′ per year or 5′ per month.

If e.g. the *Sun* in the birth-horoscope is placed 7° ♈ and Mars 14°

♌ then the △-direction (120°) of the ☉ with ♂ will be complete in 7 years; for in that time the ☉ has progressed to 14° ♈.

On an average the **Moon** moves 12 degrees in 1 day so in the progressed horoscope 12 degrees in one year or 1° per month or 2′ per day.

If at birth the Moon is placed 3° ♓ and ♅ 29° ♍, then in about 26 months the opposition of the progressive ☽ to ♅ will begin to operate, for the Moon is then, namely after those 26 months, in 29° Pisces.

If the *Moon* is 2° ♈ and ♄ 20° 30′ ♋, then — seeing that the distance from 2° ♈ to 20° 30′ ♋ is 108° 30′ — the ☌ will take place after 108 months and 15 days.

Our calculation will be more accurate, if we look up the exact motion in Veen's Tables.

The ☉'s	motion varies in a day from	0° 57′	to	1° 1′	(per progressed year)
The ☽	„ „ „ „ „ „	11° 50′	„	15° 17′	(„ „ „)
The ☿	„ „ „ „ „ „	0° 12′	„	2° 13′	(„ „ „)
The ♀	„ „ „ „ „ „	0° 6′	„	1° 14′	(„ „ „)
The ♂	„ „ „ „ „ „	0° 4′	„	0° 48′	(„ „ „)
The ♃	„ „ „ „ „ „	0° 02′	„	0° 13′	(„ „ „)

On an average the ♄ motion is 0° 2′ per day.

☿ is retrograde during 24 days.
♀ „ „ „ 42 „
♂ „ „ „ 80 „
♃ „ „ „ 120 „
♄ „ „ „ 140 „

From the rule that the motion of the planets during *one day* (24 hours) is the measure of life's experiences during *one year* (12 months) we may conclude

that the motion of the planets

during	**24 hours**	**coincides with that of**	**12 months**
„	**2 „**	„ „ „ „	**1 month**
„	**1 hour**	„ „ „ „	**15 days**
„	**4 minutes**	„ „ „ „	**1 day**
„	**1 minute**	„ „ „ „	**6 hrs.**

Since the positions in Veen's Tables are given for *12 o'clock noon* Greenwich time, it is clear from the foregoing that each hour's difference from that in time means a difference of *15 days* in those positions.

We must note two possibilities, viz.

1. If a person is born **before** 12 o'clock Greenwich time, then the positions of the planets mentioned in Veen's Tables are for a **later** date than that on which the birth took place.
2. If a person is born **after** 12 o'clock Greenwich time, then the positions of the planets mentioned in Veen's Tables are for an **earlier** date than that on which the birth took place.

XIV

Example of Calculating a Progressive Horoscope.

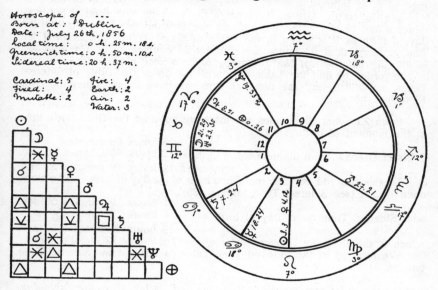

Horoscope of ...
Born at: Dublin
Date: July 26th, 1856
Local time: 0 h. 25 m. 18 s.
Greenwich time: 0 h. 50 m. 10 s.
Sidereal time: 20 h. 37 m.

Cardinal: 5   Fire: 4
Fixed: 4   Earth: 2
Mutable: 2   Air: 2
              Water: 3

In our specimen horoscope the birth took place on July 26 1856 at
0 h. 50 m. 10 s. Greenwich-time or
12 h. 50 m. 10 s. after noon Greenwich-time on July 25 1856.

The positions of the planets are given in Veen's tables for noon
Greenwich time.

1): The birth took place 11 hrs. 9 m. 50 sec. **before** July 26. noon, so
that the positions of the planets mentioned in Veen's Tables are meant
for a **later** date than that on which the birth took place. This **later** date
is the Table-day for the progressed horoscope. 11 hrs. 9 m. 50 s. will count
for 5 months, 17 days — (see the table on the preceeding page). The
positions on July 26. 1856 and every following day are therefore 5 months
and 17 days later than July 26. i.e. Jan. 13. 1857.

As Table-day for this progr. horoscope we find thus Januari 13. for
each year.

In this calculation for convenience sake we assume each month to
have 30 days; but because this is not correct, the table-day may in reality

be a couple of days earlier or later than the date thus found. For greater accuracy as well as this one, we might make use of another method of finding the table-day; any difference resulting being divided. The second method is as follows.

We deduct the Greenwich time of the hour of birth from 23 hours 60 minutes and to this difference we add the Sidereal time — noon — of the day of birth as it is given in the Table of Sidereal Time on p. 25. If the sum is more than 24 hours, we subtract 24 hours from it. The resultant is *the Sidereal Time of the Table-day at 12 o'clock noon.*

In order to find the Table-day, we look up in the Table of Sidereal Times, on which day the Sidereal Time we have found is mentioned for 12 o'clock noon.

From 23 hours 60 minutes we therefore subtract the Greenwich time at the moment of birth. Thus

	23 hours 60 minutes
Subtract Greenw. t. of the moment of birth =	12 hours 50 minutes 10 sec.
remainder	11 hours 9 minutes 50 sec.

To this we add the Sidereal Time hour of the day of birth — 12 o'clock noon — i.e. (see Sidereal Time table p, 25)

	11 hours 9 minutes 50 sec.
add: Sidereal Time noon, day of birth =	8 hours 16 minutes
	19 hours 25 minutes 50 sec.

which is therefore the *Sidereal Time of the Table-day* 12 o'clock noon.

We look up in the Sidereal Time Table (p. 25) and find Sidereal Time on Jan. 12.

As the difference is not important we shall fix Jan. 13. as the *Table-day.*

In order that when calculating this progressed horoscope, we deal *without further reduction* with the position of the planets at 12 o'clock Greenwich time as given in Veen's Tables, we draw up a list of dates as follows:

age 0 year, the positions on July 26. 1856 are those of Jan. 13. 1857 progressed
" 1 " " " " " 27. " " " " " 13. 1858 "
" 2 " " " " " 28. " " " " " 13. 1859 "
" 3 " " " " " 29. " " " " " 13. 1860 "
" 4 " " " " " 30. " " " " " 13. 1861 "
" 5 " " " " " 31. " " " " " 13. 1862 "
" 6 " " " " Aug. 1. " " " " 13. 1863 "
" 7 " " " " " 2. " " " " " 13. 1864 "
" 8 " " " " " 3. " " " " " 13. 1865 "
" 9 " " " " " 4. " " " " " 13. 1866 "
" 10 " " " " " 5. " " " " " 13. 1867 "

If we continue the list of *table-dates* of the progressed positions of age 60 year, the positions on Sept. 24. 1856 are those of Jan. 13. 1917 progressed
" 61 " " " " " 25. " " " " " 13. 1918 "

age 62 year, the positions on Sept. 26. 1856 are those of Jan. 13. 1919 progressed
" 63 " " " " " 27. " " " " " 13. 1920 "
" 64 " " " " " 28. " " " " " 13. 1921 "
" 65 " " " " " 29. " " " " " 13. 1922 "
" 66 " " " " " 30. " " " " " 13. 1923 "
" 67 " " " " " Oct. 1. " " " " " 13. 1924 "

f we wish to know the progressed positions of the planets on Jan. 13.
1921 we copy from Veen's Tables the position of ☉, ☽ and planets on
Sept. 28. 1856. The progressed positions for Jan. 13. 1922 are those on
Sept. 29. 1856.

In Veen's Tables we find the ☉ on Sept. 28. 1856 5° ♎ 26' [1])
the ☽ " " " " 28° ♍
☿ " " " " 0° ♏
♀ " " " " 24° ♎
♂ " " " " 8° ♐ 36' [2])

In order to have a clear survey of the way in which the directions
succeed each other, we write down the planets of the birth-horoscope next
to each other, according to the sequence of the number of degrees, thus:

⊕	☉	♀	♄	♃	Asc.	☿	♆	☽	⛢	♂
26' ♈	3° 3' ♌	4° 12' ♌	7° 24' ♋	8° 51' ♈	12° ♊	18° 24' ♋	19° 33' ♓	21° 29' ♉	23° 35' ♉	27° 21' ♎

The average motion of the Sun is one degree daily, therefore in a
progressed horoscope **one degree is one year** i.e. 60' in a year or 5' in
a month.

At birth the ☉ is placed 3° ♌ 3', thus in the next years the following
directions are formed:

☉ [3]) 1856 at Birth 3° ♌ 3'
☉ 1857 Progressed 4° " 12' ♂ ♀ 4° ♌ 12'
   1860 "   7° " 24' ⊻ ♄ 7° ♋ 24'
   1862 "   8° " 51' △ ♃ 8° ♈ 51'
   1865 "   12° "   ✳ Asc. 12° ♊
   1872 "   18° " 24' ⊻ ☿ 18° ♋ 24'
   1873 "   19° " 33' ⊼ ♆ 19° ♓ 33'
   1875 "   21° " 29' □ ☽ 21° ♉ 29'
   1877 "   23° " 35' □ ⛢ 23° ♉ 35'
   1881 "   27° " 21' ✳ ♂ 27° ♎ 21'
   1885 "   0° ♍ 26' ⊼ ⊕ 0° ♈ 26'
   1887 "   3° " 3' ⊻ ☉ 3° ♌ 3'
   1889 "   4° " 12' ⊻ ♀ 4° ♌ 12'
   1892 "   7° " 24' ✳ ♄ 7° ♋ 24'

---

[1]) In the table: "Differences in minutes for the year 1856" we find that for 1856
after Febr. 29. we must add 27' to the positions mentioned in the Standard-Sun-table.
Thus we get 4° ♎ 59' + 27' = 5° ♎ 26' for the position of the Sun on Sept. 28. 1856.
[2]) ♂'s position Sept. 1. 1856 is 19° ♏ and Oct. 1. 1856 10° ♐.
♂'s motion in 30 days 21° or in 1 day 42' and in 2 days 1°24'.
♂'s place Oct. 1. 1856 = 10° ♐; ♂ place Sept. 28. 1856 = 8°36' ♐.
[3]) The ☉ directions remain valid during three years, viz. the year in which they
are complete, one year before and one year after.

In the next table we have noted the place of the ⊙, ☽, ☿, ♀ and ♂ from Sept. 28. '56 to Oct. 8. '56 (see Veen's Tables).

We know that the motion during these *ten days* is the motion of these planets during *ten years* in the progressed horoscope, thus from Jan. 13. 1921 to Jan. 13. 1931 (see above).

	⊙ pr.	☽ pr.	☿ pr.	♀ pr.	♂ pr.
Jan. 13. 1921 . (Sept. 28. 1856)	5° ♎ 26′	28° ♍	0° ♏ 0′	24° ♎	7° ♐ 51′
„ 13. 1922 . (Sept. 29. 1856)	6° „ 25′	10° ♎	1° „ 21′	25° „ 12′	8° „ 33′
„ 13. 1923 . (Sept. 30. 1856)	7° „ 24′	22° „	1° „ 54′	26° „ 24′	9° „ 15′
„ 13. 1924 . (Oct. 1. 1856)	8° „ 23′	4° ♏	2° „ 23′	27° „ 36′	9° „ 57′
„ 13. 1925 . (Oct. 2. 1856)	9° „ 22′	15° „	2° „ 46′	28° „ 48′	10° „ 39′
„ 13. 1926 . (Oct. 3. 1856)	10° „ 21′	27° „	3° „ 3′	0° ♏ 0′	11° „ 32′
„ 13. 1927 . (Oct. 4. 1856)	11° „ 20′	10° ♐	3° „ 15′	1° „ 12′	12° „ 5′
„ 13. 1928 . (Oct. 5. 1856)	12° „ 19′	22° „	3° „ 19′	2° „ 24′	12° „ 47′
„ 13. 1929 . (Oct. 6. 1856)	13° „ 19′	4° ♑	3° „ 16′ Retr. 1)	3° „ 36′	13° „ 30′
„ 13. 1930 . (Oct. 7. 1856)	14° „ 18′	17° „	3° „ 5′	4° „ 48′	14° „ 13′
„ 13. 1931 . (Oct. 8. 1856)	15° „ 18′	1° ♒	2° „ 47′	6° „	14° „ 56′

If we wish to calculate and judge a progressed horoscope it is advisable thus to make a list from birthday up to the time for which we want the judgment.

It will be clear that $1/12$ of the motion in a year is equivalent to the motion in one month, and $1/30$ of the motion per month is equivalent to the motion of one day. In this way we can calculate the dates on which the directions are fully active:

⊙'s motion from Jan. 13, 1921 till Jan. 13, 1931: from 5° ♎ 26′ to 15° ♎ 18′.

⊙'s direction during that period:
⊙ pr. 7° ♎ 24′ □ ♄   7° ♋ 24′.
„   8° ♎ 51′ ☍ ♃   8° ♈ 51′.
„ 12° ♎   △ Asc. 12° ♊.

The Moon (☽).

☽'s motion from Jan. 13, 1926 till Jan. 13, 1928: from 27° ♏ to 22° ♐. ☽'s directions during this period:

---

1) See ☿ Retrograde table.

☽ pr.	27° ♏ 21′	⊻	♂	27° ♎ 21′
„	0° ♐ 26′	△	⊕	0° ♈ 26′
„	3° „ 3′	△	☉	3° ♌ 3′
„	4° „ 12′	△	♀	4° ♌ 12′
„	7° „ 24′	⊼	♄	7° ♋ 24′
„	8° „ 51′	△	♃	8° ♈ 51′
„	12° „	☍	Asc.	12° ♊
„	18° „ 24′	⊼	☿	18° ♋ 24′
„	19° „ 33′	□	♆	19° ♓ 33′

☽'s place on Jan. 13. 1926 : 27° ♏
Jan. 13. 1927 : 10° ♐

So in this year the ☽ advances 13°, that is 1°5′ in a month or 2′10″ a day.

If we want to know when the progressed ☽ forms a △ direction from 3° ♐ 3′ with ☉ 3° ♌ 3′ we find that the distance from 27° ♏ to 3° ♐ 3′ is 6°3′.

So it will be about 6 months after Jan. 13 or in the midst of July 1926 when this △ direction will be complete. The ☽ directions remain valid for three months, viz: the month in which they are complete, one month before and one month after.

Mercury (☿).

Problem: When is ☿ pr. ☌ ♂ 27° ♎ 21′ Radix?
At birth ☿ was posited 18° ♋ 24′.
In Veen's Tables we find:

Mercury July	30. 1856	26 ♋	corresponds with	(a day = a year)	Jan. 13. 1861
Aug.	9. „	17 ♌	„ „	(„)	Jan. 13. 1871
Aug.	19. „	6 ♍	„ „	(„)	Jan. 13. 1881
Aug.	29. „	23 ♍	„ „	(„)	Jan. 13. 1891
Sept.	8. „	8 ♎	„ „	(„)	Jan. 13. 1901
Sept.	18. „	21 ♎	„ „	(„)	Jan. 13. 1911
Sept.	28. „	0 ♏	„ „	(„)	Jan. 13. 1921

Thus the motion of ☿ in the 10 years, from Jan. 13. 1911 till Jan. 13. 1921 is from 21° ♎ to 0° ♏ or 9° = 540′ = 54′ in a year = 4′ 30″ a month.

The distance from 27° ♎ 21′ to 0° ♏ is 2° 39′ or 159′.

☿ pr. accomplishes this distance in $35^1/_3$ months, thus $35^1/_3$ months before Jan. 13. 1921, or in Jan. 1918 ☿ pr. will be in ☌ ♂ 27° ♎ 21′ Radix.

Venus (♀).

Problem: When is ♀ pr. ☌ ♂ 27° ♎ 21′ Radix?

When we look at the table of ♀'s motion during Jan. 13. 1921—Jan. 13. 1931, (See table p. 156),

we see that on Jan. 13. 1923 ♀ is in 26° ♎ 24′
Jan. 13. 1924 ♀ „ „ 27° ♎ 36′

Thus the motion of ♀ during this year is 1° 12′ or 6′ in a month.

The distance from 27° ♎ 21′ to 27 ♎ 36′ is 15′, i.e. $2^1/_2$ month before Jan. 13. 1924, so at the end of Oct. 1923 ♀ pr. will be in ☌ ♂ 27° ♎ 21′ Radix.

Mars (♂).

Problem: When is ♂ pr. 8° ♐ 51' △ ♃ 8° ♈ 51' Radix?
Looking at the table (p. 156) of ♂'s motion during the period from
Jan. 13. 1921 till Jan. 13. 1931 we see that

Jan. 13. 1922 ♂ is in 8° ♐ 33'
Jan. 13. 1923 ♂ „ „ 9° ♐ 15'

The motion of ♂ during these 12 months is 0°42' or 3$^1/_2$' in a month.
The distance from 8° ♐ 33' to 8° ♐ 51' is 18'.
So in 5 months and 4 days after Jan. 13. 1922, or in the midst of
June 1922 ♂ pr. 8° ♐ 51' will be △ ♃ 8° ♈ 51' Radix.
Jupiter and *Saturn* very seldom form progressive directions in the
space of a man's life; but they form *transits*.

The Transits.

Besides the directions we must take into account the *transits*, among
which those of *Jupiter* and *Saturn* are the most important.
The *actual motion* of the planets across the positions in the nativity
are called transits. The transit-conjunction (♂) and the transit-opposition (♂)
have an especially strong influence.
If we look up *Jupiter* in *Veen's Tables*, we find that for our specimen
horoscope in 1884 ♃ transits through the third house ⊙ 3° ♌ 3' and ♀
4° ♌ 12'. In 1914 ♃ transits the 10th house etc.

If we look up the table for *Saturn*, we see that for our specimen
horoscope in Nov. 1896 ♄ transits through the sixth house in ♍, in opposition to ☽ 21° ♉ 29' and ♅ 23° ♉ 35'.

In order to manifest clearly, the directions must usually be strengthened by analogous transits. The latter are a stimulus to the directions,
which often do not become active, until the concurring transits take place,
although the pinnacle of the direction may already have passed.

If ♅ and ♀ directions are not by themselves very strongly posited in
the horoscope they require a stimulus from similar ⊙ and ☽-directions
in order to manifest their activity. Thus also in astrology the saying holds
true that „union is strength". (See Ch. *How to judge the Transits*.)

Transits of ♄, ♂ and ♅ strengthen the effect of inharmonious directions
and prevent the native from profiting adequately by harmonious directions.

Transits of the ⊙, and ♃ weaken inharmonious directions and strengthen
favourable directions which happen to come into activity simultaneously,
thus rendering them all the more advantageous.

XV

How to judge a Progressed Horoscope.

When we have calculated for a certain year (or shorter or longer period) according with the method given all the directions which occur, we draw up a list of those various directions *in the order of the dates on which they are complete* and proceed to judge from this according to the time in which they are active. We also put in the transits, so that we get an exact picture of the succeeding (or possibly simultaneous) occurrences for the special year we wish to study. We also notice *in which houses* the directions and transits of the ☽ occur.

Whereas in judging a nativity we must never lose sight of the mutual connection of the aspects etc., in reading a progressed horoscope this is even more vital. For in judging each direction, we must take the radical positions into account as well as other directions which may be effective *simultaneously*. E.g. if in a birth-horoscope the ☽ is the ruler of the 3rd house and the progressive ☽ moves through the 11th house, where it forms a ♂ with the ☉-radix [1]), an animated correspondence with one or more friends will ensue. If the pr. ☽ in 11 forms a △ with ♀ radix in 7 the element of love will come to the fore; if on the other hand the pr. ☽ forms □ to ♅, ruler M. C. the native's character will suffer and his social reputation will be lessened by the friendly relations. (See Ch. The meaning of the Houses, (p. 10).

As has already been seen, a ☉ direction lasts ± 3 years and a ☽-direction ± 3 months; usually the effect is strongest and most pronounced in the middle of these periods, although some modifications may take place, chiefly through the transits.

E.g. if the pr. ☉ 8° ♐ is in the 6th house and there forms a □ with ♃-radix 8° ♈, and a transit of ♄ in 8° ♎ (thus □ pr. ☉ and ☍ ♃) is about to take place, it is possible that the effect of the inharmonious ☉-direction will at the transit ♄ ☍ ♃ be evident as gout, articular rheumatism and (or) a kidney abcess, stone in the kidney, accompanied by headache. But if in the nativity the ☉ is strong and harmoniously aspected, or if it is supported e.g. by a △ aspect to ♀-radix in ♉ M.C., the unpleasant effect

---

[1]) Radix (= root) means birth horoscope.

may be mitigated or speedily overcome; in that case the illness will not be of a serious nature or soon take a favourable turn.

A person with a strong occupation of the 12th house will not be able suddenly to reach fame and respect through a single harmonious direction in the 10th house, nor will a person with a well-occupied 2nd house become indigent through a single inharmonious transit in 5.

Therefore one· should be cautious in drawing conclusions and *keep an eye on all the factors.*

XVI

The Directions.

Directions of the Sun (☉).

Pr. ☉ ☌ ☽. This direction gives a strong feeling of *animation,* a sense of being suffused with new vitality; this will be a time during which the physical body feels strong. The native will rise in general estimation; the interest of influential people may be expected. With this direction a union — marriage if the person concerned is marriageable — is often made. If the ☽ is not strongly posited in the nativity — and with women — there is a likelihood that during this direction the "fire of the sun" may cause feverish symptoms.

Pr. ☉ ⚹, △ ☽. These derections bring *sunshine* both in physical life and into the life of feeling. They cause good health, animal spirits and calm, cheery thoughts. A business-like, clear view of economic conditions in society will lead to favourable management of finances. Respect and cooperation make work much easier and pleasanter and a fixed tie or regular appointment may bring much happiness.

Pr. ☉ ☐, ☍ ☽. These directions are *not favourable to health* nor reputation. There is a possibility of loss through death; opportunities will pass unused through *hesitation,* laxity or dishonesty of partner or purveyor entail disadvantageous consequences. Conflicts of feeling with the other sex may be expected. These directions bring a change of circumstances, and generally symbolise separation and alienation.

Pr. ☉ ☌, ⚹, △ ☿. *Active thinking is enhanced.* New schemes are drawn up promising success in business and it becomes easy to put down one's thoughts in writing. There is much love of travelling, for pleasure as well as in order to extend one's connections. This is a good time in which to advertise and start a new study or business. „Nothing ventured, nothing won."

Pr. ☉ ☐ ☿. There is a great likelihood of being *mistaken* through a certain nervousness. This direction seldom occurs, only at a great age.

Pr. ☉ ☌, ⚹, △ ♀. This may become a time of *beauty and love in its highest expression* and may be very favourable for contracting a happy marriage, entering an artistic society or something of the sort. Artistic expression is sought.

All that is connected with feeling and emotions gives joy. Without himself knowing it, during this direction the native will be a radiant centre of love and warmheartedness.

Pr. ⊙ □ ♀. This direction renders somewhat *discontented, slovenly*; in financial matters the native acts too carelessly; troubles will arise with women and friends. There is little inclination to undertake anything fresh or — for an artist — to create new work.

Pr. ⊙ ♂ ♂. This will be a *very critical time,* during which the personality will incline towards astoundingly energetic, or adventurous-romantic deeds.

If, however, the powers then at work, can be *sublimated,* the native will obtain *knowledge* and *physical strength* which will be a great help in later life. For thus strengthened the *spirit* will be able to make the *body* a healthy servant, instead of the temperament ruling through tempestuous moods. It will give the native great happiness and satisfaction to test his actions by Truth and Purity and to enter the service of a strong personality who aims at a definite goal in life.

Pr. ⊙ *, △ ♂. Stimulated vitality tends to energetic action. This direction will therefore be favourable for *starting a new enterprise* which has an adventurous and rather speculative side. The resolute manner will force respect from many. Partnerships, entered into when under this direction will usually not be of a lasting nature, since they will have their source in passion rather than in love.

Pr. ⊙ □, 8 ♂. When *the will* (⊙) and *desire* (♂) strive for mastery it makes the native reckless, adventurous, blind to all danger. Being cantankerous both in his own home and among friends estrangements are sure to result. He should avoid all exaggeration both in his work and daily life, and so far as possible evade accidents e.g. during this time he should be more particularly careful with regard to fire and fire-arms and all sharp-edged tools.

Diseases of an inflammatory nature, infections and *fevers* often occur under these directions.

Pr. ⊙ ♂, *, △ ♃. These directions will strengthen in a great measure faith and trust in God and men. The bond between the native's own higher Self and the Universal Principle, the mutual harmony of much that formerly was considered contradictory, illogical, helps him to realise the unity of all that exists. The realisation that man's evolution runs along *a fixed line,* will add help and give direction to his own life and insight into his task in life.

This will be a time of extraordinarily favourable opportunities both for *spiritual* and *material* work. Health, finances and social circumstances are as one wishes them to be; popularity increases. These directions give much satisfaction from the work achieved.

Pr. ⊙ □, ⚹ ♃. These directions render it difficult to give or to receive exact conceptions of things, so that troubles will arise both with legal and spiritual authorities. Through *lack of tact* alienation or separation will take place from a person who is otherwise much attached. The native should try to act only after calm deliberation. Someone will give advice in a friendly way which may turn out rather unfavourable for the finances. But if the mind can keep sufficiently calm, intuition will at the right moment denote how to act better. Then the native's own faculty will grow (here intended not so much in a material sense but as the faculty of the Ego) very strong.

Pr. ⊙ ⚹, △ ♄. These directions make the native *more serious,* more sedate than otherwise; sober, steadfast and patient. They will urge him to continuous labour — which will be a great help for example when unfavourable directions of ♀, ♃ or ♅ happen to occur at the same time and by this the native will gain the help and sympathy of older people, superiors in rank or experience.

If the 2nd or 5th house plays a part in it, such a direction is especially favourable to financial matters. Persevering work will be blessed.

Pr. ⊙ ♂, □, ⚹ ♄. A *time of loneliness,* in which a feeling of *discontented rebelliousness* will again and again assert itself. The native will go through *much depression.*

These directions cause a worrying attitude of mind, render pessimistic and inclined to give in in the battle for existence. Little encouragement will be experienced from others. When something has to be done, something else will always interfere — death, financial troubles or opposition of the partner. Losses and disappointments of all kinds almost take away all joy of life.

With regard to health such a direction manifests as inadequate circulation of the blood, numbness, and catching of colds; there is little recuperative power. Poisonous remedies and drugs should be avoided; it is advisable to see to regular metabolism and to use hot baths to help the kidneys to function. A dry sunny house is desirable.

During this time the conscience will be very insistent. The native feels as if he were touched by *"the Watcher on the Threshold"*. He recollects and feels as guilt whatever was not pure and true in life. Acknowledgement of error as a necessary means of learning — there is no teacher like experience — will enable him to see this evil as needful on the road to greater realisation. The native is advised to keep as many as possible optimistic, religious, philosophical thoughts, which will enable him to look upon and value temporarily difficult circumstances as an indispensable link in the chain of life.

Pr. ⊙ ♂ ♅. This direction brings radical changes in social and spiritual insight and owing to these changes renders irritable and abrupt. The field of vision is extended by original and exceptional ideas which give others an impression of arbitrariness (or wishing to have one's own way). Through this, alienation from friends and relatives arises and connections are made with people of a more idealistic character.

Pr. ☉ ⚹, △ ♅. These directions will give an *extraordinary illumination* to consciousness; this increases the possibility of gaining metaphysical insight and the inner power of adjusting material life to the newly-obtained knowledge. Hypotheses of astrologers, theosophists, and occultists will be ratified by personal experience so far as this is possible. It will be well for the native to acquaint himself beforehand with the teachings of occultists such as H. P. Blavatsky and others, so that during the time that these directions are in action, their ideas may be elaborated and become personal knowledge. Extraordinarily interesting discoveries in the region of natural science, related to ancient, occult teachings might then be made. New thoughts will suddenly arise as it were by intuition and new points of view in various problems. A friendship with an original person will be entered into, broadening the outlook on life. This time, extremely favourable to all that is planned, is full of surprises.

Pr. ☉ □, ☍ ♅. These directions lead to unexpected, strange actions, whereas unexpected occurrences make the schemes planned fall through. They give a tendency to act impulsively, thoughtlessly, contrary to one's own reasonable insight and bring many inner and outer conflicts to the person concerned. The patience of friends and relations will be put severely to the test; alienation or separation from them is very likely. This period will be a time rich in unknown experiences, but not favourable to reputation. During these directions obstinacy is altogether wrong, because it will only increase the difficulties.

Pr. ☉ ☌ ♆. This direction brings *peculiar dreams* and *psychic experiences,* but when the person concerned wishes to tell others about them he will not be taken seriously. Contact with some one peculiar, mystical or poetical is very likely. Love of beauty and a tendency to day-dreaming are also characteristics of this time.
One should be careful of poisons and narcotics.

Pr. ☉ ⚹, △ ♆. This will render the *domestic surroundings more comfortable.* The view of life becomes *more poetic,* the constitution stronger, vitality will increase and the work be done with greater cheerfulness, spare time will be agreeably spent. These directions promise material welfare. For those who are more evolved it will be a time of *spiritual awakening* and for the artist a time of *inspiration.*

Pr. ☉ □, ☍ ♆ denotes gossip and slander, loss of rank or authority. These directions make over-sensitive; the lower tendencies will assert themselves, all kinds of queer, unhealthy phantasies arise. If the nativity is weak, such a person may be possessed by spirits which search for a medium to gratify their lower desires. Unless the morality is strengthened as much

164

as possible, the suffering will have no end. *Purity* alone can be the saving angel.

Directions of the Moon (☽).

Pr. ☽ ☌ ☉. This conjunction will bring new, promising circumstances, because during this time physical and mental capacities can be used to the utmost. It is a time of great confidence in the attainment of the aim in view, *vitality* increases, there is more *energy* and *inclination to occupy a leading position*. This direction will contribute to self-confidence and belief in the matter in hand, and is particularly suitable for entering into partnership. A change of abode is probable; at any rate it will be a serious point of discussion. The desire some day to occupy a good position in the world will become stronger.
"Desire and love are the wings to great deeds".

Pr. ☽ ⌄ ☉. This gives a desire to see and experience something new. There is a likelihood of financial promotion and of an increase in general esteem. If rightly tackled this direction may effect something good, but one should beware of allowing discontented moods to dominate one's feelings. To think of and wish to live for some one else will strengthen spiritual capacities more than to limit oneself to the material side of life. This direction will bring more light and life, hope of social and spiritual progress and a favourable change of circumstances, which augur well for the future. Kindness will be shown by those higher in rank.

Pr. ☽ ✳ ☉. This direction is *good for health,* it renders *cheerful,* gives the pleasant feeling of having grown *stronger* and has a good influence on both personal and domestic life. Self-reliance increases and more and more one feels most attracted to an optimistic view of life. The power of concentration becomes stronger and at the same time confidence in success. Life will be regarded in a happier light and *social* and *moral progress, promotion and welfare* are very probable. Much strength for the future both physical and moral, may be gained during this period! Things thrive in which one is interested, well-to-do people of standing enter into connection with the person concerned. Appreciation by a superior of work done for him will stimulate to even better work.

Pr. ☽ □ ☉. *Anxiety* and *disappointment* regarding cherished wishes will cause difficulties and opposition. Unfair *criticism* and interference by someone who is more meddlesome than friendly are not easy to bear. The person concerned will be touchy and hasty, therefore the following saying is most applicable "Think before you act and while you are acting still continue to think." Troubles will also arise in domestic matters. During this direction, which is apt to render melancholy and reserved, it is advisable to seek the beautiful in nature and in outdoor life, to read good, uplifting books, to see fine works of art and to disregard one's own reflections, listening rather to what others have got to say whose view of life is enthusiastic, though maybe somewhat superficial. *Depression* must be fought during this time, for "so long as there is good to be done and evil to be redressed, life is important and to live is a duty."

This influence is apt to render too liberal in buying tools and articles of daily use. Financially this will not be a favourable time, it is hard to cut one's coat according to one's cloth; debts, anxiety about family relations cause a good deal of unpleasantness. Extraordinary self-control will be necessary in order to prevent these aspects from having a prejudical influence on health. The best is to be absorbed in thoughts along a mental-religious line which exercise a favourable influence on physical well-being.

Pr. ☽ △ ☉. This will be a time during which the spirit is particularly clear, fit to start new enterprises. There is an uncommonly sane outlook on things which augurs much for success in material and spiritual development. Financial success is sure to come and work will more than ever be a pleasure. It is a time of original and well-balanced creations, of constructive work; people of high position will show their appreciation and approval. New plans are made, new enterprises started which, if not begun too speculatively, will meet with success. This constellation enables much to be achieved, but might cause overstrain, therefore *"be moderate in all things"*.

Finally this period gives the opportunity to cultivate hope and confidence and to realise and value the affection of really helpful friends.

Pr. ☽ ⊼ ☉. This direction causes a *discontented,* uncertain attitude towards things which previously were tolerated. Objections arise about these which result in irritability and little is born from people who were hardly noticed before.

Pr. ☽ ☍ ☉ gives a tendency to *extravagant actions,* to put forward and defend untenable hypotheses and to risk imprudent speculations.

One should take heed to check oneself as much as possible in these matters during this direction, not to act impulsively or carelessly and to take no risky trips, before accurately investigating the soundness of possible vehicles (if one can do this oneself as is e.g. the case with a bicycle, motorcar etc.) One should be careful of one's health, especially avoiding fever and catching colds, as the lungs are more than usually sensitive to inflammation; this holds especially good if the opposition takes place in ♊. A warning must be given against excessive physical exertion, the eyes especially should be saved.

Difficulties in public work may be expected, it seems better to avoid all public actions. *Conduct can hardly be sufficiently cautious and diplomatic.*

This direction brings *separation,* an old tie is broken and a sad mood follows. Bereavements will make a deep impression; thoughts about the death of well-known people, and one's own attitude towards death will often be prominent. Some loss will probably be sustained, about which one will be more at peace later when a broader view has been gained than at first seemed possible.

One should cultivate a calm, serious trustful attitude to life; then a stronger inner life will be built up from the lessons of adversity; then *loss* will turn into *gain.*

Pr. ☽ ♂ ☽. An opportunity will arise to *come more into the foreground,* one gets a chance to express one's feelings, to serve others freely. Gradually "limitations" will be less felt.

Pr. ☽ ⊻ ☽. This gives an inclination to make *new plans,* although it will still be hard to carry them out satisfactorily. One seriously will consider what attitude to adopt in the world which has the greatest chance of success.

Pr. ☽ ✳ ☽. This influence brings *new emotions* and consequently also new ideas, particularly concerning the arrangements of a house, furniture and dress. There is a great desire to *order, regulate,* to make practical use of things deemed useful for the future; thus providing a sound basis for further constructive work. During this time contact will be made with a sensitive person with lofty ideas concerning life, with whom one likes to talk about religious experiences.

Pr. ☽ □ ☽ easily leads to *misunderstanding with a female friend.* A certain jealousy between two feminine acquaintances will affect the feelings unpleasantly. One will overcome the opposition by fighting with the conviction that the battle will contribute to the development of one's own powers. "Without wind and storm, water would stagnate and become foul, turbid." One should take heed lest passion lead him to make the same mistake with which he blames others.

Pr. ☽ △ ☽. This direction favours growth — therefore *health* — and gives also much joy of life. Things are done most willingly for the sake of another. To help others, to cooperate in bringing about a desired end — or at least to bring it nearer for the time being — will give much satisfaction.

This direction teaches one to distinguish clearly between reality and unreality, it will increase the *love of enterprise* and render practical, business-like. This opens the way to develop self-consciousness and promises much from one's own occupation, to which one is devoted, probably in imitation of some one who is adored and admired. It will be well to profit as much as possible by this influence which leads to greater *self-confidence* and to retain faith in the final victory.

Pr. ☽ ⊼ ☽. All kinds of *mental difficulties* will obstruct friendly relations. One should be careful lest too resolute a way of saying or acting give rise to unpleasant relations. There is a tendency to speculative action which cannot lead to the favourable results one should expect. It is there-fore advisable, during the action of this direction to make good use of intellectual critical faculties in order to be saved from great disappointments.

Pr. ☽ ☌ ☽. This is an *unfavourable direction* giving rise to a tendency to judge rashly and superficially, to allow oneself to be guided by vague feelings. *Mistakes* will easily be made, whilst there is much likelihood of breaking or spoiling something through clumsiness e. g. through an inkstain about which one will feel sorry for long. Also an accident may lead to some one else suffering an unpleasant loss.

Pr. ☽ ♂ ☿. This period will be characterised by a certain *business spirit* and gives a particular aptitude for valuing goods. There is a great liking for real estate, fields, houses — the work of a solicitor.

Practical, businesslike element becomes more pronounced, renders diligent and methodical, and will bring a time in which it will be especially easy to work accurately which among other things will benefit the social position. An active mind and personal exertion promise success; friendly discussion will be pleasant, little windfalls in business and correspondence may be expected. The way in which a subject is defended will be sympathetic and lead to a rapprochement. This is a splendid opportunity to plan a journey, write a book, or extend one's business connections etc.

Pr. ☽ ⩖ ☿. Rapid thought and active observation enable work to be done with great assiduity and satisfaction. This will be a time of many good opportunities of which one should make good use. With this direction good help and advice from friends or sympathisers and people in a high position may be expected. If through other influences one should come into contact with spiritual phenomena, this ☽-☿ direction will cause one to preserve enough critical sense to regard these neutrally and only to accept as true those things which without prejudice must logically be acknowledged to be so.

Intellect will be keener, more alert than usual. More correspondence will be carried on, a journey will be undertaken. Opinions of men and things will be reliable and may be made use of productively; sound judgment will enable various enterprises to prosper.

Pr. ☽ ⚹ ☿. This direction acts favourably on *mental capacities,* it renders clever, observant. It will be a favourable time for study, for making and carying out a plan that is sure to meet with success from a business point of view. Business negotiations with an honourable contractor will be carried on to their mutual satisfaction. A man of business will be pleased to make use of the advice offered. His appreciation will have a very favourable influence on the native's social position.

The native has fixed opinions, not likely to be easily influenced or altered. This direction is favourable for correspondence, and makes for quick and accurate observation, broadens the outlook on various conditions of life and awakes the desire to be practical and businesslike in everything. In conversation he will like to point out the results of experimental science, and he shows great respect for the knowledge of facts.

Pr. ☽ □ ☿. During this position caution is advisable in ☿'s sphere (commerce, travelling, administration). Subordinates should be most carefully watched and instructions be very clearly and calmly worded, since there is a great probability of *misunderstanding,* which will entail *sleepless nights.* One should keep as calm as possible and be a great deal in the open air, so that the nervous system may suffer as little as possible from the unpleasant consequences of this inharmonious direction. *Timely accuracy* may help to raise one above the nervous, uncertain effects which this direction otherwise has. This time will also influence home life, which will not be "rosy"; unpleasant *correspondence* with some one who is otherwise attached will be of brief duration. Some expressions seem somewhat rash, incautious. It is not a favourable time for correspondence about a difference of opinion, in fact all disputes will be bad for the nervous system. The best thing will be to try and regard contrasting opinions as poles of a higher unity and to appreciate them as such. *"True love bears with what is unbearable."* (Robertson.)

It will be difficult to have a right opinion of people and things; much opposition occurs which can only be overcome by ignoring it. Fighting it simply increases the trouble and makes one rebel against the feeling of being limited by circumstances. During this time it is best to take regularly sufficient physical rest and to find peace by keeping only worthy ideals before one and meditating on them. One should apply oneself to consciously serving ideas of Truth and Peace.

Pr. ☽ △ ☿. Work will go very smoothly, it will be a joy to study and to talk about what has been studied. There is great interest in the study of nature in relation to cosmic laws. One will be spell-bound by the beauty of cosmic happenings and their subjection to law — especially if ♀ is also playing a favourable part in this direction. Time given to these studies will not be regretted.

Further this direction renders resourceful, favours the invention of systems, methods, instruments for work. *There is great versatility of interest.* Work will always be a pleasure, and one will complain of lack of time. If ☿ is placed in 8 psycho-analytical research will especially attract attention; if in 3 literature and education, etc.

This direction bestows an increase of mental harmony through conversations with a strong, impressive logical personality. The native likes to exchange views with an intellectual person, and as this direction renders attentive and cautious it will easy come to him to concentrate and to express his thoughts. His mind is clear, active, accurate, investigatory; and does not only give momentary success but also the possibility of experiences by which spiritual progress may be made and which are less favourable for the after life.

Pr. ☽ ⊼ ☿. This influence will make it difficult to *weigh* one's words sufficiently *beforehand*. Mind and mood will become *critical* and this will increase according as Mercury receives more aspects in the nativity.

Pr. ☽ 8 ☿. This causes a great inclination to *disputes,* it makes sarcastic, harsh at times and continually in *opposition.* There is a desire to overtrump others, to be one too many for them and to throw obstacles in their way. Although the mentality is active, one should attempt to consider things in a businesslike way before acting, for during this influence one is restless, nervous, rather undecided, troublesome, exacting, not easily satisfied. It is hard to be fair to subordinates, and this causes a nervous irritability in one's environment.

☽ ☌ ♀. The feeling is pleasantly affected by this direction. *Artistic inspirations* assert themselves, intellectual and artistic talents get an opportunity of developing. Much enjoyment will be found in the pure and beautiful; closer study of the fine arts will prove to be of great influence on the further life. There is a great *love of nature* and much liking for walks in beautiful surroundings, by the side of ponds, in woods, in sunny restful spots where an intense contentment will fill the heart. Interest lies chiefly in things related to pleasure, also for others. It is a pleasant time for travelling, for animated social life and for forming new friendships. Circumstances will lead to a bond of friendship being drawn closer with someone who fulfils the spiritual requirements; and in course of time this relation will also prove to be financially favourable. Successful endeavours of a philanthropical kind may be expected.

☽ ⊻ ♀. A friendly relation will make the life of feeling more important. The desire for something lasting, beautiful in life grows, but one doubts the possibility of its realisation. This direction often gives an opportunity of making one's home more comfortable by buying objects of beauty, or of rendering life more valuable by the acquisition of new theories. Feeling will endeavour to express itself more consciously; congenial people, beauty and joy are sought. To an artist this will be a time of renewal of inspiration.

Pr. ☽ ✶ ♀. Feelings of love seek to express themselves by *devotion* and *helpfulness;* to have given pleasure to another causes great satisfaction. Friendly meetings will be held in surroundings different from those in which one had hitherto moved.

This direction renders sensitive, sympathetic, beloved and promises an *agreeable time.* Artistic performances, art-galleries etc., are enjoyed. One will try to find an artistic circle in which to move and shops with beautiful objects of art are very attractive. Attraction to the *other sex* will be *strengthened,* but a tendency to *flirt* will also assert itself.

Pr. ☽ □ ♀. This will give rise to difficulties with respect to the houses of which in the nativity ♀ is the ruler (e. g. in 2 with regard to finance, in 10 to profession, in 7 to marriage and partnership etc.). There is lack of insight and confidence in the partner's way of living and aims, which causes all kinds of disappointments, miscalculations in business, arouses opposition from the environment and from society in general. Plans will arise aiming at a complete change of direction. A certain amount of irritability causes misunderstanding and estrangement in friendship, and a conflict in domestic and financial matters may be expected.

Pr. ☽ △ ♀ brings a time of much love, helpfulness, disposition to sacrifice. This influence brings contact with someone in whose vicinity one likes to linger, with whom one likes to exchange views, and whom one likes to tend with great devotion. All this gives a pleasant, cheerful mood, makes for good temper and more interest in art than usual. One can often indulge in the desire for pleasure; much progress may be made in one of the fine arts — if the rest of the horoscope cooperates — arousing appreciation and affection from others. "Art reveals friends".

Happiness and good fortune may be had so to say for the asking. Life will be viewed more cheerfully and optimistically; a happy time may also be expected in *family life*. Business, enterprises thrive and on various sides the happiness experienced will be shared. If the 3rd or 9th house play a part in it, after a pleasant journey there will be an agreeable correspondence with one's former travelling companions.

Pr. ☽ ⊼ ♀. This brings an *element of distrust* in a friendly relation. On the other hand there is a tendency to rely on friendships which do not come up to the expectations cherished. Affection and doubt will each in turn be pre-eminent. One should strive to keep feelings as pure as possible. A longing for relaxation, for leisure manifests, but is immediately followed by misgivings and doubts whether the time should not be spent to more purpose. Naturally by so doing little is achieved.

Pr. ☽ 8 ♀. This direction influences feeling, it brings a revolution in the affections; a preference for something or somebody different from that which was felt before. If the direction occurs in 10—4 there is a possibility of change of abode or work, in 1—7 disappointments in personal affections may be expected etc. The circumstances relating to this should be regarded soberly and an eye should be kept upon the future. This direction brings separation, loss, disappointment in one's feelings and therefore requires special self-control. The income will be damaged by the jealous behaviour and extravagance of a woman.

Pr. ☽ ♂ ♂. This causes an *active, impulsive way of acting*. Questions concerning sexual life demand an answer, physical passion is stimulated. But as the spiritual faculties also receive powerful impulses it will be a time during which, by sublimating the lower tendencies, such spiritual and mental faculties may be built up as will in later life give the demeanour a most pronounced character.

This direction enhances energy, the magnetic radiation also grows stronger, perseverance and self-reliance increase. ♂ promotes courage and joy of life — and this attitude will make for success and social well-being.

During this time, all *overexertion* must be avoided, the higher spiritual capacities should suffuse the physical impulses and social enterprises with their purifying strength. Recklessness or impatience are altogether wrong.

Pr. ☽ ⊻ ♂. This strengthens the inclination to talk about something which one thinks ought to be set right. But for the time one will go no further than planning and *scheming,* the opportunity of carrying it out will only come later. A firm resolution is taken to keep to regular habits, to work in an orderly way, neatly, methodically and this is actually carried out.

This direction augments energy, strengthens the power of resistance, renders resolute, less doubtful than usual, there is more desire to become conspicuous; one should take heed not to allow lower tendencies to dominate reason; one should *remain reasonable* and not indulge in antipathy against people or things. Physical strength and the wish for action increase; there is great inclination to travel in order to broaden one's consciousness and knowledge — especially if the 9th house plays a part in it — but it will be wise to guard against too much exertion.

Pr. ☽ ✳ ♂. This direction brings activity of thought, makes *courageous,* and increases one's *self-reliance,* urges one to take the *initiative* and *lead,* and to be of service to others by word and deed. It is favourable for travelling, for bringing changes into less pleasant circumstances and for diligent work. This is a good time for starting a new work, to instal oneself and get affairs set right. The public will approve of energetic, sound enterprises; also a rather speculative matter will be considered which promises well.

Pr. ☽ □ ♂ renders *inclined to dispute.* Those whose manner is somewhat rough, materialistic and martial will provoke others. One should try to keep as calm as possible and not be mastered by vexations, for this direction tends to reckless action, trouble with a superior from which an uncertain position arises. It will be well during this time to avoid intercourse with those who are superficial, materialistic and critically inclined, to try and stand above conflicting opinions, to suffer this influence to pass without any wilful excitement. This direction brings new, difficult problems, according to the nature of the houses involved in it. One will be more than usually inclined to press one's own limited opinions on to others and take too little notice of each individual disposition. There is a tendency to exaggeration and to pass judgment too rashly. Some work once started enthusiastically will end in disappointment which induces a manner that is intractable, thoughtless and rebellious.

If, however, preceding harmonious directions have enabled one to acquire an inner attitude of serenity, peace and trust, this positive power will greatly help to overcome the temporary opposition. Walks in nature, amidst flowers and birds, are far better during this time than spontaneous actions or exciting talk. Only an *inwardly balanced* attitude will prevent indispositions caused by infections and attended by fever. All quarrels and overstrain should be avoided. One should take care to purify the blood, for example by a vegetarian diet, lemon juice etc., because there is a danger of illness of an inflammatory nature with feverish symptoms.

Pr. ☽ △ ♂. This constellation gives devoted energy, noble courage, and an inner trust making for the success of all enterprises. Former schemes devised, (that is when there was a weaker ☽-♂ direction) and plans discussed with others, will now meet with success. If the nativity falls into line, this progressive position might bring an inheritance, but only if one of the two is placed in 8 or is its ruler. It is a favourable time for cooperation and promotion, making propaganda for some association.

This direction endows with the strength necessary to keep in bounds other, unfavourable influences, it increases the courage to life and brings the firm resolve not to be discouraged should difficult circumstances arise. One will be strong enough not to yield to moods of discontent but — at any rate for the time being — keep one's eyes fixed on the aim of work and life.

Pr. ☽ ⊼ ♂. This direction promotes the desire to be actively employed, to live and work for an ideal. There will be a good understanding with one's subordinates even resembling friendship. But this relation will prove in fact to be shortlived; the cooperation which was at first expected will not be forthcoming. During the action of this direction it is advisable not to be provoked and not to get excited at disappointment. It is best simply to take things as they are.

Pr. ☽ ☍ ♂. It will be difficult to control oneself when opposed either really or in fancy. Before this time one should do well to take much exercise in the open air but not too fatiguing, in order to keep the blood pure and thus prevent the unpleasant consequences of this direction which in addition to conflicts of soul are often externalised as inflammatory abcesses. Some clumsy handling of fire is likely; subordinates, inmates of the house etc. should be warned to be careful in this respect.

Pr. ☽ ♂ ♃. This direction will give a far *more optimistic* outlook on life and bring into contact with a cheerful person. This time is very favourable for all enterprises both social and financial. Everything which is striven for in the spirit of love will meet with success; many good opportunities for development will arise. Difficulties brought by life will be regarded in a new light and be conquered; cheerful, energetic people will render aid most willingly. The means used to reach a certain aim will be successful. This is a time during which it is a joy to live, during which both to give and to receive will be blessed.

Pr. ☽ ⊼ ♃, especially if the 3rd or 9th house is concerned in it, will lead to discussions about *propaganda for new principles of life,* also to spreading articles or books among seekers or those who doubt. This is a rather *weak* direction, and therefore will not lead further than to the making of various plans, which are discussed with congenial people, and corresponded about; direct results do not follow. It will be easier to bring oneself into harmonious circumstances if one has a good understanding with others.

This influence is also good for financial affairs, gives a feeling of wealth, i.e. having sufficient for oneself; renders contented, even if others do not consider the fortune to be of much account.

Intercourse with a religiously inclined friend and a journey will do much good inwardly.

Pr. ☽ ⚹ ♃ indicates that there will be much reason to feel uplifted and strengthens the element of confidence given by religion and philosophical thought. One likes to exchange views about the problems of life with cheery energetic people; an aesthetic expression of one's emotions is sought; there is a tendency to somewhat romantic-philanthropic enterprises. Without looking for a reward nothing is better liked than to help the weak and suffering.

This direction strengthens one's *self-consciousness* and gives also much influence for good on others. Consequently pleasant friendly relations are entered into, and one gets a chance of being of service in divers ways to various greatly respected personalities by which one rises in their esteem.

Pr. ☽ ☐ ♃. This direction causes an *indifferent, extravagant, careless attitude* both in inner and outward matters. There is danger of deception through being too trustful and it will therefore during this time be wise to avoid all intercourse with those who are not in all respects reliable and attached. One should take no notice of slander and false accusations. If ♃ is placed in 6 or is its ruler, difficulties with domestics will arise; one should take care not to talk about intimate affairs and also not behave arrogantly. Business should be dealt with in a business-like manner; for there is much probability of loss in financial matters. *Do not throw good money after bad,* do not undertake things that have no sound foundation, "*do not build on sand!*"

This time is also unfavourable for domestic circumstances and intercourse with others. Change of abode is not desirable. One should follow a vegetarian diet, be temperate and limit oneself in all respects.

Pr. ☽ △ ♃. *This is one of the most favourable directions,* it brings *spiritual* and *social* progress. On all sides fortune smiles, the emotional life can develop to the well-being of all concerned. Misgivings, isolation, criticism — according to the nature of the nativity — disappear before a growing faith in the guidance of God, whilst this knowledge may also be gained by study, for instance of astrology. A revival of moral and physical power may be experienced.

Some plan that was conceived in former years and since long time had been relegated to the shelf of vain hopes, bids fair to become successful. But it will be necessary to have kept faith in that ideal, in times when a pessimistic mood strove to prevail. A taste for philosophical thought increases and this arouses a desire to stand for what is acknowledged to be right and true.

This direction is favourable for a long journey. If ♃ is in 2, the fortune is concerned, also power and both thrive i.e. financial profit and a higher self-realisation may be expected. New connections are made with strong, cheerful people and much help will be experienced.

This is a fortunate time generally, making for increase of energy and a large inflow of "*prana*" and therefore a healthier condition of body and soul.

This particularly fine direction may be put to better use by "tuning" oneself for it beforehand and by keeping that atmosphere of devotion and joy as long as possible afterwards.

Pr. ☽ ⚻ ♃. This will bring *desillusion* with regard to the houses concerned. During this time it will be difficult to form a right opinion of people and things with whom one comes into contact and consequently disappointments are sure to follow. It is advisable to take a somewhat passive expectant attitude, not to allow feelings to assert themselves too much, but to observe things with logical discrimination; not to start anything that may lead to discord and in no wise to sign a contract or in any other way to bind oneself.

This direction will cause some doubt, arouse misgivings. The taking of regular walks and periods of rest, the reading of ethical-uplifting books will prove to be of much help during this somewhat uncertain nervous mood.

Pr. ☽ ☍ ♃ urges care whilst travelling, and special heed to health. During this time one is indifferent to material possessions, reckless, going to extremes and consequently is likely to get into trouble. Words and deeds will be misunderstood. Anything that might lead to legal proceedings should be avoided. Difficulties may arise in solving a legal problem. This aspect inclines to act rather irresponsibly in order to hide momentary indecision or ignorance. "Look before you leap" is a warning which should be kept well in mind especially during that time, because in the long run peace cannot be found where there are rash decisions and insufficiently considered words. If at birth ♃ is placed harmoniously, sufficient self-control to face the temptations will prove to be present. Trouble with relatives and business friends may be expected under this direction; connected with this disputes about religion will do more harm to the nervous system than one can stand. One should beware of being confidential or too intimate with acquaintances who are not quite trustworthy.

The liver will make itself felt; attacks of rheumatism may be expected. Act with *moderation* in all things!

Pr. ☽ ☌ ♄. This has a depressing influence on the feelings, the power of growth and therefore also on *health.* One should take heed not to catch cold. If ♄ is placed in a mutable sign there will be a tendency to rheumatism and tuberculosis; in a cardinal sign ♄ will cause the activity of the stomach to be slack and one should masticate one's food well (Fletcherise). Colds in the head, deafness, kidney disease often occur. One should always see to dry and warm clothing.

Some disappointment will be experienced, (presumably in monetary matters) which may be regarded as temporary. Not many cheerful things may be expected to happen, most satisfaction will be got from the faithful performance of duty. One should try to tune oneself as peaceable as possible through rest and meditation on uplifting books.

Pr. ☽ ⊻ ♄. The sense of responsibility and of duty will gradually take deeper root. The relation of the ☽ to ♄ renders earnest, calm, careful, economical, help one to realise that it is not desirable to allow spontaneous emotions to gain the mastery. This direction causes serious and thoughtful resignation to life's circumstances. Older people will show their high opinion. A sensible, older counsellor will assist the person concerned.

Pr. ☽ ✱ ♄. This influence makes well-balanced and very accurate, the sense of responsibility and of duty are prominent and arouse the sympathy of a more conservative looker-on, an older superior will think highly of the dutiful work done and be willing to second his promotion. This leads to a peaceful, controlled, purposeful mood which gives also more confidence in one's social position. One will gladly take upon oneself the care of an older relation or congenial person and much appreciation will be gained by this. Some doubt which is still felt about the future — possibly also about life beyond the grave — will be removed by this influence. There is a possibility of setting right by means of quiet meditation (♄) certain disappointed hopes and of understanding seeming contradictions as necessary elements for inner (♄) growth (☽). This direction gives satisfaction from strenuous, persevering work, whilst it renders ready to persist in a direction proved right by experience and to recognise sobriety of life as a means of development.

One may count on the help and affection of an older friend.

Pr. ☽ □ ♄. This will be a time of depression, critical and anxious in domestic matters. Financial deceptions may be expected, disappointments in old acquaintances. One should beware of catching cold, rheumatism and sciatica. If the pr. ☽ moves through the 8th house, some death will occur that will bring about a change in environment and cause a feeling of loneliness. Pessimistic views of life predominate, thoughts of illness and death occupy the mind. This earth is called indeed a vale of tears.

It is a time of *many temptations. Conscience* is particularly sensitive and admonishes to *self-examination*. There is a greater tendency to "throw up the sponge" than to persevere, but this mood should not be indulged in, since perseverance alone leads to success.

Pr. ☽ △ ♄. This direction gives steadfastness and persistance and renders fit for serious, practical work, e.g. cooperating in a solid social institution. It promotes accurate fancy — from the business point of view — among other things correct valuation of building plots, interest in the building of houses etc. If ♄ is placed in 2 or is the ruler of the 2nd house, this direction will contribute to the formation of a *sound financial basis*. It will be a matter of great satisfaction to invest money out of one's own earnings in some well-known firm and to look back upon results hitherto achieved.

After hard struggle some talent will become open to development which before was probably merely latent. The feeling (☽) of being at last able to be oneself (♄) to develop according to one's own ideal, will give great satisfaction, although a tremendous effort is required. Success may be expected of everything done with persistence, enthusiasm and fidelity. *Lasting sympathy* will be obtained from an older person, attracted by the serious attitude to life.

This direction provides a fixed position in which one will be assured of the necessities of life, so that daily duties will be performed faithfully and without hesitation. The ♄-influence, however, cannot be called altogether fortunate, the more is the pity. Work will be done from a sense of duty rather than out of the love of it.

Pr. ☽ ⊼ ♄ causes *misgivings* to arise, *regrets* for past action of which at the time one approved. The frame of mind threatens to become *dismal* and health is not all one could wish. This constellation renders troubled about the future and fixes attention more than usual on saving. It is better not to have too many irons in the fire. All difficulties would be borne better if one realised that this time will only be a passing cloud. Seriously meant good projects may contribute much to deepen life.

Pr. ☽ ☍ ♄. Under this direction it will be difficult to keep up one's courage. There will probably be anxiety about one's condition of health, the death of an old friend. One should especially beware of *gloomy moods,* of catching colds and all physical over-exertion. Under this direction the vital power will diminish and one will feel *depressed, disappointed* and *listless.* The conviction that *there is a silver lining to every cloud,* and times of rain will be followed by sunshine, will help to overome this difficult period and prevent energy from flagging too much.

The kidneys are the sensitive part if the direction takes place in ♈-♎; in ♋ it is the stomach, in the mutable signs the lungs or the muscles (rheumatism) etc. A *serious but trustful* way of living is advisable.

Pr. ☽ ☌ ♅. Old conceptions are pushed aside, *fresh ideas* take their place and the newly acquired knowledge is imparted to others. *Unexpected changes* will take place and ways of looking at things which were formerly rejected will be aroused by sudden, peculiar experiences.

The mind is inventive, memory and the imagination very lively; there is a tendency to sarcasm. Quite new outlooks — *inspirations* — may improve a position quite suddenly.

Pr. ☽ ⊻ ♅. Consciousness obtains the opportunity to widen, to lift itself to a higher level, to attain *new ideas.* The actions are well considered; intuition and inventions give calm pleasure. Theosophical and astrological thoughts become more attractive. This direction will bring unexpected profit, also change of circumstances. The native will probably become *acquainted with an original person;* and if the 3rd or 9th house is connected with it there will very likely be a journey, which will modify the material and the mental life. An invention will keep the mind occupied.

Pr. ☽ ✱ ♅. This direction strengthens interest in *occult study* and brings new conclusions, gives a clearer understanding of life's school and its difficulties. Some one whom most people consider eccentric, who has theosophy etc. as a hobby will be of much help and support in his contemplations. It is in every way a pleasant time for widening the sphere of thought. The real will quickly and intuitively be distinguished from the unreal, new thoughts will arise as inventions. The native will like to discuss astrological and kindred subjects with congenial spirits, interesting ideas will be propounded, *clarity of spirit* and *inventiveness* will be coupled to *seriousness* and *perseverance.* This direction brings an unexpected happy occurence in friendly relation to a spiritually eminent personality whose thoughts will be of much influence to the native's further life.

Pr. ☽ □ ♅ makes *impulsive in action and speech;* inclined to say more than one can answer for, and fly off at a tangent, before the consequences are well considered. Wellmeant words may be taken in quite a wrong spirit. Eccentric actions, incomprehensible to others may lead to alienation. It is advisable not to allow oneself to be tempted to disputes but rather to retire and keep the nervous system *as quiet as possible.*

A critical attitude will be the cause of a — probably temporary — materialistic view of life; the native is rather *ill-tempered* and *irritable.* By being provoked in small things, the larger ones are lost sight of. Life gives unexpectedly new forms, which always contain new meanings. There is danger of some *accident* or an unexpected, unfortunate occurrence which will leave a deep impression.

This ♅ affliction inclines to unpremeditated action, which will be regretted later.

Pr. ☽ △ ♅. As ♅ is the planet that rouses new ideas, makes original and inventive, its contact with the "sensitive" ☽ causes unconscious knowledge — knowledge gained formerly, in former lives — to appear. The intuition is pure; it will be easy to scheme plans and find means to carry them out. Congenial people will cooperate and give unasked for their benevolent criticism of which good use may be made. Success in material matters may be expected, especially through the friendship of an uncommonly originally inclined person. It is a direction under which in a certain sense may be reaped what was sown in former, more difficult times. What is now undertaken, after being well-considered will succeed and carry fruit for years to come.

There is more faith again in the connection of the personal life and the life of the Macrocosmos; the metaphysical theses sensed will also be recognised in the scientific and occult spheres and interest in astrology especially will much increase.

Ideas about life beyond will become clearer and strengthen the belief in the presence of metaphysical worlds. This influence leads to the acquisition of insight into occult planes, the worlds of causes.

Pr. ☽ ⊼ ♅. It will be difficult to retain one's faith in occultism, astrology etc. Various criticisms by others of these subjects must be worked out, and it will be rather difficult to affix the true value to them.

The native is inclined to *impulsive attempts at reform* and to somewhat *risky actions.* During this direction more than at other times it is desirable not to throw over old things before one has the certainty that the new ones are as sound and reliable. Attempt only that which you can do. It is safer not to risk much, than to set about boldly and thoughtlessly.

Pr. ☽ ☍ ♅ makes very touchy; many troubles may be expected in one's affections. The retiring, quite unexpectedly, of a partner, friend, congenial spirit, or the exposure of a much admired person will bring such an eye-opener as may easily give rise to a *cynical mood.* It will be best during this direction to retire modestly as much as possible, not to ask much of oneself, to try and serve one's neighbours and in silence remain faithful to Truth, Love and Beauty. One should try and limit oneself and confine oneself to the nearest duties, without interfering with others.

"In der Beschränkung zeigt sich der Meister" (The master shows himself in limitation.) (Goethe).

Pr. ☽ ☌ ♆. Uncommon metaphysical experiences will bring an agreeable time of a *calm serene attitude* to material circumstances. It would however be good not to allow oneself to undergo these experiences too passively, but rather to use one's intellect and analyse logically the super-physical things experienced in dream-state. And this not in order merely to weigh these experiences critically, but to obtain from them knowledge analogous to scientific research of higher states of consciousness.

The native likes to move in a mystical atmosphere, enjoying harmony of feeling and art. The acquaintance of romantic, peculiar people may be expected. Life is regarded *poetically,* he feels withdrawn from all earthly cares, happy in the enjoyment of affection and music. All through life the experiences of this time will be kept in pleasant memory.

Pr. ☽ ⊻ ♆. The inner necessity for art will be very strong here and is coupled with the desire to study and write about these things. Peculiar artistic taste will manifest, vague inspirations occur which will in part be retained, partly thrown over later. The doubting, critical element constantly asserts itself. This influence renders imaginative, sensitive to peculiar impressions, able to psychometrise. Some experiments will draw the attention of the native's own circle of friends, a meeting will take place with an extraordinarily talented person, religiously mystically inclined whose ideas will remain a great influence in life. He would do well to keep unexplained experiences of sensations controlled by his brain and not to lose himself in them.

Pr. ☽ ⚹ ♆ gives an interest in metaphysical problems, makes *poetic,* fond of being in a mystically dreamy mood of *intimate beauty.* The stronger the sense of unity the more powerful the effect of that which, without one's own cooperation, constantly helps to build that unity. This influence makes artistic, leads to better comprehension of the syntheses of seeming opposites, inclines to *peacefulness.* It is a time of remarkable dreams. probably prophetic mystical religious subjects are studied in order later to be able to speak about them. New ideas of friends with a special spiritual nature will help to increase interest in spiritualistic phenomena which leads to the acquaintance of a mystically inclined person. Consciousness will be extended in a remarkable way by intuitive impressions. It is a time during which one feels one's own personal life to be enriched.

Pr. ☽ □ ♆. During this direction one should beware of too great communicativeness, seeing that expectations turn out differently from what was first supposed. This is a time in which much accurate reflection is necessary in order to distinguish the true from the false. There will be disappointments in the direction from which excessively high expectations have been cherished. Personal enterprises are vaguely idealised rather than considered in a businesslike way. It renders somewhat queer, self-indulgent; there is danger of *slander* and one should beware of *infections,* especially of lungs and kidneys. The taking of alcoholic drinks, narcotics and tobacco should be avoided, however much others may incite thereto.

This direction gives a possibility of becoming the victim of deceit or theft. One will not receive all one counts on, and be disappointed in one's debtors. In this time it would be better to postpone any journey one may have proposed. Goods sent to or from the native should be thoroughly insured. It will be well to be more than ordinarily active in administrative work, also to control feelings and affections by reason and so find out in *quiet observation* whether there is anything dishonest or insincere about their aim. One should be careful when confiding in people, because others will easily make use of information genuinely given. The native needs a harmonious, healthy environment, where his somewhat nervous mood may come to rest. He should also refrain from meditating on super-physical things, to which he is much inclined, and spend much time in the open air. During this period a somewhat *ascetic* way of living will be the best surety that this difficult time will bring a *deepening of consciousness* and an *inner experience of religion* which may be of great help through the rest of life.

Pr. ☽ △ ♆ will quicken the feelings and lead to experience of more ideal conditions. A heavenly dreamworld — as in a narcotic state — is considered possible as a dwelling in perpetual bliss. The native's inclination to seclusion is strengthened. His interest in modern art will increase. He will form a friendship with a talented, artistic, mystically-religious person, a man of a specially spiritual nature. Thoughts on the existence of a metaphysical world are prominent. If ♆ is placed in 2, or 8, or if the ☽ moves through 2 or 8 there is a possibility of receiving a legacy or money for which one has not worked or exerted one's brain powers. This inheritance may also be experienced in a more immaterial way, especially if at the same time a strong harmonious aspect to ♅ is active in the higher regions of consciousness. Presentiments will be strong; there is a great sensitivity to the moods of the environment. Development of *psychism* becomes possible.

There will be a possibility of helping some one with very uncommon experiences of life. A high ideal stimulates to work for the upliftment of those socially worse off.

Pr. ☽ ⊼ ♆. This direction may bring discord in connection with a difference of taste about an article of art or a structure, etc. One had best look upon the matter from a humorous point of view, but of course not provoke others by so doing.

Pr. ☽ 8 ♆. This direction leads to the *breaking of unusual connections*. The native must be on his guard in giving his confidence, for in this time it is easily given to some one who abuses it. All actions should be well considered and be reasonable; he should not indulge in sentimental feelings or whims. A financial disappointment may be expected, also ingratitude from people one has helped spontaneously for idealistic considerations. In administration one should be more than usually *attentive,* because mistakes are apt to slip in during this time, which may bring about disadvantageous effect. In sleep, in dreams phantasies arise which the native will wrongly regard as prophetic and will therefore meditate on them later.

Great likelihood exists of suggesting wrong ideas to oneself which may cause a discontented mood. One is also inclined to discuss these experiences, especially with women. It is much better to *experience,* to *see* and to *keep silent.* A death may make a deep impression. It is a difficult time in which to govern one's feelings and it brings alienation from those with whom one used to be most intimate, whilst the sorrow one feels will be expressed by a kind of *indifference,* a tendency to be easy-going.

Pr. ☽ ☌, ⚹ ⊕ will cause a *happy and contented feeling.* The conviction will take hold that much success may be found in the direction of which one is most fond and for which one has the greatest capacity. One feels oneself the right man in the right place. This direction also strengthens the longing for harmonious, simple domesticity, especially in 4. "There is nothing more beautiful on this earth than a home full of happiness and peace".

Pr. ☽ □, ☍ ⊕. A disappointment through *misunderstanding,* a misrepresentation of good intentions will occur in a direction in which one has great confidence. Expectations, soaring too high, will fall through. It will be advisable in this time to lean more on practical considerations than to build *castles in the air.* One should more than ever have a mindful eye on fellow-workers and dependents, making them attend to their duty and doing so oneself.

Pr. ☽ △ ⊕. This will have a favourable effect on all matters concerning the house in which the ⊕ is posited. It gives a pleasant, harmonious feeling and enables the native to value works of art. New plans will be schemed which promise well for the future, both materially and ideally. Under this direction the native is very likely to enter into some connection of an emotional nature.

Directions of Mercury (☿) [1]).

Pr. ☿ ☌, ⚹, △ ♀. A time during which many a cosy hour will be spent with acquaintances where instructive, educational conversations will be held. These directions are characterised by *cheerful activity,* by sensible and striking remarks. They give a certain ease of intercourse, an unconstraint which will sometimes make it difficult to draw the line between superficial sympathy and stronger personal affection. A certain artisticity will cause attraction for the other sex. There is much love of travelling, the outlook may widen in an interesting way.

Pr. ☿ □, ☍ ♀. These directions cause a conflict between affection and reasonable insight. Friends of a refined taste and sensitive nature will express *criticisms* which rather hurt. It will be difficult to achieve success and the native is inclined to *disputes,* in which his motives and aims will

1) Directions of ☿ with the ☉-radix and the ☽-radix can be judged as directions of the ☉ and the ☽ with ☿-radix.

not be rightly valued. During this time, it is desirable to avoid everyone who does not quite answer to one's own ideal.

Pr. ☿, ⚹, △ ♂. These directions render extremely keen (♂) witted (☿), diligent, enterprising, practical and optimistic. So they will be favourable for the extension of one's business, the making of contracts and compacts. The buying of goods, advertising them, and selling them at a profit will be successful, correspondence will go smoothly, in short there is an extraordinary clarity of mind. Should the native be an artist, during this time he will go in for etching or engraving.

There is just then a special attitude for all kinds of manual work, also a desire to write and courage is found to set unjust things and impure relations right by the power of one's pen. It is a favourable time for *social work,* especially *educational* and for interpreting the rights and duties of the individual by means of social institutions.

Pr. ☿ ☌, □ ☍ ♂. These directions render *irritable,* touchy, and inclines to make mountains out of molehills. They lead to all kinds of illusionary ideas, make rash and passionate. There is a great desire to be one too many for people and in reaction one will suffer from the sly practices of others. These directions are not conducive to honest dealing. It will be advisable to concentrate in quiet surroundings on some scheme so that its intuitively sensed success may not be spoiled by rash action. To be contented, and leave others free, not exacting too much from them but rather to exert oneself for their welfare and lend them a hand in another department than the one about which there is trouble, will bring satisfaction and be conducive to health. Movement in the open air should not be omitted in order to strengthen the body and maintain it in health.

Such a direction is especially unfavourable in mutable signs, in those cases one should beware of accidents and of affections of the lungs.

Pr. ☿ ☌, ⚹, △ ♃. These directions render cheerful, honest, *tolerant, optimistic.* They give true inner peace. In all kinds of things judgment is very good; it is a beneficial time. Success may be expected in all enterprises. A reliable, religious friend will be willing to cooperate to better one's position. Many plans for the future will be schemed and considered, all of which are promising. It is a period for successful study, for deepening and widening one's insight.

Pr. ☿ □, ☍ ♃. These directions cause a *conflict between the higher and lower mentality.* The native is *vain* and *sceptical,* inclined to bluster, to self-will and to give wrong representations. There will therefore be a danger of being involved in a lawsuit and suffering losses by it, financially and morally. It will be well to beware of others' too fair promises, and also to examine one's own business and personal matters accurately, without any distrustful feelings. One should endeavour to be tolerant and keep oneself constantly controlled by truth.

Pr. ☿ ⚹, △ ♄. This is the narrow path, the difficult road along which the Ego can make the best possible progress in this life by means of seriousness, setting oneself limits and sense of duty. The native knows intuitively whither life should be steered in order in the end to attain victory through trouble and suffering. These directions render reserved, enable one to think deeply and concentrate purely and are the cause that once a purpose is set it will surely be reached. The talent for business (☿) will lead one to new plans, which will be successful, supported as they are by connections of a serious older partner (♄). These directions are favourable for investing money in real estate or for obtaining a position as a mining or railroad engineer.

Pr. ☿ ☌, □, ☍ ♄. During this direction a *depressed, worried* attitude will cause loss of credit, and make one unfit for intercourse with older people. The steady older people — with or without criticism according to ☿'s position — look on with increasing displeasure and suppose that with the native all energy to shake off misery has died down. Under these directions one is exposed to wrong judgment and it will not be easy to put right, seeing that one does not oneself really know what one wants. Actual help or cooperation cannot be found anywhere, one feels handicapped.

Pr. ☿ ⚹, △ ♅. These directions give personal ideas, differing from those of others and are conducive to the study of *occultism* especially *astrology*. A praiseworthy curiosity manifests. Many of the secrets of life and death will be unveiled intuitively. The *magnetic radiation of the hands and fingertips* is increased and this magnetic fluid may be used to benefit the weak and to expel their ailments.

Pr. ☿ ☌, □, ☍ ♅. These directions prompt to *action,* make *sarcastic,* irritable, nervous and discontented. Moreover very sensitive to thoughts of the environment which will be judged severely if they prove to be dishonest. It renders recalcitrant, difficult. Misunderstandings in all kinds of relations will for a long time cause unpleasant intercourse with others. One had best do and say as little as possible that differs from the ordinary, well-known theories, in order not to encounter opposition which would be too much for the nervous system. If one could compel oneself to *work* and *meditate quietly,* for variety taking walks, this unpleasant time might be much improved.

Pr. ☿ ⚹, △ ♆. A *mystical idealistic* mood, controlled by logical thought, will bring a feeling of happiness, appreciation of beauty and harmony not before experienced. This direction renders humorous in the subtler sense of the word; helps one to understand others' difficulties and tactfully to point them out.

Pr. ☿ ☌, □, ☍ ♆. The mind is *dreamy, hesitating,* confused by vague *visions.* Sensual dreams may weaken morality and cause a temporary degeneration. Training of the logical mind, practice in concentration — not exaggerated! — more movement in the open air with wholesome hobbies, may expel these "tempters".

Directions of Venus (♀) [1].

Pr. ♀ ☌ ♂. *A combination of higher and lower emotions.* The feeling of love may rise to a higher level consciously drawing from it power to be much for others. This direction points to much opportunity to develop harmoniously with regard to ethics, makes enthusiastically sympathetic, strengthens ties of friendship, brings an agreeable cheerful time and will keep aspirations of love especially lively. It leads to uncommon actions of which the world will speak. Indifferent to others' opinions the native will act according to his own conviction. He will earnestly strive for the realisation of desires which have matured in his own life.

Pr. ♀ ⚹, △ ♂. These directions with which the ♀-vibrations become very active may contribute much to the development of the *artistic capacities* and to harmonious intimate intercourse, especially with the *other sex.* These directions bring pure appreciation of what is good and beautiful upon earth, give a healthy fruitful passion. A sympathetic person with a sensitive nature but also practical and steady, will cross the native's path. This time is favourable for health, renders cheerful and full of vitality, popular.

Pr. ♀ □, ☍ ♂. During these directions one should be on one's guard against too impulsive, passionate actions. In this inharmonious connection ♀ and ♂ easily cause a conflict between *soul* and *senses.* Occasions will then arise in social intercourse which might lead the native into trouble — so he should try to control himself.

He should further beware of catching cold, and of accidents, for this aspect tends to recklessness in this direction. It will be best to withdraw calmly during this period, to work at oneself and meditate constantly on a single hopeful thought. This may be the source of so much strength, that the unpleasant effect of these directions will be reduced to a minimum.

Pr. ♀ ☌ ♃ brings a *peaceful element* to consciousness, it purifies the feelings and thoughts, renders the intuitive and mental faculties clear and endows with the power to uplift the sick and depressed into a harmonious atmosphere and to help them by so doing. Those who are depressed will be led by the native's tactful manner to think less of their own anxieties and begin to take an interest in others and try to become like the person who with a few words, or even by his (or her) mere presence brought such a favourable change into their mode of thought. This direction will enable the native to cure the sick by realising the idea *'health'* i.e. by picturing in the mind the patient as perfectly healthy and retaining this image so continually that their ailments gradually disappear. In proportion as this picture of health can be kept pure, imperfections will disappear and improvement begin.

The ♀—♃ constellation creates the purifying power which e.g. a genuine practitioner of *Christian Science* applies. Fear and anxiety will

---

[1]) **Directions of ♀ with the ☉-r, the ☽-r, and ☿-r, can be judged as directions of the ☉, the ☽ and ☿ with ♀-radix.**

vanish before the inwardly growing power of confidence which this direction strengthens. "Faith is the substance of things hoped for".

Pr. ♀ ⚹, △ ♃. These directions bring *joy of life* and *excellent health,* helpful friendship, popularity, and increase of esteem. Whatever is undertaken during this period will promise well for the future, unless other, unfavourable influences are at work at the same time. Financially it is a fortunate time during which in every respect life will be enjoyable. Inner and outer riches increase; it is a veritable horn of gladness filled to overflowing.

Pr. ♀ □, ☍ ♃. A dispute about an aesthetical religious subject may lead to alienation from one who is disposed to be friendly. The native must deal carefully and with tact where difference of opinion might lead to a legal affair. This may also lead to *conflicts* of *feeling* and misunderstanding may arise often too on account of *theological problems.* The conflicting parties cannot realise each other's standpoint, and talk alongside and not *to* one another. These directions are less favourable for health (circulation of the blood) and enterprises generally. There is a speculative tendency, lack of *definite-ness* in thought and action.

Pr. ♀ ☌ ♄ indicates a period of *unpleasant experiences,* makes greedy and brings much disappointment and care in matters of feeling e.g. delay or giving up of marriage and danger of consequent damage to reputation. Some *loss* will make the native indifferent, unmoved by this world and inclines the native with all his sensitivety (♀) to shut himself up (♄) in his own heart. The more radiant the principle of Love can be, the less room will there be for egoism and selfcentredness.

Pr. ♀ ⚹, △ ♄. These directions render ethical-philosophic, but at the same time practical and sensible, also economical in financial matters. The native will choose a partner who is well-off financially, and by remaining faithful to him will command others' respect. Intense affection of an older person may be expected, some one who likes to assist with word and deed. This is a favourable time for serious pleasures. If there is a question of the kind for the native this direction is favourable for the purchase of a countryhouse or other *real estate* (♄) matters which will give satisfaction (♀).

Pr. ♀ □, ☍ ♄. Cherished expectations will not be realised, enterprises will fail which were started idealistically. These directions have an unfavourable influence on all things related to personal and social matters. There are constant thoughts of separation, death and deceit. It is a sad period — fortunately only temporary — during which there is little joy of life and faith in humanity; it may be termed a time of mourning.

Pr. ♀ ⚹, △ ♅ gives interest in everything that is *modern* and *original.* These directions make *idealistic, popular,* bring unexpected inspirations and progress in leaps and bounds. Astrology or some other branch of occultism will be studied with new acquaintances. The pleasant side brought by these directions in matters of love will often be followed by what is unpleasant.

Pr. ♀ ♂, □, ☍ ♅. *Eccentric, idealistic feelings* lead to all kinds of *abnormal pleasures and relations of life*. These directions bring domestic discord, often separation, and injure the reputation. Rationally overparticular considerations, due possibly to harmonious aspects of ♅, ♀ or ♄ may ward off excesses. *Women* especially should beware of rash actions under these directions.

Pr. ♀ ♂ ♆ leads to a singular engagement in a somewhat *platonic* direction, and inclines to dress in a striking and interesting manner so that extraordinary popularity will be gained. The native has taste for very peculiar things.

Pr. ♀ ✳, △ ♆. A *peaceful period* in which the native is apt to be moved to tears by his ideals of beauty of life. These directions promise material and spiritual welfare. The native likes to jest about future artistic success, fame and the acquisition of wealth through inheritance, of which there is just a very small chance. He likes to build *castles in the air* and has all kinds of phantasies.

Pr. ♀ ☐, ☍ ♆. These directions render self-indulgent, sensuous, inclined to get *intoxicated* and to take *strong drinks* or *narcotics*. There is great probability of discord with someone who otherwise is very affectionate. It is advisable to remain *pure* and *true* in everything; only an attitude of inner peace can help to overcome all difficulties.

Directions of Mars (♂) [1].

Pr. ♂ ♂ ♃. This renders nervous and irritable, inclined to recklessness. Too much confidence will be put in unworthy people, so that domestic and legal difficulties may be expected. The more intense, however, the desire becomes to let others also realise that "faith" may lead to "great power" and to the annihilation of anxiety concerning material things, the better may this direction be used for the soul's progress.

Pr. ♂ ✳, △ ♃. These directions symbolise *peace after strife* and sometimes cause *religious conversion*. Mars is tamed and so the joy of conquest follows. Some matter in which there is *great faith* (♃) will be pleaded with *enthusiasm* (♂). The native actually lives for the chosen business or line of religion, and fortune is favourably inclined towards the faithful (♃) warrior (♂).

Pr. ♂ ☐, ☍ ♃. These directions arouse enthusiastic sympathies which

---

[1] Directions of ♂ with the ☉-r, the ☽-r, ☿r, and ♀-r can be judged as directions of the ☉, the ☽, ☿ and ♄ with ♂-radix.

will lead to *reckless action*. Domestic troubles and financial losses may be expected. In order to prevent much disappointment it will be advisable not to confide too quickly nor absolutely in people with whom one comes into contact. Many changes arise through thoughtless actions. The saying of an unpremeditated word or the doing of an impulsive action causes unpleasantness and leads to alienation and separation. Some degree of slander may be expected in connection with pleasures which are envied. Strength (♂) and faith (♃) in *one's own nature* must grow so that there is no need to seek refuge with others. By listening to Truth and acting accordingly the conquest of self will be attained. In this way step by step self-confidence will be able to grow and with it the power to rule earthly troubles. Then true Freedom, so often desired, will be gained.

Pr. ♂ ✳, △ ♄. A time of *strong, persevering* attempts notwithstanding a less optimistic view of life. The manner is very *serious, energetic, practical* and suited to harmonious cooperation with older people. These directions also increase the faculty to put theological problems clearly and have discussions about them, give strength and the energy necessary to face difficulties, so that honour and respect will be gained.

Pr. ♂ ♂, □ ♄. The temperament is irrational, violent, thoughtless, reckless. Conflicts, contact with accidents or crime are very likely. It will be best not to cherish strong desires, but *to sacrifice one's own will with confidence*. By so doing the troubles will turn into better things.
Anger and embitterment may cause obstruction of the passages of the bile which probably leads to jaundice. The constitution is liable to impure blood, feverish affections. Difficulties in the social position may be expected. One had best keep as patient as possible and seek and retain the sunny side of life, which will be a difficult matter but makes the victory all the greater.

Pr. ♂ ♂ ♅. The native is inclined to act *impulsively* and to be *vindictive*, to do things unexpectedly, so that plans will be suddenly thrown over and alienation follow. There is great likelihood of *accidents,* it is therefore advisable not to act too rashly or without control — an accident is always round the corner. There is a tendency to throw old habits and methods overboard which — if otherwise also the horoscope cooperates — may awaken anarchistic tendencies. During these directions, one should consider everything carefully before acting, exercise patience and not allow oneself to be disheartened by disappointment. Many roads lead to Rome. Confidence in the purpose aimed at will surely in the end lead to its fulfilment.

Pr. ♂ ✳, △ ♅. These directions render extremely enthusiastic and are favourable for starting a new business or for *bringing new inventions into use*. Whatever is undertaken is carried on resolutely, the native keeps his aim clearly before him and works very hard. ♅ furthers quite new lines and gives a good outlook on those with whom one has to come into contact, besides deep insight into occultism and astrological problems. The idealistic nature and confidence in success are helped by these.

Pr. ♂ ✶, △ ♆. During these directions the native seeks energetically (♂) or some specially artistic (♆) expression. The imagination is strong and he likes to show it to people.

Pr. ♂ ♂, □ ☍ ♆. These directions between two such heterogeneous planets will of course lead to mutual degeneration; they render *oversensitive,* uncertain, nervous, put the psyche under a severe strain, try to bring the native into society he had better avoid and incline to excessive, unnatural sexual habits. Under these circumstances one is likely to become the victim of delusion and incalculable deceit. To cultivate and practise love for natural philosophy will ward off much evil. It is an excellent time just to enjoy life in the sunshine and open air and so not be troubled much by these inharmonious directions.

Jupiter, Saturn, Uranus and Neptune seldom form a progressive direction, because they only move slowly. But they form transits.

XVII

The Transits of Jupiter, Saturn, Uranus and Neptune.

Transits of Jupiter (♃).

Tr. ♃ ♂ ☉. This transit gives a *more optimistic view of life* and greater *love of life,* so that the native's health will improve and he will become able to do more than usual, if this does not turn into over-estimation of self. Under this transit some *social success* may be expected.

> "Believe in your mission,
> Greet life with a cheer;
> There's a great deal to do
> And that's why we are here."

Tr. ♃ ☍ ☉. One should not pay much attention to, at any rate not be disappointed by *mistakes, losses, indisposition* or misplaced confidence in subordinates. Experiences of this kind should rather be looked upon as occasions to learn under difficult circumstances to remain tranquil, calm and confident.

Tr. ♃ ♂ ☽. *Agreeable cooperation* and *appreciation* will cause joy in an intimate circle; the improving health or convalescence of one near to the native will make him thankful.

Tr. ♃ ☍ ☽. Some *misunderstanding* may cause alienation, there a battle will be fought against *slander.* One should guard against inaccuracy and recklessness, for they bring unpleasant consequences.

Tr. ♃ ♂ ☿. The native will look at life from the sunny side and will make a plan for a journey or for business with great gusto. He will realise that the greatest chance of success lies in an optimistic mental attitude.

Tr. ♃ ☌ ☿, ♀. The *joy* ♃ gives is coupled with the *harmony* and *aestheticism* of ♀ and the *clear mentality* of ☿. These moods are reflected in the environment, in intercourse with congenial people.

Tr. ♃ ☍ ☿. During the activity of this transit it will be well to mind one's business affairs attentively and to be on one's guard against *deceit;* goods sent should be well insured. Inharmonious ♃-transits incline to *extravagance* through insufficient business-knowledge and through too little serious consideration. It is necessary to make time regularly for rest and for thinking over what has been done and what still remains to be done. Through many disappointments confidence in higher guidance will be severely put to the test. The native should force himself to do with all his might whatever his hand finds to do.

Tr. ♃ ☌ ♀. This transit brings appreciation and sociability; more than usual a circle will be sought and prized which is harmonious, artistic and full of devotion. Peaceful thoughts of charity and growth of soul awaken in the native's consciousness.

Tr. ♃ ☍ ♀ indicates misunderstanding in the intimate circle, and somewhat reckless tendencies. Some disappointment — ideally — in business or a financial deficit may be expected. The native must be careful in monetary matters and should heed the details even if the income is so ample that economy seems altogether unnecessary. Some indisposition of a relative may occur, but this will soon pass.

Tr. ♃ ☌ ♂ makes somewhat *whimsical* and *undecided,* but they are passing qualities. This transit renders irritable on account of other people's unsympathetic attitude — at times only surmised for instance by their arrogant, catechising way of giving advice. The native's own views are quite contrary to those of these people who say "they mean so well". All kinds of things will be exaggerated, although the native's intentions are good. Disputes with orthodox-conservative people about religious subjects prove to be waste of time and cause estrangement. All unnecessary excitement should be avoided. Yet sometimes quite unexpectedly the native will be able to restore the right relation in some unpleasant conflict.

Tr. ♃ ☍ ♂ causes the native's excessive pliability to be abused, so that his nervous system will be severely tried. This transit may cause legal troubles the nature of which will be defined by the houses in which these planets are placed e.g. 2—8 in connection with legacies and inheritance; 4—10 with promotion, 6—12 possibly with confinement in hospital or prison.

Tr. ♃ ☌ ♃ gives great cheeriness, so that work will go particularly pleasantly. Life itself is regarded as a privilege, the native *feels himself grow* spiritually and physically and is more than ever inclined to put this to the service of others.

Tr. ♃ ☍ ♃. A certain *discontented indifference* will try to master the feelings. It seems to the native that everything is about the same, nothing much better or worse.

Tr. ♃ ☌ ♄. This transit will give an opportunity to relieve some old acquaintance in difficult circumstances. The native can help both spiritually and materially with word and deed. Some sacrifices are needed, but looked at clearly the *loss* will prove to be *gain*. If trust and faith are retained and also a strong conviction that all things work together for good, the native will later look back with great satisfaction to this time when joy and sorrow strove for the mastery. If ♃ is parallel to ♄ the feeling of being as *solitary as Job* will become balanced by the strength of *Job's confidence.*

Tr. ♃ ☍ ♄. The native will be ridiculed because of a serious intention, communicated to others. This leads to unpleasantness and a *distrustful attitude.* This transit will bring into contact with some one who charms by outward appearance and courtesy, but whose inner nature is less desirable for lasting intercourse. It will therefore be well to prepare oneself in time by purifying the faculty of perception, which will then be able to discern the motives of others, without taking refuge in distrustful feelings. It is advisable to beware of catching colds, because this transit may influence the native's health (liver complaint or deafness). This transit passes quickly and as a rule need not leave harmful consequences, but "prevention is better than cure".

Tr. ♃ ☌ ♅. Conscioussness will be led to a higher level and therefore give a harmonious solution. A certain mental attitude will enable the native to obtain *cures* along the lines of *suggestion* corresponding to the method of Coué, New-Thought or Christian Science. It proves to be possible that a physically indisposed body can be cured by the activity of an invisible force. Belief in Christ's cures will now be accepted, and regarded as the willingness to be suffused by the divine spirit which is present everywhere and which cures every evil (brokenness). It is desirable to make good use of this favourable opportunity in order to be able without suffering material or moral loss to tackle the difficult aspects which will follow later in life.

Tr. ♃ ☍ ♅. This transit will cause most difficulties through a certain *pride* and *self-conceit* after some success. The value of the result will be lessened through *jealousy,* others' gossip and the tendency of the native himself publicly to defend his own achievements. He had better refrain from the latter, the good result will surely come to light some day. Therefore: *act, believe* and *be silent.*

Tr. ♃ ☌ ♆. During this transit the acquaintance will be made of a modern artistically minded person. He will give a special view of the new conceptions of art and also in a high degree enrich and deepen the native's social feeling.

Tr. ♃ ☍ ♆. This transit makes *inaccurate, indifferent, reckless.* It is desirable not to yield to these tendencies, since by them subordinates might be seduced to dishonest actions. The native should be warned against infections, intoxication etc. It is advisable to have an accurate account of one's possessions, for during this time something is apt to get lost from which legal troubles might follow. Some one who is supposedly churchy and religious will *slander* and cast *suspicion* on the native. This transit will give rise to all kinds of unexpected unpleasantness according to the houses concerned. The native will be greatly helped if he is then able to keep ♃ 's loyal attitude, as expressed in Seneca's word "How much better is it to bear the shame of injustice than to revenge oneself".

Transits of Saturn (♄).

Tr. ♄ ☌, ☍ ☉. The circumstances these transits bring are not easy and require much patience and confidence. ♄ renders discontented, gloomy, inclined to pessimism; the mind is not harmonious. The expectations cherished prove to have been too great, the native feels *ill-used.* These transits lead to disappointments in personal, intimate matters and injure health in the part of the body connected with the sign in which the ☉ or ♄ are placed. They may cause some simultaneously good aspect to be of no effect. The native should keep in mind that:

"The great sun of suns shines
With a radiance of eternal good
In front of the window of the soul that is closed
It's only the pushing open that is lacking.

(Jan Luiken.)

Tr. ♄ ☌, ☍ ☽. These transits will *dishearten* the native, and through the feelings unfavourably affect the health, especially in women. It is advisable to be careful especially in inclement weather, without, however, being exaggeratedly anxious. For fear may attract indisposition, but rational care of the body is anyway useful and necessary. If the ☽ is placed in a *cardinal* sign excessive exertion will soon cause *headache.* In *mutable* signs, the *lungs* should be specially protected; in the *fixed* signs, there will often be inflammation of the throat. These transits cause delay and opposition in enterprises and plans. It is a time during which one had best not pay too much attention to disappointments and in no case allow melancholy moods to gain the mastery.

Tr. ♄ ☌, ☍ ☿. These transits render somewhat nervous and uneasy; afraid of suffering because others — relations or subordinates — do not succeed in their work. There is a possibility of loss through insufficient activity, deception, swindle or theft.

Tr. ♄ ☌, ☍ ♀ has not a favourable influence on social affairs. Heavier burdens will be put on the native than he considers fair and right. This causes a discontented mood, which hinders the disposition to be of service to others. During this transit the native will be somewhat disposed to envy.

Tr. ♄ ☌, ☍ ♂. These transits give as it were the touchstone of life; they test what has really become a spiritual possession, and how far the higher nature wil remain untouched by disappointments and difficulties, since they tend to stimulate opposition and rebellion. Heart and head should unite in energetic (♂), well-considered (♄) action along a useful, constructive line!

Tr. ♄ ☌, ☍ ♃. ♄ limits, kills. ♃ gives the faculty of *growth* and therefore these transits will cause a doubtful, listless mood: at one moment prudent and unfit for action, at another inclined to be reckless. Optimism will prove to result more from a temporary "dépit" rather than from social fortune.

Tr. ♄ ☌, ☍ ♄. These transits cause a depressed pessimistic mood, disappointments in things material, illness, especially in consequence of colds. The liver and organs of hearing will be hindered in their functions. Troubles with older people must be overcome.

Tr. ♄ ☌ ♅. Desire for occult knowledge will be strongly aroused. The native finds it easy to concentrate his thoughts on abstract subjects. Some one who can make new ideas of life's problems and of religion acceptable will give satisfactory insight into troubles upon which no light had previously been thrown.

Tr. ♄ ☍ ♅ will mean disappointment in the confidence, placed too *thoughtlessly* in occult faculties or intuition. If a desire to practise *black magic* is felt, the native should do well to reflect that he will become poorer not richer by shutting himself off from the Universal Love, by trying to gain power over others for purely personal reasons.

Tr. ♄ ☌ ♆ promotes *harmony of thought and feeling* and *inner growth* by withdrawal from the world and self-communion. Inner satisfaction may be expected rather than outward success through public acknowledgement. Ideal impressions from without will bring to consciousness similarly harmonious qualities in one's own nature.

Tr. ♄ ☍ ♆. During the activity of this transit special watchfulness is advisable, because there is a possibility of *swindle, imposture* etc. Administration should be specially accurate, and money in cash more than ever controlled. The native will regard metaphysical experiences too critically and not appreciate them with sufficient devotion. This transit may bring into contact with inferior minds.

Transits of Uranus (♅) and Neptune (♆).

Harmonious transits of Uranus (♅) quicken a specially *magnetic attraction*. People will be met with whom questions about art, philosophy and above all astrology will be discussed. These ♅-transits will arouse great interest in life on occult planes; if ☿ is connected with them the knowledge gained will be treated as *logically* as possible and expressed in words, so as to bring it to the material world; ♀ will express the ideas in some work of *art*, ♃ along *ethical* lines, etc.

Inharmonious transits of Uranus (♅) incline to act thoughtlessly and to be of service to others, although this is detrimental to one's own interests. The native will have to listen to strange opinions, which he cannot simply push aside; the solution of the conflict will only be reached when his feelings have been permeated by them and he has *lived* them and then *put them right*. Difficulties in money matters can only be avoided by very careful administration, so that he will always have proofs in hand should difficulties arise.

Inharmonious transits of ♅ give a nervous mood and *sleeplessness,* which may be best treated by going to bed early after having read a book which leaves one in a peaceful mood. Reading rather insignificant news in the papers·may also bring some distraction and relax the nervous system sufficiently to allow of undisturbed sleep, which will strengthen for the work to be done next day. The chief thing is to *rest at regular times,* so that the physical body may become a worthy servant of the intuition. During this period it will be well to repeat Coué's formula: "Every day, in every way I'm getting better and better."

Transits of Neptune (♆) are the cause that many people do not understand the native's attitude in the world, considering it *strange* and *mysterious*. Peculiar suggestions and expressions characterise this time. The personality reflects a *mystical aureole*.

XVIII

The Progressed Moon through the twelve Houses.

Pr. ☽ through 1. The feeling of being forlorn and neglected by the world which is given by the transit of the ☽ through the 12th house, the house of trial and enemies, will give place to a *more cheerful mood*. The ☽'s entrance into the 1st house is always felt as a *relief* by astrologers. It emphasises *initiative,* a manly desire for *self-support*. The native will have to see to his own interests, which is all the better seeing that the influence of the 12th house (the one preceding) taught him to look for riches in his own inner nature and to accept outer loneliness. One must first have a quality before one can share it with others. "To him that hath shall be given, and from him that hath not, shall be taken away even that which he hath." The native will stimulate others to action and give them advice; he will take the lead and set an example in his own circle, however small it may be.

Pr. ☽ through 2. Thought will dwell more than usually on spiritual and material "possessions". This time will be chiefly characterised by care for, pondering on, regulating, finances. If there are favourable directions, business will thrive and the native will be able to consider former experiences with more insight and classify them rightly. If there is *affliction,* financial and ideal difficulties may be expected.

Pr. ☽ through 3. During this period *correspondence* will occupy much time; the taste for it will be renewed or strengthened. There is a desire to take up various businesses at a time, it is more difficult than usual to keep to one thing and the native will make many schemes and plans, for instance for trips; will seek, probe and be generally irresolute, rather than enjoy a quiet harmonious mood. On the whole *intellect* will be more prominent than feeling. It is advisable patiently to compare things so that what is essential truth may grow stronger in oneself, and finally find expression as intuition. The faculty thus gained will be full of promise for the future.

Pr. ☽ through 4. During this period attention will be chiefly fixed on household affairs e.g. furnishing. Thoughts of leaving one's home will occur more than once. If *afflicted* inharmonious relations will occur in one's own home or that of the parents.

Pr. ☽ through 5 will increase the native's love of enterprise and make him look for an opportunity to express himself more freely. The passing of the pr. ☽ through the 5th house rouses an optimistic view of life in general so that the mind can work very actively and energetically for something new. The thoughts are ambitious, moved by the *heart* and intent on the enterprise. The native likes to do things for the sake of the *pleasure* they may afford, and will have pleasant intercourse with the opposite sex, although it will not be quite definite.

An inharmonious direction causes disappointment in speculative enterprises etc. All actions should then be well considered, lest they fail. If harmoniously aspected this influence makes the native cheerful, confident, fond of life, and promotes health and success.

Pr. ☽ through 6 gives contentment and satisfaction in a *subordinate* position rather than in an *independent* one. The native likes to occupy himself quietly and devotedly with minute work, without having to concern himself much with leadership or organisation. His *thoughts* seem to be of more value than his feelings. The tendency of ♍ (6th house) to concentrate upon the faults of others, on the flaws and trifles which he would like to see changed, will not give place to a wider and more tolerant ♎ conception until the ☽ has passed on to the next (the 7th) house.

If there are inharmonious directions ♍'s discontented moods will influence health unfavourably, until in the 7th house the more rational, logical

13

element of ♎ will lead to harmony with oneself and one's environment (if not the ☽ in 7 forms inharmonious directions); if there is an harmonious influence in 6, the native will be willing to work for the recovery of his health, which will bring appreciation and affection in the 7th house.

Pr. ☽ through 7. This is the house of contact with other people — love affairs — the house of *partnership;* the progress of the ☽ through it will therefore cause a great desire to be able to cooperate with others in a spirit of good understanding. Questions regarding intimate intercourse with the opposite sex will be prominent. The native feels a great want to discuss various subjects freely with some one who is congenial. If the 7th house is well occupied this progressed ☽ greatly strengthens the contact with many and various people, but at the same time it rouses the desire to be personally admired, loved and acknowledged to be their superior. When there is affliction sorrow and difficulties arise from lack of appreciation, either real or fancied.

Pr. ☽ through 8. For a long time thoughts about life after death will occupy the native. They usually originate in the loss through death of some one out of his environment or of one who was greatly loved and admired by him. If the 8th house is an important one in the nativity, very particular views of the life beyond may be obtained through this movement of the ☽. Conceptions of religion will also be influenced by it. Riddles of life, psychism, and astral life will often be subjects of meditation and conversation. The native propounds his own views in order to invite criticism and to find out how far his own ideas are confirmed by others. There will be problems to solve concerning possessions and partnership; the division of an inheritance will bring unexpected knowledge of mankind. The temperament is very active, impatient, often passionate. The best way in which this influence may be sublimated is by regular, but not excessive, movement in the open air and by keeping to fixed hours of work. It is advisable calmly to contemplate the beauty of nature, to discuss natural philosophical subjects with people of tranquil mental type from whom a cheerful influence radiates.

Pr. ☽ through 9. This is the house of *"distant travel"*. This progression therefore denotes that journeys are constantly being planned. The native wishes for *freedom* and *movement.* The desire to get to know new circumstances is very great. Usually a dissatisfied feeling, a certain discontent with regard to his present position urges him to this change. Harmonious directions are favourable for change of abode and for meeting acquaintances. The mind is active and the horizon widens; the greatest possible extension of consciousness may be expected through thinking and travelling, while all this will lead to personal success. Decisions are quickly made and prove to be instigated by right judgment. The passing of the ☽ through the 9th house promises a pleasant time, if there are harmonious directions. Religious and philosophical ideas are discussed. This time is also favourable for expansion, extension of the sphere of influence.

If there are inharmonious aspects the journeys will not be undertaken wholly for pleasure: disagreeable relations will lead to them. The native will find his ideals thwarted in many ways and have to combat many difficulties according to the nature of the afflicting planets.

Pr. ☽ through 10. The 10th house represents the *profession* and the repute one will gain *in the world*. Therefore the work which has to be done in the world by the native for his sustenance and possibly for that of his family will require much attention; if there are harmonious aspects there is a possibility of becoming the object of *public interest*. There is a great desire to achieve something important, by which he might acquire a more respected and remunerative position and make his name in the world. So it may be expected that during this period the mind will be occupied by the question what opportunity could best be used for this. There is also a desire to act as a *leader,* so far as the circumstances permit.

If there are inharmonious directions there is danger of *slander* and *disappointment* in the social position, according to the nature of the afflicting planet.

Pr. ☽ through 11. This arouses the desire to let the mind dwell on *new ideas* (♒-♅); subjects which are slighted by the old-fashioned knowledge will fairly often come to light through intuition, to which others, especially *younger people* like to listen. The native likes to think of astrology, magnetism, mental healing, vegetarianism and similar subjects and to discuss them with congenial spirits. Friends and superiors are sure to take an interest, if the ☽ aspects other planets favourably (especially ☉ and ♃). Some good friend and master will prove very useful. The native can honestly and freely discuss his own difficulties with superiors.

If the pr. ☽ forms *inharmonious aspects,* alienation from a friend or loss caused by over-confidence may be expected.

Pr. ☽ through 12. During the 2 or 3 years that the progressive ☽ remains in this house, *a withdrawal from the world* will give greater opportunity to *intensify the inner life.* Rest, seclusion and meditation during this time will *in later years* bring rich fruit; at the time this period sometimes seems unbearable. The native will have to pass through many moments of loneliness, and of feeling utterly forlorn. The passage of the ☽ through the 12th house symbolises the *"journey through the desert".* If the 12th house is strongly occupied, many important lessons may be learned, although the experiences in life are not easy as a rule. Material or ideal losses will be suffered and the native will have much difficulty in maintaining himself in the world. Even though at times harmonious directions or transits prevail in the progressed horoscope, which might have led to greater success and cheerfulness, there will continually be disappointments and moods of depression. The transit of the ☽ through the 12th house is upon the whole characterised by *passivity* (Cf. pr. ☽ through 1 *activity),* yielding (willingly or unwillingly) and a tendency to allow oneself to be used by others, seduced to one's physical and moral detriment and that of others also.

The native should use this time by going into retreat in order to deepen his views of life and the world. If the right attitude is acquired, this may be a period of inner enrichment; the kingdom gained is not of this world.

XIX

The Transits of Mars, Jupiter and Saturn through the Houses.

Transits of Mars (♂).

The transits of ♂ usually last only one day and consequently have little influence. They give a revival of energy or a certain passion, rashness, in accordance as aspects are favourable or unfavourable.

The transits of ♂ are not expressed through the signs or the aspecting planets so much as through the houses.

Tr. ♂ through 1 enhances the interest in sport, makes the native quick and resolute in attack but also irritable.

Tr. ♂ through 2 inclines to be especially extravagant, if well aspected it gives an idea of how to make money *productive* but this will cause a good deal of expense.

Tr. ♂ through 3 inclines to literary controversy or verbal warfare or an acrimonious correspondence which sharpens the intellect.

Tr. ♂ through 4 brings discord or excessive enthusiasm in the home and an inclination to upset things.

Tr. ♂ through 5 increases self-conceit, gives a feeling of authority and the desire to order others about and to manage them.

Tr. ♂ through 6 is unfortunate both for relations between employer and employee and for health. Difficulties with subordinates, accidents and infections may be expected.

Tr. ♂ through 7 brings an element of passion into the more intimate relations, which may be expressed as love or as hatred, according to the other positions of the horoscope.

Tr. ♂ through 8 rouses enthusiasm for experiments in things occult, may lead to risky experiments in spiritualism and hypnosis.

Tr. ♂ through 9 inspires to missionary journeys or voyages of discovery, it gives an intense certainty of being able to defeat all spiritual enemies and conquer all material difficulties.

Tr. ♂ through 10 causes a great desire for public recognition, strengthens the energy in this respect and renders the native *resolute*.

Tr. ♂ through 11 gives troubles with friends or through them, and makes the native generally eccentric and rebellious, at times inclined "to paint the town red".

Tr. ♂ through 12 causes *inner conflicts,* limitations and in consequence sorrow and embitterment. The ♂-fire is indeed smouldering.

Transits of Jupiter (♃) through the Houses.

Tr. ♃ through 1 influences *health* especially favourably. A hopeful and confident mood will cooperate to enable the native to profit by the teachings gained by reading and by his own intuition. This transit causes the development of inner spiritual power. The general position will improve in proportion as the native succeeds in making purity of truth and of love the vital principle of his life.

Tr. ♃ through 2 favours the *financial position* and gives the prospect of a happier, more hopeful time. There is great confidence in the future and in the success of enterprises. But since ♃ often inclines to live beyond one's means it will sometimes be a hard struggle to cut one's coat according to one's cloth.

Tr. ♃ through 3. This will be a favourable time for a journey of not too long duration, which will bring *spiritual* and *material profit* and lead to fortune in the future rather than at the moment. This transit gives pleasant changes and new connections; it refines the feelings and taste and strengthens the idea of brotherhood among all people. Cheerful correspondence may be expected and a pleasant time for study and the application of things learned.

Tr. ♃ through 4 gives a great desire for peace and cheerfulness and an *intimately domestic environment,* in order to study and work there quietly, occasionally discussing one's ideas with a kindred spirit. The mere thought of this will give joy. A cosy home of acquaintances will be greatly appreciated. During this transit difficulties with regard to the profession or health will probably arise but will not be too hard to bear, owing to the good understanding existing with parents and relations generally. In the native's own circle a pleasant, confident, helpful attitude usually prevails, a mood which benefits him also physically.

If afflicted disappointments may be expected with regard to the above mentioned matters.

Tr. ♃ through 5. A sensation of *"liberation"* of *"being free"* gives greater hope for the future. The view of life becomes more optimistic; the native feels a desire to *speculate.* It is an agreeable time favourable for making trips, visits and knitting new ties of friendship. The native is active and definite in his sensations and more fond of children than usual.

Affliction leads to immoderate pleasure-hunting and to all kinds of nouveau-riche-isms.

Tr. ♃ through 6 will improve health and expand the circle of fellow-workers. The work which must be done as a duty will gain in charm and make the native cheerful. Contact with subordinates and relatives is smooth and agreeable.

If afflicted subordinates will commit all kinds of pilfering, usually without being found out.

Tr. ♃ through 7 bestows or augments *matrimonial happiness,* brings profit in partnership. There is much likelihood of a righteous solution to a misunderstanding; of the renewal of a good understanding after long enmity. If ♃ is badly aspected the native should be on his guard lest he trusts others too well.

Tr. ♃ through 8 is favourable for obtaining a legacy also for the possessions of the partner in life or in business. This transit leads to a peaceful outlook on death and makes the spirit soar above its earthly limitations.

Tr. ♃ through 9. A feeling of *certainty,* of *conscious inner freedom* will support the spirit in its activity; contemplative thought is extended by the new things found by intuition. This transit promises great enjoyment through seeing new things which may increase knowledge, and is favourable for *connections abroad.*

Tr. ♃ through 10. This influence will be favourable to *social position;* popularity will increase. The native will easily gain promotion since he will be recommended and supported by persons in authority with whom he may even be only superficially acquainted.

Affliction makes the native count too much on this, with little success.

Tr. ♃ through 11 strengthens *interest in others,* mutual appreciation increases, new relations of friendship are entered into. Should difficulties arise, friends will be found willing to render any help which the native desires, whilst the native is also ready, if need be, to do the same by them.

Tr. ♃ through 12. The 12th house never brings an easy time, but at any rate ♃ will remind the native that sunshine follows after rain, that there is a silver lining to every cloud. One should keep up one's courage. *Regular times of rest* with *devout meditations* will prove to be of greater value than a nerve-raging chase after material profit. If the right helpful, trusting attitude can be found, the motion of ♃ through this house will help to brighten all things that seemed dark and difficult.

Transits of Saturn (♄) through the Houses.

Tr. ♄ through 1. Difficulties are seen ahead or are *supposed* to be, although it would be better during this transit not to pay much attention to them. This ♄-transit renders dejected, serious, sometimes listless. The physical constitution is not so strong as usual; a feeling may even arise that the beginning of the end has come. Of course this is not a favourable influence on energy; the native is inclined to sit still and let things slide. The state of mind is well expressed by the following lines:

> *Man does often suffer most*
> *From the woe he fears*
> *And although it never comes*
> *Dread that it appears*
> *Makes him oft to bear far more*
> *Than God did hold for him in store.*

If, however, ♄ receives *very strong, harmonious* influences, especially from the ☉, a particularly strong will-power will during this time emanate from the native which inspires and supports his environment.

Tr. ♄ through 2. ♄ compels to *earnestness* and *prudence* in order to keep the financial condition intact. The native will be sensible, practically and — if there are good aspects — profitably economical; *order and regularity* in his work seem to be more than ever desirable. If *no help* comes from other planets loss may be expected, which will be less extensive in proportion as presence of mind and confidence have been cultivated. Purity of faith and a firm intention to serve Truth may be acquired by this transit, if the attitude to life is sensible.

Tr. ♄ through 3. Some matter, probably related to an *older relative* causes anxiety; various small differences in the environment must be smoothed over; every one seems to be in need of the native's help and advice, so that his own work cannot make much progress. Further this transit causes *the native to be too late* in an enterprise, to miss a train on a journey; it makes him take things far from lightly and think more seriously than usual.

Tr. ♄ through 4. *Domestic circumstances* will cause special anxiety; difficulties will arise in domestic affairs which will be prolonged if ♄ is retrograde. It is very desirable not to allow a discontented mood to prevail towards those in the house who are less appreciated, but always to be careful to take *timely measures of prevention.*

Tr. ♄ through 5 causes some anxiety about the organisation of *enterprises*. It is necessary to choose a reliable counsellor, because otherwise others will speculate on the native's capital or his slight business knowledge. The motion of ♄ through the 5th house teaches however, by means of such disappointments to be thrifty. Moreover some fear for and anxiety about a child are probable. Anticipated pleasures fall through.

Tr. ♄ through 6 will bring difficulties in *activities* and *health* in relation with the sign on the cusp of this house. For example if ♎ rules the 6th house, the indisposition will be in connection with the kidneys, if it is ♋ the stomach, ♈ gives headaches, ♊ lung-diseases etc. One should not keep wet clothes on, nor allow the feet to remain wet. It is advisable to take good care of the skin by hot baths and from time to time by some means to promote perspiration in order to get rid of impure matter, also, a great deal of exercise to prevent the blood circulation from becoming sluggish. The native should not allow himself to become depressed; and not attribute value to those people and things which do not fit in with his work. During this time the best thing for the native to do is constantly to strengthen his faith in the power of Good.

Tr. ♄ through 7. If this transit is harmonious, i. e. takes place in ♎ or ♐ an intensification of the relation to intimate friends will occur; if not it causes some estrangement, cooling down. The cooperation in marriage and partnership which was expected will not then be experienced. The conviction of having done one's own duty seriously will, however, in the end bring satisfaction.

Tr. ♄ through 8. The death of some one beloved or revered will bring to the fore thoughts of the question of life after death and these will usually be pessimistic. ♄ will bring disappointment through death, in some cases also through the loss of a long cherished ideal. This transit is in a sense a *trial* to test whether the opportunity of former favourable aspects has led only to material welfare or also to spiritual development.

Tr. ♄ through 9. *Metaphysical subjects* demand attention and interest, although too little time will of necessity often be given to them. It costs the native much pains to see the truth of things and when perceived to make it acceptable to others and to lead them to value it: "le vrai peut être pas vraisemblable". He wishes to see life more beautiful and purer and therefore tries to purify and simplify his own way of thinking and acting. With inharmonious aspects life itself compels the native to do this and then his *spiritual* strength will not withstand his *material* trials.

Tr. ♄ through 10, the house of calling, will give a certain depression, a discontent with the position in the world. Very many moments of dejection and nervous pessimistic moods will be passed through by the native, due to dissatisfaction with his profession, or opposition from older people. With additional favourable conditions this transit may bring about an upheaval in spite of obstruction, a purposeful pressing onward, especially if there is strong help from ♂. But even then much is asked of the native, whilst very likely some considerations of the feelings must be put aside — which afterwards will probably be regretted.

Tr. ♄ through 11. The 11th house is related to *friends*. This transit causes coolness, calculation and unexpected critical circumstances in friendly relations. In previously superficial connections he will suddenly desire "everything or nothing". Opposition of older people will cause a mood of disappointment.

Tr. ♄ through 12. ♄ the *watcher on the threshold* by passing through the house of self-communion and examination causes the question often to arise, what may have been the cause that so often someone or something must cross one's path, who brought disturbance and disappointment. The native wishes to get things *clear* in his own mind, in relation to *himself,* and strives earnestly towards this end, in spite of the many difficulties that arise. It is advisable to retire from the world as much as possible during this ♄ transit, to *meditate quietly on the aim of life's experiences* and as recreation to read uplifting books of a religious philosophical kind and meditate on them; not to harp on disappointments but with faith keep the gaze fixed on a happier future.

"A life full of disappointment, is better than a life without an ideal."

Diurnal proportional Logarithms.

Hours or Degrees.

Minutes.

Min	0	1	2	3	4	5	6	7	8	9	10	11	12	13	14	15	16
0	3.1584	1.3802	1.0792	9031	7781	0812	6021	5351	4771	4260	3902	3388	3010	2663	2341	2041	1761
1	3.1584	1.3730	1.0756	9007	7763	6798	6009	5341	4762	4252	3795	3382	3004	2657	2336	2036	1756
2	2.8573	1.3660	1.0720	8983	7745	6784	5997	5330	4753	4244	3788	3375	2998	2652	2330	2032	1752
3	2.8813	1.3590	1.0685	8959	7728	6769	5985	5320	4744	4236	3780	3368	2992	2646	2325	2027	1747
4	2.5563	1.3532	1.0649	9035	7710	6755	5973	5310	4735	4228	3773	3362	2986	2640	2320	2023	1743
5	2.4594	1.3454	1.0614	8912	7692	6741	5961	5300	4726	4220	3766	3355	2980	2635	2315	2017	1738
6	2.3388	1.3388	1.0580	8888	7674	6726	5949	5289	4717	4212	3759	3349	2974	2620	2310	2012	1734
7	2.3133	1.3323	1.0546	8865	7657	6713	5937	5279	4708	4204	3752	3342	2968	2624	2305	2005	1729
8	2.2553	1.3258	1.0511	8843	7639	6698	5925	5269	4699	4196	3745	3336	2962	2614	2300	2003	1735
9	2.2301	1.3195	1.0478	8819	7622	6684	5913	5259	4690	4188	3737	3329	2956	2614	2296	1998	1720
10	2.1584	1.3133	1.0444	8706	7604	6670	5902	4682	4180		3730	3323	2950	2607	2289	1993	1716
11	3.1170	1.3071	1.0411	8773	7587	6656	5890	5239	4673	4172	3723	3316	2944	2602	2284	1988	1711
12	1.0792	1.3010	1.0378	8751	7570	6642	5878	5329	4664	4164	3716	3310	2938	2596	2279	1984	1707
13	2.0444	1.2950	1.0345	8728	7552	6628	5866	5310	4655	4156	3709	3303	2933	2591	2274	1979	1702
14	2.0122	1.2891	1.0313	8706	7535	6614	5855	5309	4646	4148	3702	3297	2927	2585	2269	1974	1698
15	1.9823	1.2833	1.0280	8683	7518	6600	5843	5199	4638	4141	3695	3291	2921	2580	2264	1969	1694
16	1.9642	1.2775	1.0248	8661	7501	6587	5832	5189	4629	4133	3688	3284	2915	2574	2259	1965	1689
17	1.9479	1.2719	1.0216	8639	7484	6573	5820	5179	4620	4125	3681	3278	2909	2569	2254	1960	1685
18	1.9031	1.2663	1.0185	8617	7467	6559	5800	5169	4611	4117	3674	3271	2903	2564	2249	1955	1680
19	1.8798	1.2607	1.0153	8595	7451	6546	5797	5159	4603	4109	3667	3265	2897	2559	2244	1950	1676
20	1.8673	1.2553	1.0122	8573	7434	6533	5786	5149	4594	4102	3660	3258	2891	2553	2239	1946	1671
21	1.8361	1.2499	1.0091	8552	7417	6519	5774	5139	4585	4094	3653	3252	2885	2547	2234	1941	1667
22	1.8159	1.2445	1.0061	8530	7401	6505	5763	5129	4577	4086	3646	3246	2880	2542	2229	1936	1662
23	1.7966	1.2393	1.0030	8509	7384	6492	5752	5120	4568	4079	3639	3239	2874	2536	2223	1932	1658
24	1.7781	1.2341	1.0000	8487	7368	6478	5740	5110	4559	4071	3632	3233	2868	2531	2218	1927	1654
25	1.7804	1.2290	0.9970	8466	7351	6465	5729	5100	4551	4063	3625	3227	2862	2526	2213	1922	1649
26	1.7434	1.2239	0.9940	8445	7335	6451	5718	5090	4542	4056	3618	3220	2856	2520	2208	1917	1645
27	1.7270	1.2188	0.9910	8424	7318	6438	5706	5081	4534	4048	3611	3214	2850	2515	2203	1913	1640
28	1.7112	1.2139	0.9881	8403	7302	6425	5695	5071	4525	4040	3604	3208	2845	2509	2198	1908	1636
29	1.6960	1.2090	0.9852	8382	7286	6412	5684	5061	4516	4032	3597	3201	2839	2504	2193	1903	1632
30	1.6812	1.2041	0.9823	8361	7270	6398	5673	5051	4508	4025	3590	3195	2833	2499	2188	1899	1627
31	1.6670	1.1993	0.9794	8341	7254	6385	5662	5042	4499	4017	3583	3189	2827	2493	2183	1894	1623
32	1.6532	1.1946	0.9765	8327	7238	6372	5651	5032	4491	4010	3576	3183	2821	2488	2178	1889	1619
33	1.6398	1.1899	0.9737	8300	7222	6359	5640	5023	4482	4002	3570	3176	2816	2483	2173	1885	1614
34	1.6269	1.1852	0.9708	8279	7205	6346	5629	5013	4474	3994	3563	3170	2810	2477	2168	1880	1610
35	1.6143	1.1806	0.9680	8259	7190	6333	5618	5003	4466	3897	3556	3164	2804	2472	2164	1875	1605
36	1.6021	1.1761	0.9652	8239	7174	6320	5607	4994	4457	3979	3549	3157	2798	2467	2159	1871	1601
37	1.5903	1.1716	0.9625	8219	7159	6307	5596	4984	4449	3972	3542	3151	2793	2461	2154	1866	1597
38	1.5786	1.1671	0.9597	8199	7143	6294	5585	4975	4440	3964	3535	3145	2787	2456	2149	1862	1592
39	1.5673	1.1627	0.9570	8179	7128	6282	5574	4965	4432	3957	3529	3139	2781	2451	2144	1857	1588
40	1.5563	1.1584	0.9542	8159	7112	6269	5563	4956	4424	3949	3522	3133	2775	2445	2139	1852	1584
41	1.5456	1.1540	0.9515	8140	7097	6256	5552	4947	4415	3942	3515	3126	2770	2440	2134	1848	1579
42	1.5351	1.1498	0.9488	8120	7081	6243	5541	4937	4407	3934	3508	3120	2764	2435	2129	1843	1575
43	1.5249	1.1455	0.9462	8101	7066	6231	5531	4928	4399	3927	3501	3114	2758	2430	2124	1839	1571
44	1.5149	1.1413	0.9435	8081	7050	6218	5520	4918	4390	3919	3495	3108	2753	2424	2119	1834	1566
45	1.5051	1.1372	0.9409	8062	7035	6205	5509	4909	4382	3912	3488	3102	2747	2419	2114	1829	1562
46	1.4956	1.1331	0.9383	8043	7020	6193	5498	4900	4374	3905	3481	3096	2741	2414	2109	1825	1558
47	1.4863	1.1290	0.9356	8023	7005	6180	5488	4890	4365	3897	3475	3090	2736	2409	2104	1820	1553
48	1.4771	1.1249	0.9330	8004	6990	6168	5477	4881	4357	3890	3468	3083	2730	2403	2099	1816	1549
49	1.4682	1.1209	0.9305	7985	6975	6155	5466	4872	4349	3882	3461	3077	2724	2398	2095	1811	1545
50	1.4594	1.1170	0.9279	7966	6960	6143	5456	4863	4341	3875	3454	3071	2719	2393	2090	1806	1540
51	1.4508	1.1130	0.9254	7947	6945	6131	5445	4853	4333	3868	3448	3065	2713	2388	2085	1802	1536
52	1.4424	1.1091	0.9228	7929	6930	6118	5435	4844	4324	3860	3441	3059	2707	2382	2080	1797	1532
53	1.4341	1.1053	0.9203	7910	6915	6106	5424	4835	4316	3853	3434	3053	2702	2377	2075	1793	1527
54	1.4260	1.1016	0.9178	7891	6900	6094	5414	4826	4308	3846	3428	3047	2696	2372	2070	1788	1523
55	1.4180	1.0977	0.9153	7873	6885	6081	5403	4817	4300	3838	3421	3041	2691	2367	2065	1784	1519
56	1.4102	1.0939	0.9128	7854	6871	6069	5393	4808	4292	3831	3415	3034	2685	2362	2061	1779	1514
57	1.4025	1.0902	0.9104	7836	6856	6057	5382	4798	4284	3824	3408	3028	2679	2356	2056	1774	1510
58	1.3949	1.0865	0.9079	7818	6841	6045	5372	4789	4276	3817	3401	3022	2674	2351	2051	1770	1506
59	1.3875	1.0828	0.9055	7800	6827	6033	5361	4780	4268	3900	3395	3016	2668	2346	2046	1765	1502

The use of this Table is explained on p. 30.

Table of the Signs.

Name		Symbol	The Sun	Element	Nature	Precious stone	Part of the Body
Latin	English						
Aries	the Ram	♈	March 21 —April 21	Fire	Cardinal (+)	Amethyst	Head
Taurus	the Bull	♉	April 22 —May 21	Earth	Fixed (—)	Agate	Throat and Neck
Gemini	the Twins	♊	May 22 —June 21	Air	Mutable (+)	Beryl	Lungs and Arms
Cancer	the Crab	♋	June 22 —July 22	Water	Cardinal (—)	Emerald	Stomach
Leo	the Lion	♌	July 23 —Aug. 22	Fire	Fixed (+)	Ruby	Heart
Virgo	the Virgin	♍	August 23 —Sept. 22	Earth	Mutable (—)	Jaspis	Intestines
Libra	the Balance	♎	Sept. 23 —Oct. 23	Air	Cardinal (+)	Diamond	Kidneys
Scorpio	the Scorpion	♏	October 24—Nov. 22	Water	Fixed (—)	Topaz	Genitals
Sagittarius	the Archer	♐	Nov. 23 —Dec. 21	Fire	Mutable (+)	Granate	Hips and Thighs
Capricornus	the Goat	♑	Dec. 22 —Jan. 20	Earth	Cardinal (—)	Onyx	Knees
Aquarius	the Waterbearer	♒	Jan. 21 —Febr. 18	Air	Fixed (+)	Sapphire	Ankles
Pisces	the Fishes	♓	Febr. 19 —March 20	Water	Mutable (—)	Chrysolith	Feet

Latin	IDEAL EFFECT		REAL EFFECT	
	Favourable	Unfavourable	Favourable	Unfavourable
Aries	Enthusiasm	Headstrongness	Initiative	Fits of Anger
Taurus	Confidence	Stubbornness	Respectability	Self-sufficiency
Gemini	Survey	Disintegration	Capacity	Unreliability
Cancer	Contemplation	Self-conceit	Care	Greed
Leo	Dignity	Pride	Authority	Despotism
Virgo	Purification	Scepticism	Orderliness	Narrowmindedness
Libra	Synthesis	Indecision	Benevolence	Indifference
Scorpio	Mystery	Intrigue	Creative Power	Voluptuousness
Sagittarius	Religion	Superstition	Instruction	Boasting
Capricornus	Science	Dogmatism	Organisation	Selfishness
Aquarius	Intuition	Delusion	Genius	Anarchy
Pisces	Devotion	Stupification	Sacrifice	Sensuality

Table of the Planets.

Planet		Weekday	Metal	Colour	Tone	Sense	Age	Strong	Weak	Elevation	Detriment
Name	Symbol										
The Sun	☉	Sunday	Gold	Orange	d	the Ego	23—37	♌	♒	♈	♎
The Moon	☽	Monday	Silver	Violet	b	the Soul	1—3	♋	♑	♉	♏
Mercury	☿	Wednesday	Quicksilver	Yellow	e	Eyesight	4—11	♊, ♍ (—)	♐, ♓	♍	♓
Venus	♀	Friday	Copper	Blue	g	Touch	11—14	♉ (—), ♎	♏, ♈	♓	♍
Mars	♂	Tuesday	Iron	Red	c	Taste	14—23	♈, ♏ (—)	♎, ♉	♑	♋
Jupiter	♃	Thursday	Tin	Purple	a	Smell	38—66	♐, ♓ (—)	♊, ♍	♋	♑
Saturn	♄	Saturday	Lead	Green	f	Hearing	66—	♑, ♒ (—)	♋, ♌	♎	♈
Uranus	♅							♒	♌	♏	♉
Neptune	♆							♓	♍		

Table of the Planets.

Planet		IDEAL EFFECT		REAL EFFECT	
Name	Symbol	Favourable	Unfavourable	Favourable	Unfavourable
The Sun	☉	Selfconsciousness	Boldness	Love of life	Vanity
The Moon	☽	Receptivity	Effeminacy	Sensitiveness	Sentimentality
Mercury	☿	Intelligence	Pedantry	Adaptability	Dishonesty
Venus	♀	Harmony	Lack of criticism	Charm	Indolence
Mars	♂	Righteousness	Fanaticism	Energy	Extravagance
Jupiter	♃	Broadening	Exaggeration	Mercy	Hypocrisy
Saturn	♄	Concentration	Rigidity	Reflection	Avarice
Uranus	♅	Insight	Confusion	Genius	Madness
Neptune	♆	Realisation of Unity	Blurred diffusion	Imagination	Perversity